University of
Chester

Library

This book is to be returned on or before the last date stamped below. Overdue charges will be incurred by the late return of books.

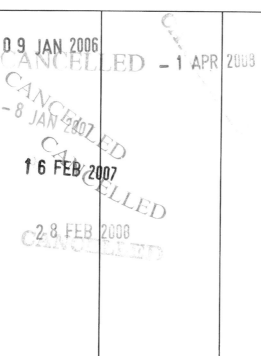
16.11.05

THE SOLIDARITY OF OTHERS IN A DIVIDED WORLD

A Postmodern Theology after Postmodernism

Anselm Kyongsuk Min

T & T CLARK INTERNATIONAL
A Continuum imprint
www.continuumbooks.com

T & T Clark International, Madison Square Park, 15 East 26th Street, New York, NY 10010

T & T Clark International, The Tower Building, 11 York Road, London se1 7nx

T & T Clark International is a Continuum imprint.

Cover art: Private Collection/Diana Ong/Superstock

Cover design: Wesley Hoke

Library of Congress Cataloging-in-Publication Data
Min, Anselm Kyongsuk, 1940-
  The solidarity of others in a divided world : a postmodern theology after postmodernism / Anselm Kyongsuk Min.
      p. cm.
Includes bibliographical references and index.
  ISBN 0-567-02570-5 (pbk.)
  1. Postmodern theology. 2. Holy Spirit. I. Title.
BT83.597.M56 2004
230—dc22
                                        2003021751

Printed in the United States of America

04 05 06 07 08 09   10 9 8 7 6 5 4 3 2 1

CONTENTS

ACKNOWLEDGMENTS

All the chapters of this book except the third and fourth have appeared as articles in journals. Chapter 1 appeared as "Toward a Dialectic of Totality and Infinity: Reflections on Emmanuel Levinas," *Journal of Religion* 78, no. 4 (Oct. 1998): 571–91. Chapter 2 appeared as "The Other without Society and History: A Dialogue with Derrida," in D. Z. Phillips and Timothy Tessin, editors, *Philosophy of Religion in the Twenty-First Century* (New York: Palgrave, 2001), 167–85. Chapter 5 appeared as "Renewing the Doctrine of the Spirit: A Prolegomenon," *Perspectives in Religious Studies* 19, no. 2 (summer 1992): 183–98. Chapter 6 appeared as "Solidarity of Others in the Power of the Holy Spirit: Pneumatology in a Divided World," in Bradford Hinze and Lyle Dabney, editors, *Advents of the Spirit: An Introduction to the Current Study of Pneumatology* (Milwaukee: Marquette University Press, 2002), 416–43. Chapter 7 appeared as "Solidarity of Others in the Body of Christ," *Toronto Journal of Theology* 12, no. 2 (fall 1998): 239–54. Chapter 8 appeared as "Praxis and Pluralism: A Liberationist Theology of Religions," *Perspectives in Religious Studies* 16, no. 3 (fall 1989): 197–211. Chapter 9 appeared as "Dialectical Pluralism and Solidarity of Others," *Journal of the American Academy of Religion* 65, no. 3 (fall 1997), 587–604. Part of Chapter 10 appeared as "Liberation, the Other, and Hegel in Recent Pneumatologies," *Religious Studies Review* 22, no. 1 (Jan. 1996): 28–33. These articles have been revised, often expanded, and included in this book with permission of the publishers.

INTRODUCTION

Solidarity of Others as the Burden of Contemporary Theology

The thesis of this book is quite simple. The globalization of the world brings together different groups into common space and produces a twofold dialectic, the dialectic of *differentiation,* in which we are made increasingly aware of differences in nationality, culture, religion, ethnicity, gender, class, language; and the dialectic of *interdependence,* in which we are compelled to find a way of living together despite our differences. The central challenge of the globalizing world is how to manage and transform this twofold, antithetical dialectic of simultaneous differentiation and interdependence into a solidarity of others, the mutual solidarity of those who are different. The task of contemporary Christian theology is to interpret this demand of the new kairos in light of its biblical and theological tradition and provide a conceptually coherent, systematic mediation between the context of globalization and the demand of its inherited faith.

The Christian tradition provides abundant resources worth retrieving for this theological purpose: the example of the historical Jesus in his solidarity with the marginalized others of society, his crucifixion and resurrection as signs of his solidarity in suffering and hope, the triune God as a communion of three persons in their difference, the incarnation as solidarity of the human and the divine in their radical difference, the Holy Spirit as the source of communion in difference, the great but neglected doctrine of the communion of saints in the body of Christ, the whole biblical trajectory of liberation and reconciliation. Using the paradigm of "solidarity of others" as the central theme of theology, it is possible and appropriate to renew the doctrine of the Holy Spirit as the Spirit of solidarity and recapture the inspiring and illuminating potential of the classical, authentically Christian metaphor of the "body of Christ" as embodiment of this solidarity.

In the course of the twentieth century we have had a succession of different theological paradigms: word, existence, hope, secularity, narrative, interpretation, rhetoric, and liberation. These paradigms have served their times quite well. By the same token, they may have already exhausted themselves. The new kairos of the globalizing world that makes different groups so interdependent demands a new paradigm. "Solidarity of others," I suggest, is that paradigm.

The book consists of two uneven parts. Part 1, which is introductory to part 2, contains four chapters presenting, discussing, and critiquing the postmodernism of difference in its philosophical, cultural, and feminist aspects. Chapter 1 is a critical, sympathetic reflection on the achievement and significance of Emmanuel Levinas, especially his critique of totality in the name of the infinity of the other. Chapter 2 focuses on Jacques Derrida's conception of the messianic and his critique of all determinacies in the name of *differance*. Chapter 3 presents an appreciative review of philosophical, cultural, and feminist postmodernisms in terms of Derrida and recent sociological and feminist discussions. Chapter 4 provides a critique of these postmodernisms and a constructive philosophical response to them in terms of expanded concepts of solidarity and human nature, ending with an anticipatory sketch of a theology of solidarity.

The postmodern emphasis on difference is a sign of the times that we may ignore only at our peril. Difference is here to stay for some time. My critique of existing postmodernism is that it absolutizes and reifies difference when difference also contains an internal need to sublate itself into the solidarity of the different. Consciousness of difference is made possible by the changing reality of the world, which brings different peoples together into common space and compels them to confront one another in all their differences. The same world also compels them to cooperate in producing a social system that will honor their differences, and to develop a minimum sense of solidarity that will make such social cooperation possible.

As an appreciative critique of difference, part 1 provides an introduction to the second, main part of the book, which is a theology of solidarity. Part 1 is titled "After Postmodernism." Part 2 is subtitled "Toward a Postmodern Theology." My contention is that difference must be *negated* in its claim to absoluteness; hence, I use the preposition "after" in the sense that its days are over. There is also something profoundly true, however, about the postmodernist obsession with difference, namely, its protest against oppression and alienation, which must be *preserved*; hence, I also use the preposition "after" in the sense of "in accordance with." The secret of both negating and preserving difference is by sublating it—in the Hegelian sense of *Aufheben*—into the solidarity of the different or solidarity of others. Thus, part 2 is subtitled

"Toward a Postmodern Theology." Postmodern*ism* as an *interpretation* of our time with its absolutization of difference may be over, but postmodern*ity* as the *reality* of our time is very much around. A "postmodern" theology, then, seeks to respond to the integral demand of the postmodern world, which "postmodernist" philosophy interprets in a one-sided way. A postmodern theology is the sublation of the philosophical postmodernism of difference into the solidarity of others.

Part 2 contains six chapters dealing with different aspects of a contemporary constructive theology based on the new paradigm. Chapter 5 presents a preliminary discussion of the biblical sources and basic philosophical categories of a theology of the Holy Spirit. Chapter 6 provides a constructive theology of the Holy Spirit as the Spirit of solidarity. Chapter 7 constructs a Christology of solidarity, chiefly by exploring the classical but neglected metaphor of the body of Christ for its rich contemporary significance. Chapter 8 broaches the subject of religious pluralism from the perspective of liberation theology. Chapter 9 completes the discussion of pluralism in terms of solidarity of others as the underlying principle of all interreligious relations and dialogues. Chapter 10 is a critical review of three recent theologies of the Holy Spirit, those of Jürgen Moltmann, Michael Welker, and Peter C. Hodgson, in light of the overriding idea of solidarity. Common to all these chapters is an interpretation of the context of contemporary theology as demanding solidarity of the different, each chapter adding a new aspect or dimension to the demand of solidarity.

For some years I have felt that various liberation theologies—Latin American, African American, womanist, mujerista, white feminist, minjung, and so on—have almost exhausted themselves. After some thirty years of fruitful, exciting, and prophetic challenges to the world and the churches, few new insights and initiatives seem to be forthcoming. With the turning of the new century and with all the breathtaking changes in the world, I have felt that we are living in a new kairos that demands a new paradigm of its own. I am convinced that "solidarity of others" is the new paradigm we need.

A word on the use of gender in this book. I refer to the first and second person of the Trinity as Father and Son, in the masculine, while using the feminine to refer to the Holy Spirit and to God taken simply as God, except where the context dictates otherwise. This has the virtue of preserving the traditional references to the triune God, balancing the distribution of feminine and masculine pronouns, and avoiding awkward neologisms such as "Godself" and stylistic infelicities such as "he/she." I also simply vary between the feminine and masculine in referring to the human being.

PART ONE

AFTER POSTMODERNISM:
A CRITIQUE OF DIFFERENCE

ONE

LEVINAS AND THE LIBERATION OF THE OTHER
Toward a Dialectic of Totality, Infinity, and Solidarity*

From Totality to Infinity

No one in recent years has done more than Emmanuel Levinas to carry on a sustained, rigorous critique of the notion of totality and the logocentrism it implies, not in order to indulge in what might appear to be a rather frivolous and nihilistic play of sheer alterity but in order to uphold the objective reality of ethical values. With passion, radicality, and absoluteness that remind us of Kierkegaard and Barth, Levinas has questioned the claims of totality and its ontology of war in the name of infinity and its eschatology of peace.[1] In an age bleeding from the "crimes of logic" (Camus)[2] unprecedented for their scale, art, and technological efficiency, in a world ever haunted by the permanent possibility of war, the only way for human beings to live together in peace and justice, he has insisted, is the ethical recognition of the infinity of the other that transcends and resists all categorical mediation and the establishment of a communion of others in fraternity and solidarity.

In this chapter I revisit Levinas's central intuition, the infinity and transcendence of the other. First, I try to bring out the philosophical significance of that intuition. Second, I confront it with certain immanent criticisms, the historical conditions of infinity and transcendence. Third, I argue for a dialectic of totality and infinity rather than a sharp opposition between the two. My argument is that we do concrete justice to the transcendence and infinity of the other not by attacking totality as such but by the praxis of creating liberating totalities. As social beings we cannot avoid the politics of totality, a system of identity binding on all such as laws, policies, institutions, and structures. The question is not whether we can avoid totality as such but

---

* A version of this paper was presented at the Theology and the Phenomenological Movement Seminar of the American Academy of Religion, Anaheim, November 20, 1989, and at the Institute for Philosophical Research, Korea University, Seoul, Korea, May 28, 1997.

only whether we are able and willing to construct a totality that serves liberation and solidarity by providing their economic, political, and cultural conditions. Totality without infinity is indeed oppressive and totalitarian, but infinity without totality is impotent and equally liable to oppression. What we need is a dialectic of totality and infinity in the interest of solidarity of others.

Levinas no doubt mounts one of the most radical protests against the destruction of human dignity. His protest is based on a stringent critique of the very roots of such destruction, the logocentrism, or the priority of reason, logic, idea, concept; and the categories of immanence that pervade the Western philosophical tradition, not to speak of a critique of the brutalities of the many political totalitarianisms of the twentieth century. For Levinas the main culprit has been the conjunction of *egolatry*, totality, and history. Whenever egolatrous reason approaches persons and things, it inevitably reduces them to a moment of the ego and the same, of totality and history, and the result is not only intellectual reduction of reality to components of totalizing ontology but also political reduction of persons to moments of omnivorous totalitarianism. The whole of Western philosophy, based on the imperialism of the same, "has been struck with a horror of the other that remains other—with an insurmountable allergy."[3] As an expression of the ego, the source of all identity and identification, Western thought has been essentially an "*egology*," a philosophy of "power" and "injustice," in fact, "an ontology of war."[4]

As opposed to this ontology of war, Levinas advocates an "eschatology of messianic peace" or "prophetic eschatology." Eschatology does not mean providing information about the future and completing a philosophy of history by demonstrating the teleology of being, which would only mean assimilating eschatology to the ontology of totality. Eschatology "institutes a relation with being *beyond the totality* or beyond history, and not with being beyond the past and the present," nor with the "void that surrounds the totality." It is "a relationship with *a surplus always exterior to the totality,* as though the objective totality did not fill out the true measure of being." It is a relationship with the infinity of being that "exceeds the totality" and is "as primordial as totality."[5]

This eschatological infinity, however, is not merely "beyond" totality and history; it is also "reflected *within* the totality and history, *within* experience," where it "draws beings out of the jurisdiction of history and the future; it arouses them in, and calls them forth to, their full responsibility." The eschatological judgment is not the "last" judgment but the judgment of history as a whole, of all the instants in time, restoring "to each instant its full signification in that very instant." For eschatology, beings still exist in relationship, "but on the basis of themselves and not on the basis of the totality."[6] Eschatology thus implies "the breach of the totality, the possibility of a *signification without a context.*"[7] In short, eschatological infinity is "in" history but not "of" history in that it judges, subverts, and transcends the totalizing and reductionist categories of history from within. In this sense, peace is possible only eschatologically, not historically.[8]

The eschatological path out of the brutalities of rationalist logocentrism and murderous totalitarianism is to root thought itself in a reality above the immanence of thought, in something "more than it can think." This reality is the infinite and transcendent reality of the other (*l'Autrui*), infinite as bearer of the "trace" of the divine infinite and transcendent over all categories of finite mediation. In retrieving the Cartesian "idea of the infinite," Levinas insists that the other is "infinite" in that she does not enter into but "overflows" the entire sphere of the same. Infinity "remains ever exterior to thought" and "overflows the thought that thinks it," while also remaining "the condition for every opinion as also for every objective truth" and "the common source of activity and theory."[9] This infinity of the other "interrupts" and "judges" totality. As such, the other is not an object of knowledge, which would immediately denature the other by degrading her as a moment of one's own *Bei-sich-Sein.* The other is appreciated precisely *as* other, in her radical alterity and irreducible singularity, only when thought renounces its totalitarian hubris and learns to think of the other on her own terms, *kath' heautē n,* not as a moment of a totality, not in terms of her relationship to others within a system, but to think "otherwise than being" or "beyond essence."

As the epiphany of the other, the "face" is "a fundamental event."[10] The other can only be "invoked" in a face-to-face conversation, which "reveals" the other "in his refusal to be contained," as "absolute being," as being "withdrawn from the categories," not "disclosed" as a theme nor "comprehended" in a category nor addressed in the violence of rhetoric.[11] The other "has only a reference to himself; he has no quiddity."[12] The other is not "constituted" by me in any way as in knowledge and vision. The alterity of the other is absolute, not relative as in the case of comparison and distinction, both of which imply a community of a genus and destroy the alterity of the other. The other remains "infinitely transcendent, infinitely foreign," and "breaks with the world that can be common to us, whose virtualities are inscribed in our nature and developed by our existence."[13] The other embodies the priority of the existent over being, of metaphysics over ontology.[14]

Ethics is the "royal road" to this metaphysical thinking of the other in her radical alterity. Doing justice to the metaphysical reality of the other requires radical humility of thought and radical transcendence of its innate egolatry.

Justice consists in recognizing "my master" in the other. The other puts the I and all "solipsistic dialectic of consciousness" in question. I truly meet the other only when I welcome the other precisely in her challenge to my freedom in all its spontaneity and arbitrariness, in its essence as "imperialism of the same," only when I welcome the "face" of the other imposing itself on me in all its destitution and hunger "beyond the manifested and purely phenomenal form," "without the intermediary of any image," "prior to all disclosure of being and its cold splendor."[15] The other is approachable only ethically, only in heeding the categorical imperative that comes to us not from the general dignity of persons as ends in themselves, but from the "face" of the singular other that "opens the primordial discourse whose first word is obligation,"[16] challenging me to justify my freedom and even my existence, my very "right to be," and keeping me in the "vigilant insomnia" of infinite ethical responsibility, the responsibility of a "hostage."[17]

The face-to-face is the "primordial event" of signification, putting into question all "constitutive freedom" and conditioning all possibility of meaning, words, concepts, *Sinngebung,* consciousness, reason itself, and the very "universality that reigns as the presence of humanity in the eyes that look at me."[18] It is the face of the other with its inviolable exteriority, not a concept, not being in general, that constitutes the *primum intelligibile.* Ethics as the sovereignty of the other is prior to epistemology, ontology, and politics, all of which require a thoroughgoing ethical critique.[19]

It is also through this ethical responsibility to the other that the ego is constituted as a true subject. The other is neither a scandal to be assimilated into the identity of the ego as in Hegel, nor a threat to be guarded against as in Sartre. Nor is the other, as in Heidegger, simply another category of beings to be encountered in one's being-in-the-world, where one's primary preoccupation remains one's own existence, especially one's own death. For Levinas, true subjectivity is not found "at the level of its purely egoist protestation against totality, nor in its anguish before death."[20] Rather, it is found only in subjecting itself to the ethical summons of the other, willing to be "obsessed" with the other, to be "accused" and "persecuted" by the other, and to "substitute" oneself and "expiate" for the other.[21]

In an unqualifiedly heteronomous account of subjectivity, Levinas insists that "it is my inescapable and incontrovertible answerability to the other that makes me an individual 'I.' I become a responsible or ethical 'I' only to the extent that I agree to depose or dethrone myself—to abdicate my position of centrality—in favor of the vulnerable other."[22] My relation to the other is not symmetrical as in Buber, but "asymmetrical": "I am responsible for the other without waiting for reciprocity."[23] As Levinas is fond of quoting from

Dostoyevsky's *The Brothers Karamazov,* "We are all responsible for everyone else, but I more than others."[24] The Levinasian subject is not the subject of traditional ontology, which reduces all things to itself, but the "me-onotological," ethical subject that recognizes the moral priority of the other and one's own heteronomous responsibility as more primordial than one's own autonomous freedom.

A genuine human community is possible only as a communion of fraternity and solidarity at the transcategorical level, only as a "religious" bond or communion of others liberated from the tyranny of immanentist categories and concepts and reconstituted beyond all ontology, at once "absolved" from all relations and radically "separated" from all by virtue of their infinity, yet also related to all in a nontotalizing way, beyond the formal unity of a genus.[25] This is where each, in Luther's language, is "a perfectly dutiful servant of all," without, however, considering oneself "a perfectly free lord of all," where the other does remain the lord. It is a relationship with the other that does not constitute or become part of a totality, human or divine, "a relation without relation,"[26] where "the terms remain absolute despite the relation in which they find themselves."[27] This "eschatological" goal of ethics is a genuinely pluralistic society where each is bound to the other by ethical responsibility, beyond all totalizing categorization, beyond the unity of genus, mutual resemblance, and even a common cause, where each is indeed an "atom" separated from all others when viewed in terms of rationalist categories, but related to others at a level beyond all objectifying knowledge and totalizing history.[28]

The Levinasian ideal, then, is a radical pluralism of egos, with each deposed from the throne of self-idolatry and recentered on the other in an equality in which "the other commands the same and reveals himself to the same in responsibility."[29] It is a solidarity of others in their simultaneous "absolute proximity" and "absolute separation," "a primordial multiplicity" "observed in the very face-to-face that constitutes it,"[30] a society of radical, not merely numerical, multiplicity of terms that are "absolute and yet in relation," with a "surplus" beyond the possibility of total reflection.[31] It is a society of simultaneous kinship and radical heterogeneity, in an "unrelating relation," which "does not fill the abyss of separation but confirms it,"[32] "a relationship without intermediary, without mediations," "beyond the categories of unity and multiplicity which are valid for things."[33] In the language of Alphonso Lingis, the eschatological community of Levinas is a "community of those who have nothing in common."[34]

Levinas echoes the attack of Kierkegaardian existentialism and contemporary deconstructionism on the logocentric hubris of the Western tradition, but his critique is based on the irreducibility to reason, not of "the existing individual" as in Kierkegaard, but of the ethically encountered other. He also echoes the attack of Barthian neo-orthodoxy on liberal theology and natural theology in the absoluteness of his denial of all mediation and his affirmation of the sovereignty of the other. But unlike Barth, Levinas includes human others among such unmediated sovereigns, not only the divine other; our primary access to the divine other is precisely through human others. In any event, Levinas exemplifies the postmodern disenchantment with the reign of reason and all its works and the pluralistic groping for a livable community in an intellectually and politically oppressive world.

Most important, Levinas echoes certain central themes from the Judeo-Christian tradition, themes forcefully recovered for our attention in recent decades by liberation theology. These are themes such as finding the "traces" of God in the marginalized others of history, the widow, the orphan, and the stranger; the primacy of the ethics of preferential option for the poor; ethics rooted in the confrontation of egolatrous egos with the concrete "faces" of others and in the selfless surrender to their appeal; the prophetic denunciation of the ideologies and instruments of domination and the prophetic annunciation of an eschatological, transcategorical utopia of liberated human community. Levinas recovers these themes philosophically, not theologically, yet with denials and affirmations whose absoluteness echoes the passion of the Hebrew prophets.

Ethics without History: A Critique

Levinas's reflections embody phenomenological freshness, metaphysical depth, and prophetic intensity to a degree that does disturb and challenge. His appeal lies in the absolute, unqualified affirmation of the infinite, transcategorical, unmediated transcendence of the other. This appeal, however, is also his weakness, I fear. In order precisely to do justice to his intuition of the other's ethical infinity, I argue, Levinas has to be *aufgehoben* in the Hegelian sense: preserved in his ethical defense of the other; negated in his dualism of ethics and history, metaphysics and ontology, infinity and totality; and raised to the positive dialectic of infinity and totality in the interest of solidarity.

Levinas is quite right in insisting that the other as other is irreducible in his ethical transcendence and infinity. However, by categorically denying all historical and ontological mediation of the other, he isolates the other from the concrete totality of constitutively mediating sociohistorical relations, which alone would provide the essential context and condition for the genesis and actualization of the ethical transcendence of the other as a *human—*

not angelic—other, and thereby also reifies and reduces the other to an ahistorical abstraction. There is an internal contradiction between Levinas's intention, the defense of the other in her ethical transcendence, and his philosophical procedure, the denial of all historical mediation, which ironically reduces the human other to ahistorical, angelic existence elevated above all contingencies of history, above all vulnerabilities, and thus neither capable of issuing the categorical imperative "Thou shalt not kill!" to devouring egos,[35] nor indeed needing protection against such murder in the first place. Let me elaborate.

It is only proper in an immanent critique to ask three key questions: (1) What conditions make possible the ethical problem as a problem: the murder of human beings and the countless acts of injustice? (2) How is the ethical infinity and transcendence of the other possible? (3) What solution makes possible the recognition, protection, and actualization of the irreducible ethical transcendence of the other?

1. How is the ethical problem possible as a problem? How is domination possible? The egolatrous domination and murder of the other is possible, one would think, because among other things the other, for all her ethical transcendence and infinity, is constitutively—ontologically—interdependent on others and *mediated* by them in such a way that the other is *intrinsically* exposed to the negativities of history, to the pressures, temptations, and opportunities for evil generated by the social structure as a system of economic, political, and cultural interdependencies, a system that is also always historically determinate, with each system (e.g., capitalism, socialism, feudalism, primitive agrarian society) generating its own kind of temptations to murder and exploitation. Certainly the global murders we are rightly concerned about—by mechanized and nuclear warfare, massive pollution of the environment, political uses of the food weapon, the bloc politics of the superpowers, and the destructive clashes of economic imperialisms, not to speak of the many racial holocausts, the great shame of the twentieth century—are inconceivable apart from our ontological and historical dependence on the systems under which we live.

It is precisely the concrete totality of historically specified ontological relations of interdependence that produces the "stranger," the "widow," and the "orphan" for whom Levinas is so concerned in all their nakedness and vulnerability. By denying all ontological and historical mediation of the other, then, Levinas renders the ethical problem of murder and injustice simply unintelligible and dissolves it as a problem. Without the many concrete mediations constitutive of the vulnerability of the other as other, we no longer have the problem of the other. At best, Levinas reduces the stranger, the widow, and the orphan to *abstract* symbols of human vulnerability *in general,* with nothing historically concrete and specific about them.

2. How is the ethical infinity and transcendence of the other possible? To this question Levinas provides a profound answer: the other is ethically infinite because he bears the "trace" of the divine infinite.[36] He is not infinite in himself but because of his "absolute" relation to the divine other. The human other shares in the transcendent dignity of the divine through that transcategorical relationship called creation, which expresses "a multiplicity not united into a totality." The creature "indeed does depend on an other, but not as a part that is separated from it." In this sense, creation ex nihilo "breaks with system, posits a being outside of every system," and makes it open to the infinite.[37]

There is, however, another aspect to the question. How is the ethical transcendence of the other possible precisely in her *humanity?* Is the other ethically transcendent only in her absolute relation to the divine infinite? Is she not also ethically transcendent in the totality of her immanent relations to persons, things, and structures of this world? Does not the problem of ethical transcendence arise precisely because the other is murdered, degraded, and exploited, which is possible only in her many immanent relations in history and society? Are we not ethically commanded by the other to feed, shelter, clothe, educate, and heal her, and in any event to *concretely* show our respect for her, by striving to fulfill her manifold needs and desires? If so, are we not also admitting that the other is transcendent not only in her absolute relation to the divine but also concretely in the totality of her many constitutive needs, desires, and relations? The ethical dignity of the other may "trace" its origin to her transcendent relation to the infinite, but that dignity is effectively destroyed or honored only in her immanent relations to history and society, and both the transcendent and the immanent relations are inseparably connected in the unity of the one person.

The other, then, is ethically transcendent and irreducible as a concrete unity of her vertical relation to the divine in her interiority *and* her horizontal relations to society and history in her externality, that is, as a totality of her constitutive relations to transcendence and history. Only as a unity of transcendence and history, only as a transcendence mediated by and mediating history, is the ethical sovereignty of the other as a *human* other possible, meaningful, and concrete. Without this constitutive mediation we denature the other to abstract, angelic existence. We murder the other not only by reducing the other to an object of violence in history but also by elevating and etherealizing the other beyond all history in thought.

The "other" of Levinas's is "concrete" only in the phenomenological sense of the lived immediacy of the face-to-face encounter. One wonders, however, how concrete such an encounter really is, whether in fact it is not an abstraction, precisely because the other is separated from all the mediating sociohistorical conditions that account for the vulnerability and degradation of the other. However ethically compelling and irreducible such an experience might be as a whole, the "face" of the other is never unmediated. Concretely, it may be the face of a Romero shot to death during the Eucharist, or the terrified faces of those fleeing from the death squads in El Salvador, or the despairing faces of the many helpless refugees turned back at the U.S.-Mexican border, or the emaciated faces of the many victims of the civil war in Cambodia languishing in Thai camps, or the horrified faces of the many millions of Jews and others waiting for their turns in the Nazi gas chambers, or the outraged faces of young Palestinians caught up in a bloody *intifada* in the occupied territories, or the lonely and despairing faces of the tens of thousands of victims of AIDS avoided by the many like plagues. The otherness of others increases its ethical challenge precisely to the degree that we encounter them in all the concreteness of their mediating social conditions, not when we abstract from them. Ironically, Levinas is guilty of the very "disdainful spiritualism"of which he was accusing Buber on account of the latter's formal conception of the I-Thou relationship.[38]

To concretize the other in this way by introducing the many sociohistorical relations into the very constitution of the other is also to raise perplexing questions about the ethical sovereignty of the other that Levinas so insists on. In concrete history, which is always a history of struggle among classes, races, sexes, religions, we encounter the other not only among the oppressed but also among the oppressors. What if the "face" of the other happens to be that of a Marcos, a Pinochet, a Mobutu, a Pol Pot, a CIA assassin, a Botha, a Hitler, a Stalin? What does it mean to "welcome" the other, to "let the other be" in these instances? As human beings they too are indeed vulnerable—in some sense more vulnerable and more destitute than many of us, but they are not just individuals in "absolute" relation to the infinite. Their very individuality is also constituted by the many historical relations that endow them with such horrendous power over the life and death of millions of others. How, then, do we still respect the ethical transcendence of these oppressive others while also trying to bring them to justice in history? Should we forgo historical judgments because all such judgments, for Levinas, are judgments in absentia and unjust?[39] Furthermore, how do we concretely discriminate between oppressive others and oppressed others except through historical mediations and historical judgments, except through categorical thinking that places them in the context of a social totality? This also leads to the next question.

3. How is the *actualization* of the ethical transcendence of the other possible? The ethical is inseparable from the will to actualization; a categorical imperative that is indifferent to its own actualization would be a contradiction in terms. The ethical, therefore, is not only a breach of totality but also a demand to become a moment of that totality in its actualization. The ethical cannot remain merely an eschatological judgment that may be "in" the world but not "of" the world; it must also be "of" the world as its transforming power. The stranger demands food and shelter, job training and green cards; the widow demands medical care and subsidized housing; the orphan demands education, foster parents, protection against drugs and pimps. In order to deliver on our infinite responsibility for the ethical transcendence of the other, we must bring the other into concretely liberating economic, political, and cultural relations in history. Without this concretizing historical mediation, which necessarily entails constitutive relations to a social totality, the ethical demand would remain only verbal and empty, a sentimental moralism that either exhausts itself in the "unhappy consciousness" of unrelieved negation or turns into cynical realism at home in the very negativities it condemns.

The ethical demand of the other requires threefold historical mediation: cultural, political, and economic. For Levinas, the "primordial" encounter with the "face" of the other puts our freedom in question, challenges all our a priori conceptions, and arouses us to infinite responsibility. However, for all its phenomenological priority to the split between theory and praxis, activity and passivity,[40] this "primordial" experience is not an isolated event independent of the totality of our social experiences. It takes developed ethical sensibility to see the "trace" of the infinite in the "face" of the other and to feel its demand and challenge. Such an ethical development is possible only through the mediation of a culture of care and respect, a social ethos of compassion and solidarity.

For Kierkegaard, the nineteenth-century bourgeois ethos encouraged "aestheticism" and speculation and enervated the will to ethical existence; it is also possible today that capitalism has been encouraging a "culture of narcissism" (Lasch), weakening not only our sense of solidarity but also the sense of the ethical as such. If the very recognition of the ethical transcendence of the other requires mediation by a socially supported culture of solidarity, the actual fulfillment of the many needs of the other requires mediation by political protection of basic human rights and by economic provision of the material conditions for human development. Without these threefold social conditions—cultural, political, and economic—the other would remain, for all her transcendence and infinity, helpless, vulnerable, in fact reduced to the immanence of a thing. By the same token, the concrete realization of the ethical imperative requires the transformation of oppressive structures, which is possible only politically, by a collective action for social change in solidarity with the oppressed.

In any event, just as the oppression of the other is brought about by a negative mediation of history, so the liberation of the other can only be brought about by a positive mediation of history, not by denying all historical mediation in the name of ethical transcendence. Such a denial might be psychologically satisfying to the moralist, but it does not really care to improve the actual condition of the other. The ethical that remains only an eschatological "judgment" on history remains an abstract negation of history, not a concrete negation: the actual transformation of history into structures and forces of liberation capable of reducing violence and murder. The "primordial" experience of the other may be a source of our ethical renewal, but such renewal must become part of a culture, and its imperatives politically recognized and economically supported. The oppressed others cannot "live" on our "primordial" experience alone.

To be true to the ethical demand that the other be respected in his irreducible transcendence "actually," not just "ideally," the primordial must be brought into a transforming relation to concrete history, where it must "dirty its hands." The eschatological must become "flesh" in history. The infinite must become part of a totality. The point of the ethical, in the final analysis, is not to preserve *my* moral purity at all costs but to actually liberate the *other* from the oppression and injustice that violate his ethical transcendence. Without this will to historical actualization and the necessary praxis of liberation, the insistence on the ethical transcendence of the other, however passionate and edifying, would lapse into impotent idealism, not indeed the idealism of egocentric logos, but the idealism of a "primordial" consciousness still incapable of action in history. It would also leave history to the "children of darkness" (Reinhold Niebuhr) and make it even more oppressive, which in turn, as Hegel's *Phenomenology* shows, would lead the "pure" moral consciousness to engage, with increasing intensity, in judgment and negation, in a vicious cycle of actual violence and rhetorical condemnation, which, however, does nothing to change the world for the better.

This project of the actual liberation of history, of course, requires appreciation of the constitutive significance of history for human existence and the positive possibilities of history for human liberation. It is precisely on this point that I find Levinas wanting, as I do also Kierkegaard and Barth. All three are uncompromising in their denial of constitutive historical mediation of human existence and all that such mediation implies. They likewise agree in their passionate denunciation of history. *History, totality, system, world:* these are essentially bad words, with no hope of redemption except through something extrinsic to history, be it individual commitment (Kierkegaard), the irruption of the eschatological (Levinas), the forgiving grace of the sovereign God (Barth).

They do not recognize, with all due seriousness, the constitutive relation of history to human existence, or if they do at all, they recognize it only in its negativity and even then only implicitly, in their furious attack on the oppressively totalizing (Levinas), enervating (Kierkegaard), or idolatrous (Barth) consequences of history on human existence. They do not, therefore, appreciate the positive possibilities of history for human transformation, proposing instead, either explicitly or by default, a solution that is essentially individualistic, the intensification of individual inwardness (Kierkegaard); the renewal of the primordial experience of the separated other (Levinas); and radical self-negation before the sovereign God (Barth). Such a solution does not come to grips with the historical sources of oppression, aestheticism, and idolatry; and thus denatures the concrete totality of human existence by reducing it to a single dimension, be it individual inwardness, encounter with the other raised above history, or the sinner before the sovereign God.[41]

Levinas's incapacity to appreciate the constitutive and positive significance of history might be located in his starting point, his critique of philosophies of egocentric subjectivity. For him, such an egocentric subject necessarily reduces the other to the same. It may recognize otherness and contradiction, but immediately reconciles them as moments in a totality of the same. The other is other only relatively, not absolutely. Levinas finds a corrective of this egocentrism in heterocentric subjectivity, the ego questioned and challenged by the irreducibly transcendent claim of the other. The ethical center has shifted from the ego to the other. Levinas's ethical metaphysics, however, remains an essentially Cartesian philosophy of the subject, albeit with a different ethical content. It still remains a philosophy of the subject as individual, without intrinsic sociohistorical mediation, where one's relation to the other as an individual "is ultimately prior to his ontological relation to himself (egology) or to the totality of things that we call the world (cosmology)."[42] The individualist subjectivism of modern philosophy is only abstractly negated, not concretely *aufgehoben.* Levinas's metaphysics remains infected by the very subjectivism it has not wholly overcome.

To be sure, his subject is not a completely solipsistic ego. He speaks of the interhuman and even calls such a relation "primary sociality."[43] This sociality, however, is just that, "primordial," "preontological," raised above all categorical historical relations, not the painfully concrete sociality of historical mediation. Distinguishing "ethics," which governs the relation of one subject to another, from "morality," which governs our social and political relations in history, Levinas considers ethics primary and morality derivative. History occurs only because there are, unfortunately, more than two people in the world. "If there were only two people in the world, there would be no need for lawcourts because I would always be responsible for and before the other."[44] Concrete history is only derivatively and secondarily constitutive of human existence; it is not a primordial existential of human being.

This ontological devaluation of history also leads to its ethical devaluation. In entering into the political world, which we cannot avoid doing, ethics "becomes morality and *hardens* its skin."[45] As soon as there are three, "we invariably pass from the ethical perspective of alterity to the ontological perspective of totality," and "the ethical relationship with the other becomes political and enters into the totalizing discourse of ontology."[46] At best, history is a necessary evil, a paradoxical necessity, a degeneration from the ethical, always a threat to the ethical integrity of the primordial sociality of the ego and the other. Levinas criticizes idealism for reducing the other to a concept and sees the completion of idealism in the reduction of ethics to politics, which reduces others to "moments in a system," absorbing all multiplicity and ending all discourse.[47] Politics reduces the human being to "the sum of his works," where the person remains interchangeable.[48] Thus, "politics left to itself bears a tyranny within itself."[49] No wonder, therefore, that Levinas defines politics as "the art of foreseeing war and of winning it by every means,"[50] as "the primal disrespect."[51] My "objective" existence in the state, in history, and in the totality "does not express me, but precisely dissimulates me."[52] History itself is our "original" or "primordial" sin. In philosophical mode Levinas repeats the early Barth's theological dialectic of pure negation between sin and grace.[53]

While, therefore, Levinas appropriately insists on the necessity of an ethical critique of politics at the "primordial" level "prior to any act,"[54] at the level of "that which stands *behind* practical morality," "the extraordinary relation between a man and his neighbor, a relation that continues to exist even when it is severely damaged,"[55] he also disclaims all concrete responsibility for political transformation. "As *prima philosophia,* ethics cannot itself legislate for society or produce rules of conduct whereby society might be revolutionized or transformed."[56] I think this means more than the banal claim that ethics as such, which has its own proper object within the scientific division of labor, cannot do the work of other disciplines such as politics, sociology, and jurisprudence. It conceals the radical claim that it does not *want* to dirty its hands by getting involved in the concrete process of political transformation. Its critique of history, therefore, remains an abstract, general critique: the world is not what it ought to be. Given the sharp, almost "Manichaean" dualism of ethics and history, one wonders why ethics should even bother with history to the point of criticizing it; after all, the world in any event *cannot* be what it ought to be. Ethics remains "always other than the 'ways of the world.'"[57]

The only answer Levinas could make, therefore, to his Latin American students who asked for actual examples of ethical praxis was, "Yes, indeed— here in this room," a reference to their conversation. Another example he cites is the commonplace gesture of saying "after you, sir" when passing through a door.[58] These acts of civility, of course, are not to be depreciated, but they also need deconstruction: they presuppose the tranquility of the academic setting and an interpersonal encounter separated from the raging or concealed tensions of the larger society. They prove utterly trivial and politically irrelevant when confronted with the bloody confrontations, say, between the Shining Path and the oppressive wealthy in Peru, between the New People's Army and the landed aristocracy in the Philippines, or between the angry African Americans and the local police in Mississippi in the 1960s. Such examples, the best Levinas could muster by way of historical hope, also only demonstrate the extent to which Levinas appreciates—or rather fails to appreciate—the intensity of historical conflicts.

Levinas's devaluation of history is seen not only in his devaluation of politics as such but also in his failure to appreciate the difference between the political and the interhuman as spheres of human existence, each with a distinctive moral requirement. The only distinction Levinas knows is the pejorative distinction between "the ethical perspective of alterity," which governs the face-to-face relationship of "one subjectivity to another,"[59] and "the ontological perspective of totality," where "morality" governs the political relationship among citizens, their social behavior and civic duty. He also reduces the political to the interhuman by trying to "found" political morality on "an ethical responsibility *towards* the other"[60] and then falling into political cynicism when such an attempt does not seem to work.

More fundamentally, Levinas fails to recognize a qualitative difference between the "public" world of politics and the "private" world of interpersonal relations, and tries to judge the former by the norms of the latter. Interhuman

relations are face-to-face relations between two individuals. Political relations, on the other hand, involve millions of people in their struggle to
establish social, not interhuman, conditions for living together, such as
institutions, laws, policies, and structures. These are, by nature, totalizing
and impersonal: they apply to all regardless of individual differences. These
conditions can be oppressive when they are imposed on the rest of society in
the interest of one group or class; they can also be liberating when they provide the basic economic, political, and cultural needs for all and come closer
to the ideal of the common good. To measure the "morality" of political
institutions by the "ethics" of interhuman relations, and then to fall into cynicism because politics will necessarily be found wanting, is to confuse the categories at best and at worst to remain indifferent to the suffering of millions
of others under so many oppressive structures in the world.

One would think that the compelling priority of the starving other is to
find food as such, not a face-to-face relationship with millions of people
whose taxes pay for the food. It would be more humane, of course, if the
other could also get the interpersonal care from as many people as possible.
But politics and interpersonal relations remain two different dimensions of
human existence: the public dimension of social interdependence for basic
conditions of life, and the private dimension of individual relations respectively. The one is not reducible to the other, and each has its own moral
requirement based on the respective structure of the two dimensions. Interpersonal "ethics" is not necessarily more compelling than political "morality."
In many instances, it may be just the reverse. Levinas's "politics of ethical difference," as Simon Critchley calls it, remains, despite claims to the contrary,
profoundly "apolitical."[61]

Levinas, therefore, is more interested in condemning the world for what it
is than in offering any historically relevant hope for becoming what it ought
to be, which he could not do precisely because the world, in his view, is fated
in any event to be what it is. The only solution he provides is "eschatological"
"thinking," learning how to "think otherwise than being," attempting to
secure isolated beachheads in the permanently occupied territories of ontological *consciousness,* and hoping thereby to effect a saving "breach" in the
otherwise permanently damned continuity of historical *reality.* Levinas's
metaphysical thinking is "critical" only in the sense of negation of ontology,
and of abstract negation at that—not in the concrete sense of unmasking the
historical origin of reified social phenomena, disclosing historical contradictions of a society and the potential of human liberation, and indicating
broad outlines of political praxis whereby those contradictions could be sublated into forms of liberation in a concrete negation of negation. Levinas

rejects all idealism because of its egolatry, but he too remains an idealist insofar as he seems to blame all the *actual* violence on the other in history on the
violent *thinking* of Western logocentric ontology, as though philosophers as
such had that much power to shape historical actuality.

In this regard, I believe that mutatis mutandis, Marx's critique of Bruno
Bauer and the "critical critiques" of his age, still retains its validity and relevance. The workers in the Manchester workshops, says Marx,

> do not believe that by "pure thinking" they will be able to argue away their
> industrial masters and their own practical debasement. They are most
> painfully aware of the *difference* between *being* and *thinking*, between *con-
> sciousness* and *life*. They know that property, capital, money, wage-labor,
> and the like are no ideal figments of the brain but very practical, very
> objective products of their self-estrangement, and that therefore they must
> be abolished in a practical, objective way for man to become man not only
> in *thinking*, in *consciousness*, but in *mass* being, in *life*. Critical criticism, on
> the contrary, teaches them that they cease in reality to be wage-workers if in
> thinking they abolish the thought of wage-labor; if in thinking they cease
> to regard themselves as wage-workers and, in accordance with that extrava-
> gant notion, no longer let themselves be paid for their person. As absolute
> idealists, as ethereal beings, they will then naturally be able to live on the
> ether of pure thought. Critical criticism teaches them that they abolish real
> capital by overcoming in *thinking* the category *capital*, that they *really*
> change and transform themselves into real human beings by changing their
> "abstract ego" in consciousness and scorning as an uncritical operation all
> real change of their real existence, of the real conditions of their existence,
> that is to say, of their real ego.[62]

The basic problem with Levinas, then, is the false dichotomy he poses
between ethical irreducibility and ontological, historical mediation, as though
mediation necessarily entailed reduction. In order to defend the irreducible
transcendence of the other in the ethical order, he feels compelled to deny all
mediation of the other in the ontological. No doubt mediating totality can
lead, and has led, to intellectual and political totalitarianism, and Levinas's
prophetic outcry in defense of the irreducible transcendence of the other serves
as an indispensable corrective against all totalitarian temptations. The result
of denying all mediation, however, is no less embarrassing. The other—ontologically isolated from, and raised above, all sociohistorical relations—is simply not a *human* other, to whom, therefore, neither the problem of murder

nor the salvation from it is relevant. Meanwhile, the other continues to be oppressed, without any hope of real liberation.

It is often said that Levinas is more a prophetic thinker than a systematic philosopher and that, as such, he could afford to be one-sided and passionate about the "one thing necessary" and forgo the responsibility of the systematic philosopher for completeness and balance.[63] My argument, thus far, has been that his "one-sided" concern for the infinity of the other to the exclusion of all historical mediation is too costly precisely for the other's own historical well-being, the one thing necessary.

Toward a Dialectic of Totality, Infinity, Solidarity

For all these criticisms Levinas's challenge remains. How restore the historical mediations of the other without *reducing* the ethical transcendence of the other? How engage in totalizing ontology without falling into oppressive totalitarianism? Or, rather, more accurately, can reason, dialectical reason, continue to engage in totalizing ontology at all after the shock of Levinas and deconstructionism? Is it possible for reason to sublate (*Aufheben*) itself into a thinking of the other in and through history, a thinking of infinity in and through totality?

Ever since Kierkegaard, "totality" has been an unremittingly bad word, especially among the existentialists, pragmatists, and deconstructionists. It has been a symbol of human hubris to be exorcised, the source of all intellectual and political imperialisms in the modern world. Without going into the thought of Hegel and Marx, the two thinkers of totality, I would like to offer the following brief reflections on totality, infinity, and the role of dialectical reason in the contemporary world.[64]

I begin with a fundamental agreement with Levinas. It is not possible to construct an ontology in the *absolute* sense of a comprehensive, exhaustive grasp of totality, holding all beings including God in the totality of their own intrinsic being and their mutual relations. Such an ontology is indeed reductionist and oppressive, as Levinas rightly insists. To all beings, especially human beings, and preeminently God, there is a certain interiority and transcendence that no finite human being can grasp, certainly not from without. This is true even of nature, an area in which Levinas was not particularly interested. All beings have their own subjectivity, interiority, and transcendence, which endows each with a certain "metaphysical" uniqueness by virtue of which "each being declines the concept and withstands totalization."[65] To grasp them as a totality theoretically would be to subordinate them to a system of human reason and deny them their interiority and transcendence. They are reduced to projections of a finite and ideologically tainted human reason, and such an ontology is readily abused as a theoretical weapon of an oppressive totalitarianism.[66]

However, an ontology in the sense of a *relative* grasp of totality is both possible and necessary. While denying the possibility of an exhaustive, final knowledge of all reality, a relative ontology would seek to grasp all reality as an at least externally interconnected and interdependent totality or system insofar as this totality is accessible to human reason. This would affirm the ultimate intelligibility of being in a relative way, and dare to explore the mystery of being ever more deeply on the basis of hope in that intelligibility. A relative totality provides the enabling horizon of finite reason. It limits itself to the external, interrelational aspects of being and recognizes thereby the ultimate otherness of being as such by appreciating the existence of a dimension of being irreducible to categories of human reason. An absolute totality is a product of indiscriminate, imperialist reason; a relative totality is a product of critical reason aware of its own limits.

A relative totality, however, is a product of critical reason not only aware of its own limits but also committed to its own historical responsibility. Looking for absolute totalities in history is both impossible and dangerous, but this does not mean leaving history alone with all its possibilities of oppression and liberation. The interest of human liberation and solidarity makes it increasingly compelling today to grasp economic, political, and cultural events, policies, and trends not in isolation but in their mutual relations, as a relative totality, and assess their respective total impacts on human well-being. The contemporary world is becoming intimately interdependent because of the globalization of capitalism, communication, and transportation, gradually but surely forming a single system of identity in economics, politics, and culture. In many instances, however, this system of identity is turning into an oppressive totality due to neoimperialism, neocolonialism, and the many contradictions among nations and classes. This is the central fact of our time that sets the fundamental limit and condition for contemporary life.[67] In such an oppressive totality, the transcendent dignity of hundreds of millions of others is being violated and most often simply "reduced." It is imperative, therefore, to grasp global capitalism as a totality, assess its systemic possibilities of oppression, and to explore the possibilities of constructing a liberating system of identity as the historical condition that would recognize and protect the dignity of others actually, not only ideally, thereby avoiding such violation and reduction.

To live in history is to subject oneself to economic, political, and cultural systems of identity or totalities. However different and other we are to one another, as long as we have to live in common social space with some degree of interdependence, we remain under the imperative of creating laws, economic structures, political systems, and cultural habits that would keep our interdependence from becoming an occasion and system of mutual exploitation. Maintaining such laws, structures, systems, and customs, however, necessarily entails subjecting and "reducing" ourselves to systems of identity. We cannot, while living in common political space, follow different laws, different currencies, or different administrative systems—one for Hispanics, another for blacks, a third for Anglos, a fourth for Asian Americans. A basic condition of living together in community is to establish a minimum system of identity.

Such a system of identity is not, as Levinas fears, intrinsically evil. It can be liberating or oppressive. The challenge of social life is precisely to create a liberating system of identity, which is also the meaning and task of "politics" in the classical, critical sense of the term. A system is liberating insofar as it provides the historical conditions for the solidarity of others in their transcendent dignity by creating a social order that concretely ensures basic human rights of all in economics, politics, and culture; that protects legitimate differences among constituent groups; and that promotes harmony and community among them. It is oppressive insofar as it violates the transcendent dignity of others by promoting social *dis*order or *anti*order that oppresses basic human rights, stifles legitimate differences, and alienates groups against one another. Our historical choice is not between accepting a system of identity and transcending it altogether. It is neither possible nor desirable to transcend it altogether because this would deny the basic sociality of human existence in history. Our choice is limited to either building a liberating system of identity or promoting an oppressive one.

What we need for this purpose is neither "transcendental" reason, interested only in the a priori, transcendental conditions of knowledge but indifferent to the historical conditions of praxis; nor "empirical" reason, only interested in the investigation of minute regions of reality but utterly negligent of the larger interconnections of things in their historical processes. Again, we need something different both from "existential" reason, only interested in the ultimate problems of the individual in isolation from the historical conditions of individual existence; and from the "*anti*reason" of Levinas and Barth, which regards history itself as original sin and insists only on eschatological thinking.

The urgent intellectual need of our time is rather a reason capable of grasping the world as a "concrete totality" of differentiated moments in the process of change, and grasping this totality not from a neutral point of view but precisely from the perspective of liberation, sensitive to the possibilities of oppression and liberation in every social change, and ready to promote the concrete praxis of liberation. That is, we need dialectical reason. As finite reason, dialectical reason guards itself against the temptation to pursue absolute totalities. As responsible reason, however, it does not escape from history by rising above the critique of oppressive historical systems of identity altogether, or engaging only in a negative critique of history as such. Its overriding concern remains that of building liberating systems as relative totalities. The difficult task and burden of dialectical reason today is precisely to live this tension of finitude and responsibility, of committing itself to history yet without falling into totalitarianism, of avoiding transcendental irresponsibility yet without committing the horrors of political fanaticism.

Human existence means interdependence among others, each with a dignity ethically transcendent and irreducible to egocentric categories; it means solidarity of others, as Levinas duly insists. It depends on the triple dialectic of totality, infinity, and solidarity. Authentic existence becomes historically actual only through a totality, a system of identity that provides the economic, political, and cultural conditions of infinity and solidarity. Without a liberating totality, infinity remains merely ideal and exhausts itself in unrelieved negation. Without it, solidarity too becomes mere talk of "community" and lapses into an ideology. Our existence also depends on infinity, which alone provides both moral encouragement for positive political praxis and moral critique for oppressive politics. Without infinity, totality indeed becomes totalitarian, and solidarity mere collectivism. Our existence likewise depends on solidarity, the conscious recognition and praxis of our mutual dependence for both the appreciation of our respective ethical infinity and the establishment of a liberating totality. Without solidarity, infinity becomes egoism absolutized, and totality a war of all against all.

Authentic human existence thus depends on the triple dialectic of totality as the actualizing principle, infinity as the idealizing principle, and solidarity as the socializing principle. Only through this dialectic can the Levinasian eschatological community of radical others become a possibility. The great challenge of human existence is to constructively maintain the tension and dialectic between totality, infinity, and solidarity; and between history, transcendence, and sociality; and create, through a politics of solidarity, totalities that liberate us for our mutual infinity. It is precisely the task of dialectical reason to illumine and promote such a politics.

Notes

1. For recent works of general introduction to the thought of Emmanuel Levinas, see John Llewelyn, *Emmanuel Levinas: The Genealogy of Ethics* (London: Routledge, 1995); and Colin Davis, *Levinas: An Introduction* (Notre Dame, Ind.: University of Notre Dame Press, 1996). Levinas's conversations with Philippe Nemo in Emmanuel Levinas, *Ethics and Infinity* (trans. Richard A. Cohen; Pittsburgh: Duquesne University Press, 1985), is a readable introduction to his thought in his own words. Sean Hand's editorial "Introduction" in *The Levinas Reader* (Oxford: Blackwell, 1989), 1–8, is also a brief but fine summary of Levinas's thought.

2. Albert Camus, *The Rebel: An Essay on Man in Revolt* (trans. Anthony Bower; New York: Knopf, 1956), 3.

3. Emmanuel Levinas, "The Trace of the Other," in *Deconstruction in Context: Literature and Philosophy* (ed. Mark C. Taylor; Chicago: University of Chicago Press, 1986), 346.

4. Emmanuel Levinas, *Totality and Infinity: An Essay on Exteriority* (Pittsburgh: Duquesne University Press, 1969), 44, 46, and 22, respectively.

5. Ibid., 22–23.

6. Ibid., 23.

7. Ibid., 23; and *Ethics,* 86.

8. Levinas, *Totality,* 24.

9. Ibid., 195, 25, and 27, respectively.

10. Robert Bernasconi and David Wood, eds., *The Provocation of Levinas: Rethinking the Other* (London: Routledge, 1988), 168.

11. Levinas, *Totality,* 194 and 70–71, respectively.

12. Ibid., 69.

13. Ibid., 194.

14. For a classic critique of Levinas's primacy of metaphysics over ontology, see Jacques Derrida, *Writing and Difference* (trans. Alan Bass; Chicago: University of Chicago Press, 1978), 134–52: "Of Ontological Violence."

15. Levinas, *Totality,* 200; also 72, 86, 195.

16. Ibid., 201.

17. Hand, *Reader,* 86, 28, and 84, respectively.

18. Levinas, *Totality,* 208.

19. Ibid., 43, 48, 201, 216.

20. Ibid., 26.

21. Emmanuel Levinas, *Otherwise than Being or Beyond Essence* (trans. Alphonso Lingis; The Hague: Nijhoff, 1981), 99–129: "Substitution."

22. Richard A. Cohen, ed., *Face to Face with Levinas* (Albany: State University of New York Press, 1986), 27. For Levinas's critique of Heidegger and Sartre, see *Face to Face,* 14–17. For nuanced comparisons of Levinas and Heidegger, see David Boothroyd, "Responding to Levinas," in *Provocation* (ed. Bernasconi), 15–31; on Levinas and Sartre, see Christina Howells, "Sartre and Levinas," in ibid., 91–99.

23. Levinas, *Ethics,* 98; idem, *Totality,* 297; Hand, *Reader,* 72–74, and Cohen, *Face to Face,* 31. For a discussion of Levinas's relation to Buber, see Robert Bernasconi, "'Failure of Communication' as a Surplus: Dialogue and Lack of Dialogue between Buber and Levinas," in Bernasconi, *Provocation,* 100–135.

24. Levinas, *Ethics,* 98; Hand, *Reader,* 182; Cohen, *Face to Face,* 31.

25. Levinas, *Totality,* 102–5, 195.

26. Ibid., 80.

27. Ibid., 180, 195.

28. Ibid., 40, 52, 214.

29. Ibid., 214.

30. Ibid., 251.

31. Ibid., 220–21.

32. Ibid., 295; also 293.

33. Emmanuel Levinas, *Existence and Existents* (trans. Alphonso Lingis; Dordrecht: Kluwer Academic Publishers, 1988), 95.

34. This is from the book title: Alphonso Lingis, *The Community of Those Who Have Nothing in Common* (Bloomington: Indiana University Press, 1994).

35. Levinas, *Totality,* 199; idem, *Ethics,* 89.

36. Cohen, *Face to Face,* 31. For a brief exposition of Levinas's views of religion, see Davis, *Levinas,* 93–119.

37. All quotations are from Levinas, *Totality,* 104–5.

38. Ibid., 69.

39. Ibid., 242.

40. Ibid., 82–90.

41. For my critique of Kierkegaard and Kant in this regard, see my essay, "Dialectic of Salvation in Solidarity: Philosophy of Religion after Kant and Kierkegaard," in *Kant and Kierkegaard on Religion* (ed. D. Z. Philips and Timothy Tessin; New York: St. Martin's, 2000), 278–94.

42. Cohen, *Face to Face,* 21.

43. Levinas, *Totality,* 304.

44. Cohen, *Face to Face,* 21; also Levinas, *Otherwise,* 157ff.

45. Cohen, *Face to Face,* 30 (emphasis added).

46. Ibid., 21–22.

47. Levinas, *Totality,* 216–17.

48. Ibid., 298.

49. Ibid., 300.

50. Ibid., 21.

51. Ibid., 298.

52. Ibid., 178.

53. In light of what has been said, Levinas's admission that "we must use the ontological *for the sake of the Other*" (Cohen, *Face to Face,* 28) sounds rather grudging and hollow, as does his claim that his moral utopianism does not prevent us from recognizing the relative progress that can be made in the morality of politics; see Bernasconi, *Provocation,* 178. Theodore de Boer's defense of Levinas against the charge that he is paying too little attention to social structures is likewise feeble and beside the point; de Boer, "An Ethical Transcendental Philosophy," in Cohen, *Face to Face,* 102–3.

54. Hand, *Reader,* 290.

55. Ibid., 247 (emphasis added).

56. Cohen, *Face to Face,* 29. Similarly, to the question of whether his discourse is "deficient in concern with concrete reality," Levinas responds: "I am neither a preacher nor the son of a preacher, and it is not my purpose to moralize or to improve the conduct of our generation" (Hand, *Reader,* 247).

57. Cohen, *Face to Face,* 32.

58. Ibid., 32–33.

59. Ibid., 29.

60. Ibid.

61. Simon Critchley, *The Ethics of Deconstruction: Derrida and Levinas* (Oxford: Blackwell, 1992), 219–25.

62. Karl Marx, *The Holy Family, or Critique of Critical Criticism* (Moscow: Progress Publishers, 1975), 63.

63. Stephan Strasser, *Jenseits von Sein und Zeit: Eine Einfuhrung in Emmanuel Levinas' Philosophie* (The Hague: Nijhoff, 1978), 370–73.

64. For an account, rather pessimistic, of the concept of totality since Georg Lukacs, see Martin Jay, *Marxism and Totality* (Berkeley: University of California Press, 1984).

65. Levinas, *Totality,* 57.

66. For a trenchant critique of universalist logocentrism, see Raimundo Panikkar, "The Invisible Harmony: A Universal Theory of Religion or a Cosmic Confidence in Reality?" in *Toward a Universal Theology of Religion* (ed. Leonard Swidler; Maryknoll, N.Y.: Orbis, 1987), 119–24.

67. For analyses of global capitalism and its trends and contradictions, see Richard J. Barnett and John Cavanagh, *Global Dreams: Imperial Corporations and the New World Order* (New York: Simon & Schuster, 1995); Robert N. Bellah, "Changing Themes in Society: Implications for Human Services: Social Change and the Fate of Human Services" (speech to Lutheran Social Services, San Francisco, Apr. 28, 1995); Robert Gilpin, *The Political Economy of International Relations* (Princeton, N.J.: Princeton University Press, 1987), 364–408; Paul Kennedy, *Preparing for the Twenty-First Century* (New York: Random House, 1993), 329–49; the whole issue of *The Nation* 263, no. 2 (July 15/22, 1996); William Pfaff, *The Wrath of Nations: Civilization and the Furies of Nationalism* (New York: Simon & Schuster, 1993); Robert Wuthnow, *Christianity in the Twenty-First Century: Reflections on the Challenges Ahead* (New York: Oxford University Press, 1993).

TWO

THE OTHER WITHOUT HISTORY AND SOCIETY
A Dialogue with Derrida

The specter of Derrida has been haunting the Western intellectual world for some three decades now. His message has been getting across. Totalities tend to totalize and oppress. Identities tend to exclude and marginalize. Dogmas dogmatize, and systems produce closure. Messianic claims spill blood. Fundamentalist claims to certainty and definitiveness create hell on earth. Hence, the need to subvert totalities, disrupt the same, complicate simplicities, problematize the complacent, contaminate the pure, and destabilize all systems and fundamentalisms—by exposing them to the shock of alterity, the demand of the other, the trauma of the unexpected. That is, to deconstruct. Deconstruction is "the delimitation of totalization in all its forms,"[1] the thought of "an absolute heterogeneity that unsettles all the assurances of the same within which we comfortably ensconce ourselves."[2]

Derrida on Negative Theology and the Messianic

In the area of religion Derrida's deconstruction has been most challenging in his treatments of negative theology and the messianic, the first showing what God should not be, the second what God should be without being.

Derrida discerns two different voices in negative theology. The first voice is hyperousiology. Even though negative theology denies the possibility of attributing names to God and places God beyond all names, it does not stop at negation but affirms God precisely in God's hyperessential reality. It is a higher, more refined modalization of ontotheology, a variation on the metaphysics of presence.[3] For all its negations, it claims deep down to "know" what God is. The God of negative theology, in fact, turns out to be "a transcendental signified, the dream of being without *differance,* of being outside the text, outside the general text, outside the play of traces."[4] Negative theology feels as secure in its possession of an object as positive theology; it is a triumph of presence over representation.[5]

There is, however, another voice in negative theology. As an irruption from the depth, it expresses a yearning, a movement, a passion for the wholly other of which we all dream and by which we feel addressed, a deeply affirmative desire for "something always essentially other than the prevailing regime of presence, something *tout autre.*"[6] It embodies a passion for the impossible, a movement of transgression over and beyond the present, a response to a primordial promise. It embodies the spirit of relentless critical negation in pursuit of an ultimate that always remains wholly other, a kind of a generalized apophatics, a "kenosis of discourse."[7] Everything must pass through "the aporias of negative theology," and only a discourse "contaminated" by negative theology can be trusted.[8]

What does deconstruction do for negative theology? Deconstruction does not provide a secure foundation or a horizon for the intelligibility of the content of negative theology. Instead, by reinscribing or resituating negative theology within the general movement of the trace, *differance,* and undecidability; within all the multiplicities and ambiguities of language and history, the basic situation of all human experience, according to Derrida—by such action deconstruction preserves faith as faith, as something "blind," without the privilege of *savoir, avoir,* and *voir,* both accentuating the passion of faith as faith struggles to take a leap and decide for the impossible in the midst of the very undecidability that constitutes its very structure; and also maintaining faith as an indeterminate, open-ended groping and hope in the wholly other. *Differance* precludes the possibility of knowledge, vision, or face-to-face union with God, since it always recontextualizes faith, exposing it to indefinite substitutions, translations, and interpretations. Ontotheology takes faith as a mode of presence outside the movement of *differance* and the play of traces and turns it into something secure, positive, and closed, thus generating the pernicious dangers of absolutism and triumphalism inherent in all fundamentalisms and all "determinable" faiths. "Closure spells trouble, . . . closure spells exclusion, exclusiveness; closure spills blood, doctrinal, confessional, theological, political, institutional blood, and eventually, it never fails, real blood."[9]

For Derrida, religion is a response to the call and demand of the wholly other, an invocation or prayer ("come!") for its advent, and the messianic praxis of justice here and now corresponding to that invocation and demand.

The "object" or "God" of this religion remains the "wholly other," resisting all reduction to a human concept, category, or horizon. It lies beyond all human imagination, credibility, graspability, or determinability; beyond all human logos, teleological, eschatological, and otherwise. In contrast to the God of ontotheology, who remains "infinitely and eternally the Same"[10] and in fact "the name of indifference itself,"[11] the God of deconstruction is "the name of *the* impossible, of novelty, of the coming of the Other, of the *tout autre,* of what is coming with the shock of an absolute surprise, with the trauma of absolute heterogeneity. Cast in a deconstructive slant, God is not the possible but the impossible, not the eternal but the futural."[12] There is no transcendental horizon within which God can be awaited, expected, or made knowable; God shatters all human horizons.

Derrida is especially insistent that the wholly other is beyond all determination or determinacy. A determinable future, with a determinable telos, is a future that can be anticipated within the horizon of a particular aim, of what is possible, and thus a future as present. Presence, possibility, determinacy: these are, for Derrida, one and the same. The future of the wholly other is an "absolute" future: a future *ab*solved from the regime and horizon of presence and identity, from whatever is presentable, programmable, imaginable, foreseeable; and beyond the traditional dualisms of essence and existence, universal and particular, ideal and real. The wholly other is "structurally" and therefore "always" to come. It is precisely the function of the wholly other to shatter and shock the horizon of the same and foreseeable and open up the promise and possibility of something wholly other. The wholly other is identifiable with neither a determinable faith nor a determinable messiah nor a determinable end of history nor a determinable degree of justice. It is also to be distinguished from any utopian or Kantian regulative ideal, which also has its own determinate content. The wholly other is simply the beyond, the *au-delà.* It is impossible to measure the extent to which the wholly other is being approximated or realized in a society.[13]

Religion addresses its prayer, its "come!" to this wholly other in response to the latter's solicitation and demand. "To call upon God, to call God's name, to pray and weep and have a passion for God, is to call for the *tout autre,* for something that breaks up the ho-hum homogeneity of the same and all but knocks us dead. The name of God is a name that calls for the other, that calls from the other, the name that the other calls, that calls upon us like Elijah at the door, and that calls for things new."[14] The invocation is a primordial affirmation based on the faith and hope that the impossible will be possible, the impossibility of a saving breach in the chain of presence and totality, of a liberating breakthrough in the oppressive horizon of the same, of the messianic emergence of the *novum* beyond all human expectations and calculations. "Outside all human mastery and control *viens* hopes for a break within the interstices of the laws of regularity, an outbreak of chance within the crevices of the continuous flow of presence." It "silently tears open lived time and ordinary language," renders them always already structurally open to what is coming," and "prohibits (*pas!*) closure while soliciting transcendence (*le pas*)."[15] It is "the order, or disorder, of messianic time, of *venir* and *avenir,* that disturbs the order of presence."[16] This messianic invocation of the wholly other embodies "a certain structural wakefulness or openness to an impossible breach of the present, shattering the conditions of possibility, by which we are presently circumscribed."[17]

For Derrida, *tout autre est tout autre.* The wholly other is every other. The wholly other is not only God but also every human being. As Levinas says, "infinite alterity" or "absolute singularity" belongs to both God and human beings. For Derrida, this invalidates both the Kierkegaardian distinction between the ethical (the finite relationship to the finite) and the religious (the infinite relationship to the infinite), and the Levinasian distinction between ethics and religion.[18] Religion is not separable from ethics nor, for that matter, from political and legal matters. Wherever infinite alterity is at issue, there is religion. This is why the hope in the wholly other is also a messianic hope for a "universal culture of singularities"[19] in which justice will be done to the other in its irreducible singularity.

Messianic time interrupts the living present with the demand for justice. Messianic time is prophetic time, the time of justice that is always to come yet issues a call for justice here and now. Justice deferred is justice denied. Deconstruction "is not meant to be a soft sighing for the future, but a way of deciding now and being impassioned in the moment."[20] *Différance* "does not mean only deferral, delay, and procrastination, but the spacing out, the extension between memory and promise or *à-venir,* which opens up the here-now in all of its urgency and absolute singularity, in the imminence of the instant. The call of what is coming calls for action now."[21] Justice does not tolerate present injustice in the name of a gradual approximation of an ideal but demands justice here and now. It is by definition "impatient, uncompromising, and unconditional. No différance without alterity, no alterity without singularity, no singularity without here-now."[22]

The freedom of the wholly other from all determinate contents makes Derrida's religion "a messianism without religion, . . . even a messianic without messianism,"[23] a faith without dogma, a religion without religion. It is a commitment to the wholly other in all its nominalist freedom and absolute heterogeneity without an equal commitment to the determinate content of a particular religion, dogma, institution, or program. Such a commitment to determinacy, for Derrida, entails totalitarian reduction of the other to the same and generates violence and war.[24] The "call for a fixed and identifiable other, foreseeable and foregraspable, . . . would release the manic aggression of a program, the mania of an all-out rush for a future-present."[25] Thus, deconstruction "keeps a safe distance from ever letting its faith be a faith in a determinate thing or person, from ever contracting the *tout autre* within the horizons of the same."[26] The invocation for the coming of the other is an apocalyptic prayer for the advent of messianic time, but it is an apocalypse without (determinate) vision, truth, or revelation, an apocalypse without apocalypse.

This description of Derridean religion should also make clear the minimal character of its content. The heart of that religion lies in its messianicity or its prophetic passion for justice, "the infinite respect of the singularity *and* infinite alterity of the other."[27] This is where religion and deconstruction converge. It is the very nature of messianicity, however, to shatter all determinate horizons with their determinate contents and thus to exclude all determinate, particular, historical religions and messianisms. Derrida's messianic hope and promise always remain "absolutely undetermined" and "eschatological."[28] To endorse a determinate religion is to spell closure and to spill blood. It is important to purify the messianic of all determinate contents by *epoche* and abstraction so as to intensify its urgency. But this also amounts to "desertification" or rendering of religion into a dry and barren desert, deprived of its specific comforts and intelligibilities and reduced to a universal, formal structure with a minimal content. It is "the messianic in general, as a thinking of the other and of the event to come,"[29] "the opening to the future or to the coming of the other as the advent of justice. But it also is without horizon of expectation and without prophetic prefiguration,"[30] a primordial idea of justice and democracy to come—to be distinguished from any of their current conceptions—as the irreducible and undeconstructible ultimate.

In this way, Derrida reduces religion to the bare minimum of an atheological, open-ended, negative, or apophatic process of justice, a movement toward a New International as "a community without community"[31] or "the friendship of an alliance without institution."[32] Particular religions are nourished by their "place," their history, tradition, nation, language, and people, and generate the "politics of place and the wars over place."[33] Derrida seeks to liberate the messianic of universal justice from such politics and wars by turning it into a desert, "a kind of placeless, displacing place—or a place for the displaced,"[34] a postgeographical, universal religion, a "religion for all and everywhere,"[35] a Derridean equivalent of the Kantian "religion within the limits of reason alone," although reason is never without faith.

Historical Relevance of Deconstruction

Living together with those who are different, especially with respect for their difference, has always been a central problem of human history. Individually and collectively, our instinct has been to subjugate them to our system of identity, which makes no room for their difference, and to reduce and violate them in their integrity as other. This occurs at all levels of human existence, individual and social; in all spheres of society, economics, politics, and culture; and with consequences in all areas of philosophy, ontology, epistemology, ethics, aesthetics, and philosophy of religion. What Emmanuel Levinas calls the "horror of the other"[36] and its correlative, the terror of the same, have been as pervasive, as destructive, and as compelling as any original sin in human history. The two global wars of the twentieth century; the many regional and local conflicts from the Korean War to Afghanistan; the countless racist, ethnic, and religious strifes from the Jewish holocaust to South African apartheid and racism in the United States to the bloody struggles between Jews and Arabs in Palestine; and the growing recognition of the sexist violation of women throughout human history—all of these have deepened our awareness, and intensified the urgency, of the problem of the other in our past century. At the turn of the twenty-first century most societies also increasingly face the problem of living together under conditions of religious and cultural plurality. Global capitalism has been bringing together different cultures and making them interdependent, relativizing all cultural absolutes, forcing the problem of the other on all, and imposing the political imperative of dialogue.

Given these historical urgencies, it is no exaggeration to say that today we cannot live without a heavy dose of what deconstruction stands for, its critique of the terror of the same in all its forms, and its vision of justice and democracy. All modern philosophies have been critical of the given, from Descartes through Kant, Hegel, and Marx, to pragmatism and critical theory. Deconstruction has few peers, however, in the single-mindedness of its attention to the problem of the other, in its universalization of that problem, and in the radicality with which it subverts all traditional ideologies from Plato to Heidegger. To enter the world of deconstruction is to enter a world without absolute principles, horizons, foundations, and centers from which to judge the other; to reinscribe or resituate all our beliefs within the general movement of *differance* that renders all identities heterogeneous and defers all presences to the play of traces; and to live accordingly, without nostalgia for absolute certainties but also with respect for difference and always with hope—in the case of messianic postmodernism—in the coming of the absolutely other. Nothing can boast of pure identity, nothing can insist on pure presence: all reality is marked by differentiation and deferral. In an age that has suffered so much from the terror of the same, at a time when a pluralist sensibility is de rigueur for survival and peace on earth, in a world where the "sacrifice of Isaac continues every day"[37]—in such a setting deconstruction should remain, even for those of us who do not accept it, a thorn in our side, a perpetual reminder of the dangers into which monocentrism can plunge the world, keeping us in a state of "vigilant insomnia" (Levinas)[38] for the cry of the other.

In this spirit, much of Derrida's philosophy of religion deserves and demands attentive and respectful meditation. His deconstruction of negative theology and determinate religions, his description of the messianic as the wholly other, his refusal to separate religion and politics, messianicity and justice—these are important antidotes against the terror of the same lurking in religion, in its claim to closure, its dogmatism, its fundamentalism, its totalitarianism. Left to themselves, religions, including believing philosophers and theologians, delude themselves into thinking that they "know" who God is, with only a lip service to the classical thesis of the "incomprehensibility" of God. Augustine's question, which is also Derrida's, remains and should remain compelling in its very challenge: What exactly is it that I love when I love my God? In this regard, Caputo is quite right in locating the specific contribution of deconstruction in providing for the religious believer "a saving apophatics, a certain salutary purgation of the positivity of belief, which reminds us all that we do not know what is coming, what is *tout autre*."[39] A periodic "contamination" of religion with negative theology should be a wholesome exercise that would also challenge each religion to transcend its determinacy and probe its own messianic depth for the impossible possibility of the wholly other.

What can we say about Derrida's "religion without religion"? Derrida's religion is deliberately minimal in its content. It consists in an existential commitment to the impossible possibility of the absolutely other; in a prayerful invocation for the advent of the wholly other beyond all human reason, calculation, and imagination; and in the praxis of justice in response to the call and demand of that other. It is a deliberate, extreme abstraction from the content of all determinate and determinable religions; their dogmas, rituals, and institutions; and therefore also an intellectual and emotional desert without the nourishing comforts of tradition and community. It places itself beyond the distinctions of theism and atheism, religion and secularism, as different therefore from the atheism of Enlightenment rationalism as it is from traditional religious faith. One could say that it is the "logical" expression of the faith of the modern Western intellectual who has been thoroughly alienated from all institutional religions as well as from all traditional rationalities, yet who cannot simply surrender themselves to sheer, destructive nihilism and irresponsible relativism. Even in thorough alienation and utter blindness, one still hopes and gropes, beyond all reason and faith, for the possibility of the impossible, for something ultimate and undeconstructible, the advent of messianic justice, without quite knowing what to call it. It is "a search without hope for hope," "in a space where the prophets are not far away."[40] Derrida's religion is perhaps the last refuge of the Western intellectual elite committed to both the protest of modern atheism and the Blochian spirit of utopian hope.

I do not say this in disparagement. The cultural situation Derrida depicts is not fictional. It is a situation that has been facing Western intellectuals for some time and that is now increasingly facing intellectuals in the rest of the world as well. It is no wonder that Christian theology has likewise been trying to cope precisely with that situation in some of its representatives such as Paul Tillich and Karl Rahner. Tillich deconstructs traditional faith into "absolute faith," which is not faith in a determinate object but a state of being grasped by the power of being-itself, which in turn is neither personal nor pantheistic but goes beyond both, which can only be called "the God above God."[41] Rahner's increasingly negative reference to God as "absolute," "incomprehensible mystery," and "absolute future" is likewise an attempt to make Christianity credible in the present intellectual climate. Serving the same purpose is his minimalist, existential definition of the Christian content as the commitment that "we are ineluctably engaged by the incomprehensible mystery whom we call God, and who ceaselessly and silently grasps us and challenges our hope and love even when we show little concern for him in the practice of our lives or even actually deny him in theory."[42]

The Other without History and Society

This is also, however, precisely where the issue lies. Neither Tillich nor Rahner goes on to propose, as does Derrida, an extreme abstraction from the concrete content of determinate Christian faith. They may try to criticize and sublate the determinate historical content of Christian faith into something more credible and relevant through existential or transcendental hermeneutic; it is not their intention to do away with the essential mediation of faith by determinate historical contents and produce a "religion without religion," which Derrida does. Granted that we cannot live *without* deconstruction today; granted that we have to reinscribe religion and politics within the general movement of *differance*; can we, however, live *on* deconstruction alone? I do not think we can. The very strength of deconstruction, the radicality of its negations, may also be its very weakness.

Let me begin with Derrida's depreciation of determinate religion. Derrida has nothing but aversion for concrete, determinate religions with their historical content. They are simply identified with reification and closure and as so many sources of absolutism, triumphalism, and bloody conflicts. It is not that *some* determinate religions are triumphalistic or that all determinate religions *sometimes* generate triumphalism and absolutism; it is rather that the very idea of determination or determinability entails presence, identity, and the imperialism of the same. Even though Derrida himself derives his concept of the messianic from existing, determinate Jewish and Christian eschatologies by bending and repeating them "with a difference"; and even though Caputo himself admits that Derrida's own messianic religion has all the marks of a determinate religion and can survive only with the support of determinate, institutionalized messianic eschatologies;[43] still, determinate religions remain only "consummately dangerous,"[44] with no positive virtues to show. As a nonessentialist Derrida may not say, but as he does imply, *pace* Caputo, "theology or religion always and essentially means bad news, the *ancien regime,* a reactionary, world-negating, and fear-driven pathology."[45]

This means two things. On the one hand, the wholly other of messianicity cannot and *should not* become actual and concrete through incarnation in a determinate religion. The only relation between messianicity and determinate messianic religions is one of relentless negation, period. The messianic is *not* what a determinate religion is. The messianic is nowhere embodied because it is not in principle embodiable. It is not only that the messianic always transcends any of its concretizing historical mediations, but also that it should *not* be so mediated because such mediation necessarily involves a fall, a corruption. On the other hand, it also means that determinate historical religions have no positive mediating function to provide precisely in the service of the messianic, the wholly other in terms of nourishing faith and praxis. As modes of frozen presence and identity, determinate religions have no principle of self-transcendence, self-criticism, and self-reform within themselves; there are no resources of a dialectic between the present and the future, the determinate and the determining in historical religions. Between the wholly other and historical religions there is no mediation, only radical otherness.

Derrida's own religion without religion, therefore, can remain pure and holy only because it is nowhere embodied or institutionalized in a determinate religion. It engages in deconstruction of *all* determinate religions from the transcendent height of pure, disembodied, angelic ideality, just as Enlightenment rationalism has been engaging in the critical dismissal of all religions from the self-legitimating height of pure, uninstitutionalized, ahistorical reason. Instead of advising concrete religions, therefore, on how to bear better witness to the wholly other under the conditions of history and necessary institutionalization, it simply says no! indiscriminately to all determinate religions regardless of their differences in the degree and kind of witnessing they do. It is a yes! to the messianic but a no! to all historical attempts to embody it. Derrida's messianic reservation, like the Christian eschatological proviso, is more interested in condemning religions for what in any event they *cannot* do, that is, achieve a perfect realization of the messianic on earth, than in empowering them to do what they *can,* that is, bear a more effective witness to the messianic even if no witnessing will ever measure up to the full demand of the messianic. Derrida's religion without religion remains an ahistorical abstraction.

The messianic wholly other impinges on our history, therefore, only in the mode of interruption, disruption, discontinuity, surprise, and opposition; and only in the experience of the impossible, unimaginable, unforeseeable, and unprogrammable. What we can do by our own power and with our own foresight and planning and what we experience within the realm of the possible and the foreseeable, within what Derrida calls, with sweeping generality, the horizon of the same—these have no messianic or religious significance. That is to say, our moral and political actions in history have no religious weight because we undertake most of them with our own responsibility, with our own knowledge of what is possible and what is not, and with our own freedom to risk the unknown but always with caution and prudence. The ancient dualism of body and soul returns in the guise of a new opposition of what is determinate and what is indeterminate, what is possible and what is impossible, what is foreseeable and what is unforeseeable. We encounter the God of deconstruction only as a matter of "absolute surprise."

What Derrida says about determinate religions also applies to determinate political praxis. The messianic as such—the "universal culture of singularities," or justice and democracy—are "structurally" and therefore "always" to come and should not be identified with any determinate present form of law or political structure. Although the perfection of the messianic lies in the "absolute" future, not in a future that can become present, its demand is for justice "here and now." The messianic provides the light in which all present forms of justice and democracy, however perfect, will be judged and challenged to transcend themselves. Messianic politics lies in the hope for "an impossible breach of the present, shattering the conditions of possibility by which we are presently circumscribed."[46]

The messianic rhetoric of "shattering," "new," "unforeseeable," creates the impression of a "radical" politics as appropriate praxis for the messianic hope deconstruction constantly evokes. When it comes to political praxis, however, it is anything but radical. Deconstructive politics involves operating *within* the conventions and rules of the prevailing order—there is no other place to operate—"bending" and "repeating" them "with a difference," and "twisting free of the same, altering it just enough to let a little alterity loose," which is different from "straightforward opposition, confrontational countering, which succumbs to dialectical assimilation."[47] Furthermore, we "can only prepare for the incoming of the other, but we cannot invent it, cannot effect it, bring it about, by a cunning deconstructive agency. We are called upon, paradoxically, to prepare for the incalculable, to prepare without calculating in advance." The "only" concern of deconstruction is the time to come: "allowing the adventure or the event of the *tout autre* to come."[48]

Deconstructive political praxis, then, comes down to "hoping" for an impossible breach of the present, "bending" and "twisting free" of the present rules and conventions to "let a little alterity loose," and thus "preparing" for the coming of justice, which we cannot "calculate" or "program" or "control." It is opposed to "confrontational countering" because it would "succumb to dialectical assimilation." At best, we have a "politics of exodus, of the émigré," "a subversion of fixed assumptions and a privileging of disorder," or "responsible anarchy."[49] Just as deconstruction reduces religion to a minimal content, so it reduces politics to the passive minimum of hoping, bending a little, and waiting. There is no substantive, systematic reflection on the dynamics and trends of contemporary history, on the possibilities they contain for liberation and oppression, on prospects for political mobilization for the liberation of the oppressed and marginalized others that deconstruction seems so much to care for, nor on political structures that mediate between the messianic ideal always to come and present political praxis that will concretize for a society and for a time at least the demand of the messianic.

This is not accidental. Politics in the classical sense presupposes that human beings can, collectively, as a community, acquire the knowledge of their historical situation and mobilize themselves to produce a political structure that will best embody their (prevailing) ideals of justice in that situation according to their knowledge. This is predicated on the faith and hope in the possibility of collective human action and collective human wisdom. This faith and hope have sometimes been vindicated by history: as witness the gradual, often uphill, but by historical standards, truly significant achievements in democratic institutions, while they have also sometimes been contradicted by history; as witness the many violations of human rights and the often incalculable suffering brought about by totalitarian regimes. We do not, however, have much choice here. It takes precisely collective action and collective wisdom to combat the terror of totalitarian oppression, as history has also amply demonstrated; the only alternative to the oppression by a totalitarian regime is to set up a democratic regime, not to do away with all regimes. In any event, classical politics presupposes this faith and hope in collective action and collective wisdom.

It is precisely this faith that Derrida lacks, as is evident in his "historical and political" investigation into the secret of responsibility in *The Gift of Death*.[50] Derrida defines duty or responsibility as a relation between a person in his or her "absolute singularity" and the other in his or her equally "absolute singularity."[51] This ethical relationship, however, immediately exposes me to the risk of absolute sacrifice because I cannot at the same time respond to the call of all the other others, an infinite number of them, who are also addressing an absolute appeal to me in their respective "infinite singularities." This is the paradox, scandal, and aporia of the concept of responsibility, which reveals the concept at its limit and finitude. As Derrida puts it,

> As soon as I enter into a relation with the other, with the gaze, look, request, love, command, or call of the other, I know that I can respond only by sacrificing ethics, that is, by sacrificing whatever obliges me to also respond, in the same way, in the same instant, to all the others. I offer a gift of death, I betray, I don't need to raise my knife over my son on Mount Moriah for that. Day and night, at every instant, on all the Mount Moriahs of this world, I am doing that, raising my knife over what I love and must love, over those to whom I owe absolute fidelity, incommensurably. Abraham is faithful to God only in his absolute treachery, in the betrayal of his own and of the uniqueness of each one of them, exemplified here in his only beloved son.[52]

Fulfilling an obligation to an other entails sacrificing and betraying all obligations to the other others, including those dying of starvation and sickness. Everyone is being sacrificed to everyone else in "this land of Moriah that is our habitat every second of everyday."[53] The aporia of responsibility is that there is no justification of sacrificing all these others, the "ethical or political generality."[54] Derrida asks, "How would you ever justify the fact that you sacrifice all the cats in the world to the cat that you feed at home every morning for years, whereas other cats die of hunger at every instant? Not to mention other people?"[55] In this sense, then, the sacrifice of Isaac, a beloved son, the infinite other to whom I owe an absolute duty, is "inscribed in the structure of our existence."[56] Likewise, behind the appearances of normality and legitimacy, of moral discourse and good conscience, society organizes and participates in the death and sickness of millions of children through the very structure of its market, mechanisms of its external debt, and other inequities. We allow the sacrifice of others in order to avoid being sacrificed ourselves.[57]

What, then, can one do about this ethical scandal? That Derrida provides no answer is perhaps indicative of the limits of his horizon. One can say that he provides no answer because "this land of Moriah" is "our very habitat," because such a scandal is "inscribed in the structure of our existence," about which, therefore, we cannot do anything. His interest is in accentuating the aporia of moral experience and complicating our moral simplicities, within the structural limits of our existence. Is such a sandal, however, really "inscribed in the structure of our existence"? Or does it point, rather, to the limits of Derrida's own deconstructionist horizon?

Derrida's horizon, as that of his two mentors, Kierkegaard and Levinas, is that of the individual in her "absolute" and "infinite" "singularity." As a moral agent, each of us is "infinitely other in its absolute singularity, inaccessible, solitary, transcendent, nonmanifest, originarily nonpresent to my ego."[58] From this perspective of the isolated individual, Derrida goes on to ask, What can *I* do, precisely *in my absolute singularity and isolation,* to avoid the suffering of millions of starving children and millions of cats other than mine, since I cannot respond "in the same way, in the same instant, to all the others"?[59] The answer, of course, has to be "not much." An individual as such cannot respond to all these moral appeals in the same way at the same time, nor does she have the resources to respond to many of them with any adequacy even if she has the time to respond. The assumption, however, is false.

Modern history amply demonstrates that in situations where what is at stake is the welfare of a large number of people serious enough to constitute the "public" interest or common good, the appropriate agent is not the isolated individual but the political community as such. Whenever our serious welfare is at stake and we cannot attend to that welfare as isolated individuals, we do so as united individuals, together, as a community. We cannot protect our security individually, so we do so as a community by instituting the police and the military as organs of the state. We cannot provide education for ourselves individually, so we do so as a community by establishing public education. We cannot guarantee minimum welfare for ourselves individually, so we do so as a community by making sure that the economy is adequately functioning through monetary, fiscal, and other policies; by establishing minimum wage laws; and by instituting social security for old age and times of sickness. This common or collective care for the common good is precisely what is meant by politics in the classical sense. What we cannot do individually, we do together, politically.[60]

If we change the horizon from that of the isolated individual to that of the political community, from the lone "I" to the "we," and ask not "What can I do *as an individual?*" but rather "What can *we* do *together?*" the moral aporia that Derrida weeps over need not be as great or as scandalous as he makes it out to be. We together, as various countries and private associations including the United Nations, have been alleviating the suffering of millions of starving and sick children. I as an individual do my part by paying my fair share of taxes and making my fair share of contributions, which will both hire and enable other individuals, relief workers and government agents, to provide the relief. If so many cats other than mine are suffering so as to constitute their relief a matter of the public interest, we can, through the government, organize such relief by setting up shelters for cats, as many communities are already doing. The fact that our existing political means are not adequate to outstanding needs is no argument against the political solution; it is an argument for improving it.

This "political" approach does not eliminate the moral aporia that so concerns Derrida. In some sense, given the existential limitations of the moral and material resources of humanity, such a moral aporia will indeed always remain. Such an aporia, however, can be exaggerated when it is approached only from the individual perspective, and can become ideologically pernicious when it is used as an argument for political fatalism and neglect of available political means. It is critical to remember how much humanity has achieved by working together, collectively, politically: elimination of hunger, illiteracy, and many forms of epidemic in many parts of the world is, by historical standards, an achievement too great and too noble to be merely humiliated by a misplaced messianic or eschatological proviso, although it is not great enough and often too ideologically tainted to justify moral complacency among us.

However, it is precisely this "political" horizon with its faith and hope in the possibility of collective action and collective wisdom that Derrida lacks. Derrida's emphasis on the "infinite singularity" of the individual and his deconstructionist distrust of totality, community, and unity for fear of "fusion"[61]—these do not provide confidence in the possibility of "collective" action: such an action is either too ridden with otherness and division to be genuinely collective or too totalitarian to respect the infinite alterity of the agents.[62] Derrida is more interested in unmasking hidden oppressions in a totality than in encouraging wholesome collective action. Likewise, his emphasis on the absolute transcendence of the messianic and its radical discontinuity with any determinable political structure or institution or law does not encourage mobilization of collective wisdom in the interest of a determinate reform or revolution as a historically appropriate institutionalization of messianic justice. Instead, Derrida is more interested in condemning current institutions for *not* being a perfect model of justice than in providing a vision of better institutions that they *can* become or judicious reflections on the *how* of the justice that must indeed be done here and now. As "infinite asymmetry of the relation to the other," as "incalculability of the gift and singularity of the an-economic ex-position to others,"[63] justice lies in principle "beyond" all right, calculation, commerce, beyond "juridical-moral rules, norms, or representations, within an inevitable totalizing horizon."[64] In this sense, it is difficult to disagree with Richard Bernstein when he accuses Derrida's idea of a "democracy to come" of being "an impotent, vague abstraction," or with Thomas McCarthy when he accuses Derrida of being more interested in destabilizing universalist structures than in reconstructing protective institutions for rights and dignity."[65]

William James once spoke of two attitudes toward truth and error. One attitude is that of the sceptic, who is driven by an obsessive fear of falling into error and does not want to believe in anything except on sufficient evidence. The other is the attitude of the pragmatist, who is more driven by the hope of finding truth than by the fear of falling into error and is therefore willing to risk even believing in error in order to find truth.[66] Deconstruction is more like the sceptic than the pragmatist. It is fundamentally fearful of all determinate embodiments of human sociality in history because of the terror of the same. It may offer prayers and tears for the coming of the wholly other and its messianic justice, but it does not want to dirty its hands by working at establishing determinate institutions of religion and politics. In the name of *differance* it flees, in neognostic fashion, from the historical determinacy of matter, body, senses, objectivity, and sociality; from the world of presence, identity, and totality; and takes refuge in the dream of the impossible. Perhaps deconstruction should inscribe itself in the quite possible dialectic of the determinable within history so as to keep its *differance* human, not angelic. Please remember: in human history all negations are *determinate* negations.

Notes

1. John D. Caputo, *The Prayers and Tears of Jacques Derrida: Religion without Religion* (Bloomington: Indiana University Press, 1997), 126.

2. Ibid., 5.

3. Jacques Derrida, *Margins of Philosophy* (trans. Alan Bass; Chicago: University of Chicago Press, 1982), 6; idem, *On the Name* (ed. Thomas Dutoit; trans. David Wood, John P. Leavey Jr., and Ian McLeod; Stanford, Calif.: Stanford University Press, 1995), 68; idem, "How to Avoid Speaking: Denials," in *Derrida and Negative Theology* (ed. Harold Coward and Toby Foshay; Albany, N.Y.: SUNY Press, 1992), 77–83.

4. Caputo, *Prayers,* 11.

5. Ibid., 6–7, 10–11.

6. Ibid., 28.

7. Derrida, *On the Name,* 50; Caputo, *Prayers,* 27–28.

8. Derrida, *On the Name,* 83, 69.

9. Caputo, *Prayers,* 6; also 11, 12, 47–48, 57, 63.

10. Ibid., 113.

11. Jacques Derrida, *Of Grammatology* (trans. Gayatri Chakravorty Spivak; corrected ed.; Baltimore: Johns Hopkins University Press, 1974), 71.

12. Caputo, *Prayers,* 113.

13. Ibid., 73–86, 118, 129.

14. Ibid., 113.

15. Ibid., 86.

16. Ibid., 86.

17. Ibid., 96.

18. Jacques Derrida, *The Gift of Death* (trans. David Wills; Chicago: University of Chicago Press, 1995), 83–84.

19. Caputo, *Prayers,* 155.

20. Ibid., 125.

21. Ibid., 124; see also Jacques Derrida, *The Specters of Marx* (trans. Peggy Kamuf; New York: Routledge, 1994), 31.

22. Derrida, *Specters of Marx,* 31.

23. Ibid., 59; Derrida, *Gift of Death,* 49; idem, "Faith and Knowledge: The Two Sources of 'Religion' at the Limits of Reason Alone," in *Religion* (ed. Jacques Derrida and Gianni Vattimo; Stanford, Calif.: Stanford University Press, 1998), 17–18.

24. Caputo, *Prayers,* 128.

25. Ibid., 99.

26. Ibid., 150.

27. Derrida, *Specters of Marx,* 65.

28. Ibid., 65.

29. Caputo, *Prayers,* 128.

30. Derrida, "Faith and Knowledge," 17.

31. Caputo, *Prayers,* 131.

32. Derrida, *Specters of Marx,* 86.

33. Caputo, *Prayers,* 154.

34. Ibid., 154.

35. Ibid., 155.

36. Emmanuel Levinas, "The Trace of the Other," in *Deconstruction in Context: Literature and Philosophy* (ed. Mark C. Taylor; Chicago: University of Chicago Press, 1986), 346.

37. Derrida, *The Gift of Death,* 70.

38. Sean Hand, ed., *The Levinas Reader* (Oxford: Blackwell, 1989), 28.

39. Caputo, *Prayers,* 150.

40. Jacques Derrida, "Deconstruction and the Other," in *Dialogues with Contemporary Continental Thinkers* (ed. Richard Kearney; Manchester, U.K.: Manchester University Press, 1984), 119.

41. Paul Tillich, *The Courage to Be* (New Haven, Conn.: Yale University Press, 1952), 182, "God above God"; 186–90, "the God above the God of theism"; 15, Seneca (the Stoic), "God above god."

42. Karl Rahner, *Prayers and Meditations* (New York: Seabury, 1980), 35.

43. Caputo, *Prayers,* 128, 150.

44. Ibid., 128.

45. Ibid., 148.

46. Ibid., 96.

47. Ibid., 75.

48. Ibid., 76.

49. Derrida, "Deconstruction and the Other," 120.

50. Derrida, *The Gift of Death,* 33.

51. Ibid., 68.

52. Ibid., 68.

53. Ibid., 69.

54. Ibid., 70.

55. Ibid., 71.

56. Ibid., 85.

57. Ibid., 86.

58. Ibid., 78.

59. Ibid., 68.

60. For an elaboration of the concept and morality of collective action as distinguished from those of individual action, see Anselm Kyongsuk Min, *Dialectic of Salvation: Issues in Theology of Liberation* (Albany, N.Y.: SUNY Press, 1989), 104–15.

61. Derrida, *On the Name,* 46.

62. Jacques Derrida, *Deconstruction in a Nutshell: A Conversation with Jacques Derrida* (ed. John D. Caputo; New York: Fordham University Press, 1977), 13–14.

63. Derrida, *Specters of Marx,* 22–23.

64. Ibid., 28; Derrida, *Deconstruction in a Nutshell,* 17–18, 134–35.

65. Richard J. Bernstein, "An Allegory of Modernity/Postmodernity: Habermas and Derrida," in *Working through Derrida* (ed. Gary B. Madison; Evanston, Ill.: Northwestern University Press, 1993), 227; Thomas McCarthy, "The Politics of the Ineffable: Derrida's Deconstructionism," *The Philosophical Forum* 211, no. 2 (fall-winter, 1989–90): 146–168.

66. William James, *The Will to Believe and Other Essays in Popular Philosophy* (London/New York: Longmans, Green & Co., 1897; repr., New York: Dover Publications, 1956), 17–19.

THREE

THE REIGN OF DIFFERENCE
*Postmodernism in Philosophy, Culture, and Politics**

We are living in an age of difference. Under the confluence of multiculturalism and French postmodernism, the North American intellectual ethos today is dominated by the philosophy, culture, and politics of difference. Identity and unity have become suspect. "Nature" and "essence" have become taboos. Grand narratives, universality, and foundations are gone. The unquestioned aim is to safeguard difference and thereby to promote justice, liberation, and inclusion. I share the aim but differ with regard to the role and significance of difference. As I argue in the next chapter, what we need today is not the absolutization of difference but its sublation into the solidarity of the different precisely for the sake of justice and liberation. Prior to my critique of postmodernism and presentation of my alternative in the next chapter, however, I devote myself, in this chapter, to describing the postmodernism of difference in philosophy, culture, and politics. First, I analyze the postmodern theory of difference in terms of Derrida's philosophy of difference. Second, I describe the postmodern culture of difference in terms of certain sociological theories. Third, I present the postmodern politics of difference in terms of recent feminist discussions. Finally, I provide a brief reflection on postmodernism in its relation to modernity and its positive contribution in a globalizing world.

Derrida's Philosophy of Difference

Postmodernism is, first of all, a philosophy of difference, and the thinker of difference par excellence today is unquestionably Jacques Derrida. I begin, therefore, with his reflections on difference, *differance,* and negative theology.

* This chapter and the next are a revised, expanded version of the Harrington Lecture I was honored to give at Saint Paul School of Theology, Kansas City, Missouri, on September 18, 2001. I would like to express my gratitude to Saint Paul School of Theology, especially its Educational Enrichment Committee, for inviting me to give the lecture for 2001.

For Derrida, as for Ferdinand de Saussure, language is a system of signs in which signs are signs of things in their absence and therefore in their deferred presence, and in which signs can signify only by referring to things other than themselves and keeping within themselves the marks and traces of the other. Signification is not a function of fixed individual elements in their separation but of "the network of oppositions that distinguishes them, and then relates them one to another."[1] Things exist meaningfully only in this network of relations to things other than themselves. No being is a pure presence to itself or a pure identity with itself, but every being is always also mediated by absence and difference, which are therefore just as universally constitutive of reality as are presence and identity. As the source of temporalizing deferral and spatializing differentiation, *differance* is the "systematic play of differences" or the "playing movement" that produces relations and differences and thus makes meaning, conceptuality, and system in general possible. *Differance* is "the non-full, non-simple, structured and differentiating origin of differences,"[2] or "the movement according to which language, or any code, any system of referral in general, is constituted 'historically' as a weave of differences."[3]

Differance is not itself a concept, a word, an essence, a being, a name, or even Being itself, but the very condition that makes each possible. *Differance* "*is not,* does not exist, is not a present-being (*on*) in any form. . . . It has neither existence nor essence. It derives from no category of being, whether present or absent."[4] All signs—sounds, words, and concepts—are made possible only within *differance,* the systematic play of differences. As the primordial disclosure of time, space, and meaning, *differance* is older than Being, older than Heidegger's ontological difference between Being and beings. In a sense, "*differance*" is a name, even a metaphysical name, as all names are, but in its reality it is unnameable, for it "is not a pure nominal unity, and unceasingly dislocates itself in a chain of differing and deferring substitutions."[5] Neither is *differance* a reference to an ineffable being, like God. It is, instead, "the play which makes possible nominal effects, the relatively unitary and atomic structures that are called names, the chains of substitutions of names in which, for example, the nominal effect *differance* is itself *enmeshed,* carried off, reinscribed, just as a false entry or a false exit is still part of the game, a function of the system."[6]

Differance questions the authority of presence and renders questionable all interpretations of the meaning of being in the categories of being, beingness, or essence. *Differance* is "that which not only could never be appropriated in the *as such* of its name or its appearing, but also that which threatens the authority of the *as such* in general, of the presence of the thing itself in its essence."[7] For Derrida, *differance* not only resists reduction to any ontotheological reappropriation, but also altogether transcends it "as the very opening of the space in which ontotheology—philosophy—produces its system and its history" and which "therefore includes ontotheology, inscribing it and exceeding it without return."[8]

The (non)essence of deconstructive critique, then, is to reinscribe all ideas and philosophies in the movement of *differance* and reveal the many differences concealed, suppressed, or marginalized in the reifying reign of identity, unity, and totality. From this perspective the early Derrida was anxious to deconstruct and dismiss the whole tradition of negative theology, that attempt within the Christian tradition to preserve the transcendence of God by denying God all attributions of finite categories. For Derrida, negative theology still remained within the propositional form of discourse, within the horizon of the metaphysics of presence. For all its critique of the inadequacy of human language, negative theology still affirmed, however beyond being, a superessential reality, and remained in fact a metaphysics of presence in a more refined form. As long as one speaks in the element of logic and ontotheological grammar, negative theology contains a movement to ontotheologically reappropriate the hyperessential, a movement that is irrepressible but whose ultimate failure is just as necessary. Finally, the apophatic voyage often contains the promise, the possibility, of an intuition of the hyperessential presence, a genuine "vision" and a genuine "knowledge," without, however, containing "the principle of its interruption."[9]

In spite of all these negative criticisms, however, Derrida has also been haunted by the possibility that "perhaps there is within it [negative theology], hidden, restless, diverse, and itself heterogeneous, a voluminous and nebulous multiplicity of potentials to which the single expression 'negative theology' yet remains inadequate."[10] What, then, are these potentials of negative theology that Derrida has been retrieving in recent years?

For Derrida, the phenomenon of negative theology is contradictory and complex. It is voiceless insofar as God is beyond being, but it nevertheless remains a voice in speaking of God. It is atheistic in speaking of God (who is) beyond being, but it is an atheism that also contains the most intense yearning for God. It is negative, but with a negativity that hides the greatest affirmation. Negative theology thus spells the end of all monologism. This atheistic trait of negative theology consists in the boldness to go beyond whatever is given, in "going further than is reasonably permitted, . . . passing to the limit, then crossing a frontier, including that of a community, thus of a sociopolitical, institutional, ecclesial reason or raison d'être,"[11] in going toward the "absolute other" in the extreme tension of a desire that also knows how to suspend and renounce its own momentum.[12] As a movement that both negates and affirms itself, negative theology is a "stranger to knowing, thus to every determination or to every predicative attribution."[13] It exists only in its performance as a discourse: only as a prayer, an address, an apostrophe (to God), a confession. As "the very experience of the (impossible) possibility of the impossible,"[14] negative theology introduces "an absolute heterogeneity" and "an absolute interruption" in the order, modality, and regime of the possible.[15] Negative theology is a discourse of this "absolute" heterogeneity and interruption.

Of the "unknowable God" nothing can be said that might hold, save his name, save the name that names nothing that might hold, not even a divinity. "God" "is" the name of this "bottomless collapse," of "this endless desertification of language."[16] Negative theology is the very "kenosis of discourse,"[17] an experience of the desert. In mandating going where one cannot go, "toward the name, toward the beyond of the name *in* the name,"[18] the language of negative theology contains "this sweet rage against language, this jealous anger of language within itself and against itself," a passion that leaves the mark of a scar or a wound in that place where the impossible takes place. The event takes place at the edge of language where there is nothing but reference, and all history of negative theology plays itself out in the question whether the referent—everything save the name—is or is not indispensable. Every authentic statement of negative theology must bear the trace of the wound, the stigmata of its own proper inadequation, of its own proper disproportion, of its hubris countersigned.[19]

Negative theology contains a hyperbolic movement of transcendence that carries or transports beyond being or beingness *epekeina tēs ousias,* precipitating not only beyond being or God insofar as he is the supreme being, but also beyond God even as name, as naming, named, or nameable, insofar as reference is made to something. This "beyond" is not a place but a movement of transcendence that surpasses God himself, being, essence, the proper or the selfsame. The movement radically dissociates being and knowing, existence and knowledge. It fractures the cogito as it cracks even the analogy between God and creatures. The analogy does not repair or reconcile but "aggravates" the dissociation.[20] In effect, negative theology "launches or carries negativity as the principle of auto-destruction in the heart of each thesis; in any event, this theology suspends every thesis, all belief, all doxa."[21] As "a movement of internal rebellion," the impact of negative theology reaches further: it entails "the interruption of a sort of social contract, the one that gives right to the State, the nation, more generally to the philosophical community as rational and logocentric community."[22] This rupture of the social contract programs a whole series of analogous and recurrent movements such as Plotinus, Heidegger, and Levinas.

It is, then, as a ceaseless movement of negation, interruption, dissociation, rebellion, and heterogeneity that Derrida applies and universalizes negative theology to all areas of life. Says Derrida: "I trust no text that is not in some way contaminated with negative theology, and even among those texts that apparently do not have, want, or believe they have any relation with theology in general. Negative theology is everywhere, but it is never by itself."[23] As "an absolute transcendence that announces itself within" every reality, negative theology is not only a theological discourse but the power of self-critical negation found "everywhere." It is "never by itself" but always and "everywhere" where human beings struggle for liberation and transcendence over all arbitrary limits, wherever there is a yearning for the "beyond" as well as a protest against confinement.

At its root negative theology contests the very idea of identity or self-interiority of a tradition, such as the one metaphysics, the one onto theology, the one phenomenology, the one Christian revelation, the one history, the one history of being, the one tradition, or self-identity in general. As one of the most remarkable manifestations of this self-difference within the interior of the history of Christianity, apophatic theology has been anxious to render itself independent of revelation, of all the literal language of the New Testament, of the coming of Christ, the passion, the dogma of the Trinity, etc. "An immediate but intuitionless mysticism, a sort of abstract kenosis, frees this language from all authority, all narrative, all dogma, all belief—and at the limit from all faith. At the limit, this mysticism remains, after the fact, independent of all history of Christianity, *absolutely* independent, detached even, perhaps absolved, from the idea of sin, freed even, perhaps redeemed, from the idea of redemption." Negative theology is the language of this "subversive marginality."[24]

From now on, then, there can be no politics, morals, or law that is not the politics, morals, or law of negative theology, not in the sense of positive legal, political lessons to be drawn or deduced from negative theology as from a program but in the sense that negative theology obliges us to put "politics," "morals," and "law" between quotation marks, and "tremble" at their sense. How many millions have been murdered in the name of "politics," "morals," and the "law"? Derrida asks, "How dare we speak of it [religion] in the singular without fear and trembling, this very day?"[25] All social ideals, for all their promises, must be passed through "the aporias of negative theology,"[26] and never be identified with any determinate form in which they are realized at any one time. Democracy, then, means "neither the Idea in the Kantian sense, not the current, limited, and determinate concept of democracy," but always the idea of democracy as such or democracy "to come." In the same way Derrida also speaks of "religion" in the sense of the always self-transcending but also self-negating yearning for the beyond but never identifiable with any concrete, determinate religion; of "justice" as an ideal always to come, never identifiable with any determinate form of justice; and of the "messianic" nowhere concretely incarnated in a particular form of messianism because it is in principle transcendent of all finite realizations. Likewise, Derrida is suspicious of "community" because it connotes "participation, fusion, identification," in which he sees as many threats as promises; he would prefer a "gathering together of singularities," of "absolute singularities."[27]

It is in the name of this *differance* and in the spirit of this negative theology that Derrida has been proposing to deconstruct all claims to identity, unity, universality, community, totality, and system; and has been subjecting all claims to ultimacy in the form of religion, faith, messianism, and justice, to the critique and contamination of negative theology. Deconstruction means to differentiate the identical, complicate the simple, contaminate the pure, destabilize the complacent, and to subvert all reigning totalities and systems by subjecting them to the shock of alterity, the demand of the wholly other, the trauma of the unexpected. The only thing that is undeconstructible is a certain idea of justice because its affirmation and promise remain irreducible in all deconstruction. With regard to all else, deconstruction means "a radical and interminable, infinite . . . critique," because such a critique "belongs to the movement of an experience open to the absolute future of what is coming, that is to say, a necessarily indeterminate, abstract, desert-like experience that is confided, exposed, given up to its waiting for the other and for the event."[28]

It is no wonder, then, that deconstruction, a philosophy of difference with a vengeance, leads to fateful consequences. Mark C. Taylor defines deconstruction as "the 'hermeneutic' of the death of God,"[29] at least the God of ontotheology and its radical implications: the disappearance of the self as a self-identical substance, the end of history as a unified teleological process, and the closure of the book in the sense of an ordered totality.[30] The attempt of Western reason to "secure presence and establish identity by overcoming absence and repressing difference" defeats itself because of the ubiquitous presence of the "disruptive other" it can never assimilate.[31] Jean-François Lyotard defines the postmodern rather succinctly simply as "incredulity toward metanarratives"[32] or grand narratives that seek to unify the totality of history according to an Idea such as those of Christianity, Hegelian idealism,

Marxist materialism, and capitalism. The category of totality is not merely a metaphysical or an epistemological category; it is also a political category; and the politics of totality, recent history tells us, is essentially totalitarian and terroristic. Thus, Lyotard ends his book on *The Postmodern Condition* with an exhortation: "Let us wage a war on totality; let us be witnesses to the unpresentable; let us activate the differences and save the honor of the name."[33]

For Richard Rorty, postmodernism includes the "sheer contingency" of language, the self, and community along with an ironical consciousness and a purely historicist and nominalist pragmatism.[34] According to Zygmunt Bauman, postmodernism means disbelief in universality and foundation.[35] According to Calvin Schrag, postmodernism means dismantling of modern reason and a turn to practical reason, hermeneutics, and narrativity, which in turn entails the decentering of the subject as an epistemological foundation, the recognition of the social sources of rationality, the embeddedness of power and desire within the claims of reason, the undecidability of meaning, inscrutability of reference, and the congealing of the dichotomy of transcendentalism and historicism.[36]

This deconstructionist critique of totality has also had its impact on liberation theology, as seen with Enrique Dussel, who places the destiny of the poor and oppressed as others completely *outside* the totality of the prevailing system, not as others *within* the system. It is also having its impact on feminist theology, which, like the liberation theology of Latin America, has been a theology of the other and has had to struggle to maintain that otherness against the possibility of being coopted into the totalizing discourse of "malestream" theology, thus not to be a pawn in a predominantly patriarchal politics of otherness. For Elisabeth Schüssler Fiorenza, the feminist practice of focusing on "the feminine" as a hermeneutical key in biblical interpretation is "in danger of recuperating the totalizing discourse of Western gender dualism."[37] Furthermore, feminists have also succumbed to the "logic of identity," the urge to think things together in a unity and place all particulars as parts of that unity. This "drive to unity and essence" becomes clear in the search for a feminist "canon within the canon" or a liberating "organizing principle" as the normative center of Scripture, to which then the historical particularity and pluriformity of biblical writings could be reduced. The imperative for contemporary feminist theology, therefore, is

> to shift the focus of feminist liberation discourse on the Bible away not only from the discourse on "women in the Bible" to the feminist reconstruction of Christian origins, but also from the drive to construct a unifying biblical

canon and universalist principle to a discussion of the process of biblical interpretation and evaluation that could display and assess the oppressive as well as liberating functions of particular biblical texts in women's lives and struggles. Concern with biblical positivity, normativity, and authority is in danger of too quickly foreclosing such a critical analysis and feminist evaluation of particular biblical texts and traditions. It neglects the Bible and its interpretation as the site of competing discursive practices.[38]

Postmodern Culture of Difference

So much for the philosophy of difference. Let me now turn to the postmodern culture of difference. Cultural postmodernists, including many feminists and postcolonialists, have accepted from philosophical postmodernism the rejection of foundationalism and essentialism. There are no fixed essences in terms of which different groups can define their identities and provide a foundation for behavior, which would only lead to the terror of the same. There is no essence or nature to women that can define women's identity and prescribe certain behavior as appropriate to women. There are no "women" as such, only different groups and kinds of women, such as white women, black women, Asian women, none of which has a fixed identity either and each of which must be subdivided into heterosexual women, lesbian women, bisexual women, transgendered women, just as each of these in turn must be subdivided into wealthy women, middle-class women, and poor women. No cultural or ethnic group is a homogeneous entity either but contains similar divisions and subdivisions within itself. It is dangerous to speak of a community of "we" in the singular because it is likely to impose a false unity, marginalize some who are included, and exclude others altogether. Moreover, even individual persons have multiple identities with multiple connections with different groups. The clear imperative, then, is to shift from a politics of identity to a politics of difference, from an insistence on sameness to a celebration of difference.[39]

I think it is enlightening to put this philosophical and political drive toward difference in the general context of postmodern culture.[40] For sociologists Stephen Crook, Jan Pakulski, and Malcolm Waters, postmodern culture is neither a simple extension of modern culture nor a simple contradiction of modern culture but something of both: a reversal of modern culture precisely through the extreme development of its characteristic tendencies such as differentiation, rationalization, and commodification, which further fragments and transforms modern into postmodern culture.

First, with regard to commodification: Modern culture is known for its tendency to reduce all things to a commodity with cash value. However, modern culture still tried to maintain some distinction between aesthetic and commercial value as well as some balance between the two through government and private subsidies. Likewise, cultural tastes were differentiated with class differences. In postmodern culture, all such distinctions are undermined by a proliferation of "taste," which itself becomes a principle of proliferating divisions. We no longer seem to consume goods and services but meanings and signs, with the television industry as the paradigmatic agent of this change. With the erosion of institutionalized cultural authorities as judges of standards, tastes and styles prevail. The areas such as the family, class, community ties, and religious affiliation, which used to remain relatively impervious to commodification, are no longer so immune. Such family-based activities as eating, cleaning, and leisure pursuits are increasingly governed by the norms of the market and the images produced by advertising. Even the refusal of commodification—such as organic food, fresh food, and so on—is subjected to packaging and commercialization as a matter of "lifestyle." This hypercommodification pervades all areas of life, eroding the distinction between commercial and noncommercial. The images and dreams that link commodities to identity and status no longer have to refer to an area of intrinsic meaning. Commodified meanings become "self-referential." Just as taste is a product of an earlier phase of commodification, style is the product of contemporary hypercommodification and operates within the self-referential universe of commodified meanings, with little external constraint.

Second, with regard to rationalization: The drive for consistency and calculability has been a characteristic drive of modern culture. One aspect of this drive is the endogenous development of the formal possibilities inherent in each division and subdivision of culture, to the point of becoming impenetrable to even an educated audience, like Picasso's art and Joyce's writing, to which I would not mind adding Derrida's own writing, in a phenomenon that Habermas calls "the 'elitist' splitting off of expert cultures." The other aspect of rationalization is the technicization of the instruments of production and reproduction such as the reproduction of great paintings in books and of classical music in phonographs. It is through this technicization of reproduction that the great traditions of literature, art, and music have been invented and maintained. In its postmodern development, however, technical rationalization tends to domesticate or privatize cultural consumption, displacing public cultural spaces such as theaters, music halls, and opera houses with television, video, CDs, and other marvels of digital technology, to which live performances have become occasional supplements. As cultural consumption becomes increasingly private and individual, so the medium has become the message, where the image masks the absence of a basic reality. Technologies collaborate in eroding the distinction between representation and reality, surface and depth. Television has become the real world of postmodern culture.

Third, with regard to differentiation: A typical tendency of modern culture had been to differentiate society into a multiplicity of spheres of life, each with its own autonomous function, activity, and value; beginning with the division of society into economy, polity, and culture; and subdivision of each into further internal differences. In postmodern culture this differentiation has become excessive or hyper. The catchword has become, "Let a thousand flowers bloom." Irreducible pluralism and incommensurable diversity reign in place of the rule of Reason, History, and Value in the singular. Strangely, however, this hyperdifferentiation leads to dedifferentiation. The proliferation of excessive specializations and boundaries tends, in fact, to blur, erode, and transgress the boundaries, as religious scholars today can easily testify. How do we draw a sharp boundary between critical theory, Christian social ethics, liberation theology, and theology; or between theology, theology of religions, comparative theology, history of religions, and study of Buddhism? In the area of the distinction between high and popular culture, an image, a musical theme, or a format can be separated off from its classical matrix and decontextualized through hyperdifferentiation and fragmentation and can be recontextualized in any number of ways. A Mozart aria, separated from its original context, can be reappropriated as background music in film, television drama, or even advertising. This promiscuous openness of a fragment from high culture to an endless variety of reappropriations in the commodity market blurs the distinction between high and low culture, and renders postmodern culture a culture of fragmentation and bricolage, which erodes the sense of culture as a lived unity of experience. Sheer difference of taste and style so different as to be in fact indifferent is not conducive to a sense of cultural integrity and coherence. It is more likely to produce what Michael Walzer calls "the pluralism of dissociated individuals," isolated from a group and its culture, alienated, lonely, and unstable, forced to make an agonizing existential choice at every point in her life.[41]

Feminist Politics of Difference

It is in this context of postmodern culture with its pressures for differentiation and fragmentation that I would like to locate both the philosophy and politics of difference. How, then, is a politics of difference possible with all its ethical claims in a world without foundations and essences?

Iris Marion Young poses the question sharply: In a world where identity politics has become impossible because of the discovery of disidentity within the very identity of women, and where sheer heterogeneity seems to exclude all politics, how is it possible to refer to all women or women as a whole despite all their differences in class, ethnicity, religion, and culture, yet without essentializing them either? Some proponents of feminist politics argue that unity and solidarity among women is a product of political discussion and struggle among women of different backgrounds and interests, not a reality that exists antecedently to such discussion and struggle. The identity of women is not that of fixed nature but that of temporary coalition. For Young as well as Judith Butler, this approach may avoid the danger of substantializing gender, but it does not avoid that of normalizing and privileging certain experiences peculiar to the coalition. The question of solidarity and identity should always remain unsettled, subject to deconstruction in a play of possibilities that does not exclude anyone. For Young, however, the idea that the group identity of women is only a construct of feminist discussion and politics seems to make feminist politics quite arbitrary. In that case, asks Young, on what basis would some women want to come together at all? Wouldn't there be some social conditions that motivate their coalition? Should feminism also exclude those who do not join such coalitions because they do not identify themselves as feminists? Isn't there a need, therefore, for some conception of women as a group prior to the formation of self-conscious feminist politics, as at least a certain set of relations that may motivate some women, if not all, to engage in such politics?

How, then, describe women as a group without being normalizing and essentializing? On this point, Young suggests that we look at women as a "series" as distinct from a "group" in Sartre's sense. A group is a collection of persons who come together for the conscious purpose of undertaking a common project. The unity of a group is derived from the recognition of one another as sharing in a common purpose. A series, on the other hand, is a collective of persons who happen to have a common relation to a material object under conditions of social facticity, such as the bus rider standing in line for a bus, a worker in a factory, a consumer in a supermarket, and a listener to a radio. The only community persons have in these instances is their relationship to a particular material object or objects—the bus, the factory, the consumer goods, the music from the radio—and their common subjection to the social structures and conditions that make such a common relation possible even while also conditioning and constraining them—the commuting system, the system of production, the market economy, and the system of modern communication. Individuals of a series do not even know one another. Each of them has her own actions and goals. In this sense, the series imposes common conditions without defining the identity of each individual in terms of a determinate purpose, project, or sense of self. Seriality refers to a certain level of social existence, the level of routine, habitual action, and subjection to structures—the prereflective background for conscious action. The series provides a certain unity insofar as it defines the prereflective, common conditions of life, but without imposing determinate, identifying attributes on individuals. In this sense, the series is a blurry, shifting, and amorphous unity. It is from this series and as a response to some of the conditions it imposes that self-conscious groups will arise.

For Young, thinking of women as a series, not as a group, makes it possible to still think of women as some sort of a social unity without essentializing them all into a single group with a determinate identity. Women as a series, of course, are much more complicated and multidimensional than bus riders or radio listeners. They refer to individuals who have been subjected to social conditions that require them to behave in similar ways as "feminine" in relation to the same structured objects. These conditions, which Sartre calls "practico-inert realities," include the physical structure of the female body along with the social rules regarding the body (e.g., heterosexuality), linguistic practices, visual representations, and the sexual division of labor. These conditions provide some sort of a loose unity to women without defining their identity. Furthermore, details of these conditions vary from one social context to another, and it is up to each individual woman to shape her own identity within these structures and contexts.

It is also out of this serial existence of women that feminist groups will emerge, trying to politicize gender and change the power relations between women and men. What brings women together, however, will not be gender alone but also other aspects of the social conditions that may give them affinity, such as class, race, nationality, neighborhood, religious affiliation, and occupation. As subject to these particularizing conditions that do not pertain to all women, women's groups will not be coextensive with all members of the series, just as no group will encompass in its purpose all the problems inherent in the totality of the conditions of women as a series. This is why feminist politics will always be coalition politics; as such, it must also refer beyond itself to conditions and issues not yet reflected upon and included in its purpose, including those of women who are not feminists.[42]

Linda Nicholson is faced with the same challenge of finding something common as a basis of feminist politics, but unlike Iris Young, who finds that community in the common conditions of enforced heterosexuality and the sexual division of labor, Nicholson appeals to Wittgenstein's theory of family resemblance. She too rejects as biological fundamentalism any theory that certain characteristics common to all women across cultures are given simply on the basis of a certain biology of women, what in fact turn out to be projections of the traits of white, middle-class, Western women. With most postmodern feminists, she holds that women's traits are all socially constructed. Nonetheless, it is still possible to speak of women as a whole with a determinate meaning. Just as siblings of a family are not all alike in every respect yet possess certain family resemblances, and just as there are certain similarities to all games, although there may be no one characteristic shared by all games— so women do share a complex network of overlapping and crisscrossing similarities, although there may be no one trait common to all women.

This allows for the fact that some characteristics such as possession of a vagina may play a dominant role within such a network over long periods of time as well as for the fact that we can speak of "women" in the case of transsexual women before the medical operation who may have no vagina but still feel themselves to be women. This approach denies that there is any one specifiable meaning to "woman" and that the contemporary Western definition of woman is universally valid; but it does not deny that there will be patterns over a long stretch of history or that there is meaning to "woman" at least in the sense of "a map of intersecting similarities and differences."[43] The body does not disappear in this approach but becomes a historically specific variable. This eliminates the politics of identity on behalf of all women, yet it still allows a politics of coalition among women who temporarily share a common interest and come together for particular, temporary projects, which is what women in fact have been doing during the last quarter of a century. For this purpose "woman" does not need to possess a single meaning. For temporary purposes we can lift up one meaning and make claims on behalf of women from that perspective, fully recognizing that such a meaning is only provisional and that it is stipulative of what we want women to be rather than descriptive of what women perceive themselves to be. In any event, we must recognize that "our claims about women are not based on some given reality but emerge from our own places within history and culture; they are political acts that reflect the contexts we emerge out of and the futures we would like to see."[44]

Postmodernism and the Heterological Imperative

I can best summarize the postmodern philosophy, culture, and politics of difference in four respects. First, postmodernism is based on a will to justice and liberation and thus to a critique of all injustice and oppression. In this sense it continues to be animated by the same spirit of critique and liberation that is characteristic of modernity.

Second, in execution of this will to liberation it accentuates difference, sometimes elevating it to the level of *differance,* the universal power, source, and movement of all deferral and differentiation, and subjecting all things to the proviso of negative theology. In this aspect it also perpetuates the typically modern penchant for universalizing certain insights and discoveries such as "critique," "will to power," "praxis," and "existence."

Third, in the name of this *differance* and negative theology, it denounces *all* tendencies to unity, totality, universality, system, grand narrative, and community, as well as claims to reason and truth. In its critique, it is as universal, as sweeping, as totalitarian, as any system of ontotheology it tries to deconstruct, reducing all, not just some, traditional philosophies from Plato to Hegel to a metaphysics of presence and logocentrism, just as Kantians would dismiss all traditional philosophies as "precritical," and as Marxism used to reduce all philosophies from Plato to Heidegger to "idealism." Postmodern thought, ironically, continues this modern penchant for reducing all to the same without internal differentiation.

Fourth, in the name of *differance* it criticizes all ideas of fixed, unchanging nature or essence, rejecting all metaphysics and all claims to foundation and essence. No metaphysical explanation is acceptable; only sociohistorical genealogy and contextual pragmatism will do. In this insistence on sociohistorical and linguistic explanation, postmodernism likewise carries to its logical consequences the anthropocentric, historicist logic of modernity from Descartes through Kant, Hegel, Marx, and Nietzsche to existentialism and pragmatism.

Postmodernism, I am inclined to think, is more the completion of modernity than its transcendence or reversal. Its accentuation of difference along with its rejection of totality may appear contrary to modernism, but such accentuation can also arguably be regarded as the culmination of the logic of modern subjectivism and capitalist individualism, as the above brief description of postmodern culture seems to show. This also indicates a certain internal tension in postmodernism itself, between its will to justice, which presupposes a certain human value irreducible to political or commercial manipulation; and its accommodation to the capitalist ethos that worships unprincipled, aesthetic variation for its own sake. Perhaps a clearer distinction is in order between difference in the ethical sense of resistance to all arbitrary oppression and manipulation, and difference in the nonmetaphysical metaphysical sense of irreducibility to the same, to identity, unity, and totality. The two senses are not simply identical. Ethical resistance indeed follows from the metaphysical irreducibility of human dignity to the same, but not every such irreducibility necessarily dictates such ethical resistance. Desires are different from person to person and are encouraged to be different in a capitalist society, and they are different from time to time even within the same person and are encouraged to be so in the "decentered" postmodern nonsubject. Certainly, not all of these desires deserve honoring. Many of them in fact would only deserve discipline and purgation, and these include all desires that seek to manipulate and oppress the dignity of other human beings.

The most historically relevant contribution of postmodernism today, I think, is its will to justice and its deconstruction of all ideas of totality and nature in the name of *differance* and negative theology. For centuries and increasingly in recent decades, global capitalism, through all the trade, transportation, communication, and technology it promotes, has been bringing different peoples together into common social space and compelling all to find ways of living together with those who are different, creating appropriate economic, political, and cultural conditions under which different human groups can live with a minimum of justice and peace. In this process the encounter between different groups has always been, at best, fraught with tension, while some of these tensions have often become bloody conflicts ending in the horrors of genocide and mass destruction. In all these tensions and struggles the common formal factor has been the inability to live together with the different, and the subjection of the other to the same, with all its economic, political, and cultural consequences.

Perhaps it is not unreasonable to consider the exclusion of the other from one's own system of identity—whatever this system might be: tribal, religious, ethnic, cultural, political, economic, sexual, or other—as the original or primordial sin of humanity, of which all other sins may be regarded as expressions and consequences. In this propensity to reduce the other to our own identity, it is also quite true, as postmodernists have been arguing, that we have been appealing to the concepts of essence, nature, and foundation, often forgetting the ideological contamination of these concepts and practices, but also often doing so knowingly and deliberately. Whether one ultimately agrees or not with the postmodernist critique of totality, essentialism, and foundationalism—and I have some serious disagreements, which I will discuss shortly—it seems clear that the times call for some sort of a heterological imperative as an essential condition of living in a multicultural, pluralistic world.

By the "heterological imperative" I mean the willingness to subject all our convictions to the challenge of others, their views, their needs, their identity; not in the sense of giving up our convictions and beliefs as condition of dialoguing with others, as some pluralists tend to argue; but in the sense of a culture of readiness to live in the tension between our own ultimate beliefs and the challenge of those who differ, with the willingness to modify our views and behaviors if necessary, and otherwise always to take the other into consideration. As postmodernists argue, we do not indeed possess God's vision of totality, and we must learn to live with the challenge of the other, sometimes in the *light* of others so that we may learn from them, often in the *shadow* of others so that we may be challenged to repentance and conversion.

Another name of this heterological imperative would be "pluralistic sensibility," the recognition that, at least for some time, we are going to live in a world of mutually irreducible ultimate belief systems, and that we have to learn to live with such pluralism. This sensibility will be especially imperative for two kinds of persons: politicians, who make laws, the system of identity par excellence, with the greatest potential for the violation of the other; and theologians, who if truly theologians will have to talk about God, the ultimate of all foundations, and must do so in a way that is not oppressive but liberating, and therefore always subject to the proviso of negative theology, lest the name of God become "the name of indifference itself."[45]

Notes

1. Jacques Derrida, *Margins of Philosophy* (Chicago: University of Chicago Press, 1982), 10.
2. Ibid., 11.
3. Ibid., 12.
4. Ibid., 6.
5. Ibid., 26.
6. Ibid., 26–27.
7. Ibid., 25–26.
8. Ibid., 26–27.
9. Harold Coward and Toby Foshay, eds., *Derrida and Negative Theology* (Albany, N.Y.: SUNY Press, 1992), 81.
10. Ibid., 82.
11. Ibid., 36.
12. Ibid., 37.
13. Ibid., 38–40.
14. Ibid., 43.
15. Ibid., 43.
16. Ibid., 55–56.
17. Ibid., 50.
18. Ibid., 59.
19. Ibid., 60–61.

20. Ibid., 63–67.

21. Ibid., 67.

22. Ibid., 67.

23. Ibid., 69.

24. Ibid., 71.

25. Jacques Derrida and Giovanni Vattimo, eds., *Religion* (Stanford, Calif.: Stanford University Press, 1998), 1.

26. Derrida, *On the Name* (ed. Thomas Dutoit; trans. David Wood, John P. Leavey Jr., and Ian McLeod; Stanford, Calif.: Stanford University Press, 1995), 83.

27. Ibid., 46; Derrida, *The Gift of Death* (Chicago: University of Chicago Press, 1995), 68.

28. Jacques Derrida, *Specters of Marx* (trans. Peggy Kamuf; New York: Routledge, 1994), 90.

29. Mark C. Taylor, *Erring: A Postmodern A/theology* (Chicago: University of Chicago Press, 1984), 6.

30. Ibid., 19–96.

31. Ibid., 15.

32. Jean-François Lyotard, *The Postmodern Condition: A Report on Knowledge* (trans. Geoff Bennington and Brian Massumi; Minneapolis: University of Minnesota Press, 1984), xxiv.

33. Ibid., 82.

34. Richard Rorty, *Contingency, Irony, and Solidarity* (Cambridge: Cambridge University Press, 1989).

35. Zygmunt Bauman, *Postmodern Ethics* (Oxford: Blackwell, 1993), 1–15.

36. Calvin O. Schrag, "Rationality between Modernity and Postmodernity," in *Life-World and Politics: Between Modernity and Postmodernity* (ed. Stephen K. White; Notre Dame, Ind.: University of Notre Dame Press, 1989), 81–106.

37. Elisabeth Schüssler Fiorenza, "The Politics of Otherness: Biblical Interpretation as a Critical Praxis for Liberation," in *The Future of Liberation Theology: Essays in Honor of Gustavo Gutierrez* (ed. Marc H. Ellis and Otto Maduro; Maryknoll, N.Y.: Orbis, 1989), 313.

38. Ibid., 314–15.

39. See Jodi Dean, *Solidarity of Strangers* (Berkeley: University of California Press, 1996), 47–74.

40. For an excellent overview of certain postmodernist cultural trends, see Steven Seidman, ed., *The Postmodern Turn: New Perspectives on Social Theory* (Cambridge: Cambridge University Press, 1994), 1–23; for a genealogy of postmodernism and a Marxist, critical theory-oriented critique of postmodernism, especially the politically nihilistic consequences of its rejection of systematic analysis, community, utopia, and agency, and its celebration of sheer diversity, see Steven Best and Douglas Kellner, *Postmodern Theory: Critical Investigations* (New York: Guilford, 1991), first and last chapters; for a socialist critique of postmodernism, especially its textual idealism and capitalist aestheticism, see Christopher Norris, *The Truth about Postmodernism* (Oxford: Blackwell, 1993); for a critical encounter between critical theory and postmodernism, see Craig Calhoun, *Critical Social Theory: Culture, History, and the Challenge of Difference* (Oxford: Blackwell, 1995).

41. Michael Walzer, *On Toleration* (New Haven, Conn.: Yale University Press, 1997), 100. For further discussion of the three characteristics of postmodern culture, see Stephen Crook, Jan Pakulski, and Malcolm Waters, *Postmodernization: Change in Advanced Society* (London: Sage Publications, 1992), 47–78.

42. Iris Marion Young, "Gender as Seriality: Thinking about Women as a Social Collective," in *Social Postmodernism: Beyond Identity Politics* (ed. Linda Nicholson and Steven Seidman; Cambridge: Cambridge University Press, 1995), 187–215.

43. Linda Nicholson, "Interpreting Gender," in *Social Postmodernism* (ed. Nicholson), 61.

44. Ibid., 63.

45. Jacques Derrida, *Of Grammatology* (corrected ed.; Baltimore: Johns Hopkins University Press, 1974), 71.

FOUR

FROM DIFFERENCE TO
THE SOLIDARITY OF OTHERS
Sublating Postmodernism

We are indeed living in an age of difference, but what the age calls for, paradoxically, is not reification or absolutization of difference but its sublation—in the Hegelian sense of negation, transcendence, and preservation—into solidarity, not the solidarity of the same but the solidarity of the different, of strangers, of others. What we need is a paradigm shift from difference to the solidarity of others, precisely for the sake of justice and inclusion.

I proceed in four steps. First, I present a detailed critique of the postmodern absolutization of difference from the philosophical, historical, and strategic points of view and argue for the equal importance of coherence, solidarity, and totality precisely for the sake of the integrity of difference and otherness. Second, I argue that nominalist empiricism that simply rejeccts natures and essences cannot provide the ethical justification for human solidarity across the many boundaries of difference; we need a human solidarity at a level more universal, more profound, and more enduring than purely contingent and temporary coincidence of interests. Third, I try to retrieve human solidarity as the solidarity of human nature by dialectically synthesizing the classical conception of nature and essence as something objective and intrinsic to a being and the modern conceptions of historicity and sociality. Finally, I introduce an outline of a theology of solidarity by tapping three Christian sources, the Trinitarian doctrine of God as the ultimate theological source of all solidarity, the inspiration of the historical Jesus as the paradigm of human solidarity in action, and the tension between the logic of the incarnate God and the logic of the incomprehensible God, between the incarnational dynamic of determinate praxis and the self-transcending dynamic of the critique of all determinacy as a guarantee of the commitment to both the praxis of liberation and the heterological imperative. This will prepare us for Part Two of this book, "Solidarity of Others: Toward a Postmodern Theology."

Toward a Critique of Difference

Postmodernism is a philosophy of difference. It universalizes difference and accentuates it so as to denounce naive assumptions of unity, universality, and totality. Postmodern feminism and various liberation movements likewise divide and subdivide the categories of "woman," "African American," and "homosexual," in order to avoid essentializing and normalizing. While I am thoroughly committed to the cause of justice and liberation of all in their diversity and integrity, I also see three fundamental problems or self-contradictions in this approach: philosophical, historical, and strategic.

Philosophically, a philosophy of difference such as that of Derrida ignores the equally important role of coherence and solidarity both in semiotics and in social existence. According to Derrida, who in turn depends on Ferdinand de Saussure, the meaning of a sentence depends on the relation of the signs to things other than, or different from, themselves. If a sentence consisted only of the same signs—like "a," without spaces, punctuation marks, and certainly other letters—a sentence would have no meaning. In this sense, difference is essential to the meaning of a sentence. It is this constitutive role of difference in semiotics that Derrida projects and universalizes to all realms of life, including history, politics, and philosophy.[1]

What is overlooked is the fact that the meaning of a sentence depends not only on difference but also on coherence among the different. The mere enumeration of difference, like "azwxode," will have no meaning. Meaning also requires mutual coherence of the different parts of a sentence, where the parts refer to, and cohere with, one another in an appropriate way, as they do when I say, "Saint Paul School of Theology is a seminary of the United Methodist Church," but not when I say, "Saint Paul is a city in the British Museum"; this is what grammar, syntax, punctuation, diction, and style are concerned with. Derrida himself uses the language of "system," "chain," and "network" in his many discussions of language, all of which indicate some sort of mutual coherence or ordered relationships, not a purely accidental collection of merely different things or signs placed together in chaotic ways. Says Derrida: "Essentially and lawfully, every concept is inscribed in a chain or in a system within which it refers to the other, to other concepts, by means of the systematic play of differences." Signification is possible because of "the network of oppositions that distinguishes them, and then *relates* them one to another."[2] It is very unfortunate that he developed the nonconcept of difference with a vengeance while totally neglecting the other side of difference, coherence within a system, a totality of ordered relationships of different signs. This neglect of coherence is not a harmless philosophical oversight.

Mutual coherence is crucial not only in semiotics but also in our social existence. Every form of being-together and acting-together is a form of a whole, a totality, which presupposes a minimum of mutual order, coherence, and identity. Take the elementary situation of a conversation between two persons. If the conversation is going to make sense, the two persons must be ordered to each other in some way, for example, as speaking and as spoken to, as mutual friends. They must also be ordered to each other in a coherent way, such as saying and responding to what is said, telling a joke and laughing at it, and so on. This mutual ordering and coherence are themselves possible only because of some shared identity, such as a common concern that brings them together in a conversation in the first place, a common horizon and interest that makes continuing conversation possible and important, a common language or system of signs through which they can communicate, a common physical space or cyberspace they occupy. The same is true of a conversation even among mortal enemies, as it is true of all forms of social existence and interaction. The content of the common concern, horizon, interest, language, and space will differ from one form of interaction to another, but all forms of social existence do presuppose not only difference but also mutual order, coherence, and identity, which are essential to a solidarity of the different. From this perspective, it is compelling to ask what sort of solidarity is required for a common struggle for justice and liberation, and whether the kind of solidarity mentioned by postmodern feminists—the act of common discussion and struggle, the common conditions of enforced heterosexuality, the sexual division of labor, and family resemblances among women—are broad and deep enough for the kind of cause they are trying to achieve. I'll return to this issue shortly.

Derrida and many of the French postmodernists like Lyotard and Foucault have likewise concentrated on language, discourse, and history of ideas; in the process they have no doubt contributed many valuable insights into the many subtle and unexpected ways in which prejudice, discrimination, and oppression are built into the structures of our many systems of signs. It becomes problematic, however, when they apply what is essentially an insight in the sphere of linguistics and philosophy to all realms of life, including history and politics, and reduce all reality to that of signs, to the level of "signs," "discourse," "writing," "language," and "knowledge," often becoming complacent about their semiotic solutions to concrete social problems. As long as we live in the self-referential, self-contained world of signs and discourse, where signs only refer to other signs, we can indeed afford to

engage in the play of differences endlessly, infinitely, forever, with all its consequences of scepticism, relativism, and the proviso of negative theology.
Signs as signs cannot put a stop to such an endless play. We can also afford to
abstract from, and ignore, the problems of real oppressive institutions, structures, and global trends in the name of an intellectual critique of totality and
universality. In this vein, Derrideans play all sorts of semiotic tricks—such as
words crossed out, words spelled without capitalization, and triple columns
on a single page—which may shock and enlighten for a while, but which
also start to become boring nuisances when one finally realizes that reality
remains unchanged when all the fascinating semiotic fireworks are over.

Exaggerated confidence in semiotics and linguistics leads to sheer idealism
separated from the real world. Semiotic reductionism, like the good classical
idealism of old, reduces human existence to that of the thinker, the knower,
the signifier, while reducing the world to the world as thought, known, and
signified; this often eliminates the difference between the objective reality of
the world and the world as semiotically constructed by human beings. Semiotic reductionism is not always sufficiently aware of the irreducible difference between objective reality on the one hand, and thought, knowledge,
discourse, and signs on the other. Ultimately, signs make sense not only
because they are different, not only because they are coherent among themselves, but also because they are *about* and refer to realities that make sense
themselves. Signs are not autonomous but parasitic on reality. As Paul
Ricoeur clearly demonstrates, our being-in-the-world is the source, condition, and criterion of all our significations. Ontology precedes and conditions semiotics.[3] There may be no "transcendental signified," something
signified completely independently of all systems of signs, although Derrida's
recent reflections on negative theology discussed earlier seem to refer to precisely such a transcendental reality. There remains, however, an irreducible
difference between a signifying sign and a signified reality. We may live *in* the
world of signs and discourses, but we do not live *on* signs and discourses; we
live on real food, real recognition, real meaning, however mediated these
may be by signs and discourse.[4]

In this regard it is crucial to distinguish between mediation and reduction. It is one thing to say, as practically all modern and postmodern Western philosophers have been saying, and rightly, that we do not have an
unmediated access to objective reality in itself, which is the error of objectivism and what postmodernism calls "realism"; and that our relation to
objective reality is always mediated by our thought, knowledge, language,
and other myriad culturally produced signs. In many ways, this is the distinctive contribution of modern Western philosophy and social thought. It

is another thing altogether, however, to say that there is nothing to objective reality other than what we interpret it to be; that we can simply reduce that reality to our interpretation and thus to a world of humanly constructed signs and mediations; and that in our dealings with the world we have only to do with our own thought, knowledge, and signs, not with objective reality *through* such mediations. This reductionist temptation is all the stronger in modern societies where we are indeed immersed in socially mediated signs and artifacts.

Our views will radically change, however, if we shift from the essentially idealist paradigm of thought, language, interpretation, and construction to the concrete, dialectical paradigm of action; if we stop thinking of the human being as primarily a thinker, writer, or interpreter, the model so popular with Western intellectuals; and if we start thinking of the human being as primarily a person who has to act in the real world, struggling to make a living (economics), acquire a minimum of recognition and respect (politics), and search for a meaning of life that transcends sheer contingencies (culture).[5]

To act is to engage in a determinate action in a particular natural environment and a particular society at a particular time, subject to all the real, not merely imagined or interpreted, constraints, contradictions, and possibilities of that nature and society. To act is to make a relevant choice under determinate conditions and determinate possibilities. The possibilities are not infinite, and the choice one does make has very determinate consequences one cannot simply undo. Faced with the necessity of concrete action, then, one cannot afford the luxury of engaging in an infinite play of differences. In relation to determinate situations, some differences are more relevant than others. I am indeed constituted at any one time by an infinite number of differences by virtue of my infinite number of relations with persons and things in the entire universe; but for the purpose of acting in a particular situation, I can and should ignore all relations and differences other than those relevant to the situation. It is simply impossible to act in a world of infinite, imagined possibilities because such a world renders all choices and decisions equally relevant and therefore equally irrelevant.

Some postmodernists also adulate sheer difference in the constitution of a subject—the fractured, multiple, protean self of the modern Western consumer society—as a protest against rigid self-identity; but from the standpoint of action such a multiple self would be only the stuff out of which an individual must forge and shape a coherent, unified self through self-discipline and consistent action, not something simply to be celebrated. Such a celebration would be precisely an accommodation to the capitalist adulation of the free-floating, other-determined, aesthetic self, created and manipulated by the market, a reversion to Kierkegaard's aesthetic stage of existence. Faced with the necessity of living and acting in the world where actions have consequences, such a multiple self would be at best a source of contradiction and anxiety, certainly a task to work on and integrate, but hardly something to celebrate.

Historically, the real challenge of our globalizing, multicultural world, from the standpoint of action, is not so much how to recognize and appreciate difference, although its importance is not to be denied, as how to find ways of living *together* with all these differences. In order to promote recognition and appreciation of difference, we even have to do so *together* through some public means, especially by instituting policies and laws that will promote tolerance, spread information about other cultures, and penalize crimes of hate. If different groups were to live in isolated spaces, admiring their difference from a distance would be sufficient. The historical reality, however, is that they have been thrown together into common space, compelling them to find a mode of living together that will assure a minimum of justice and peace for all. We cannot simply leave one another alone in all their differences. The differences—such as differences in the cultural attitudes toward gender, sex, family, time, politics, religion—themselves must be integrated and adjusted for the common good. There are likewise many issues facing the community as a whole, not just a particular group, which will have an impact on all groups, and which therefore require the mobilization of all groups as citizens of the community, regardless of their differences. These civic actions require transcendence of difference and organization of solidarity. An internally differentiated community requires varying degrees of solidarity of civic action if it is not going to disintegrate under the weight of sheer difference.

Political actions and the making of laws seek to institutionalize systems of identity. Laws are made for all and binding on all, not just for a particular group. They are indeed systems of identity par excellence. Precisely because they are systems of identity, there is also a great and constant danger that the laws may be oppressive to some. The alternative here, however, is not just to denounce all systems of identity indiscriminately, as postmodernists tend to do, for never measuring up to the messianic ideal of justice, but rather to struggle to establish a less oppressive and more liberating one. Merely to denounce all determinate systems of identity as oppressive may be good idealism and immensely pleasurable to a disembodied intellect in search of an uncontaminated perfection, but it fails to respond to the imperatives of action in civic solidarity in a demanding and imperfect world. We cannot afford either pure idealism or cynical realism, which are, in fact, dialectically the same, as Hegel insightfully pointed out. In a world where collaborative civic action is so much demanded, accentuating difference both further fragments the community and enervates the energy for needed cooperative action.[6]

Furthermore, it is the very demand of action—of informed action—for justice in the world that requires analyses of economic, political, and cultural trends in an increasingly interconnected world. Liberating action entails studying all the relevant facts and statistics, putting them in reasonable relationships with one another, and getting a picture of the *whole,* that is, grasping the world as an interconnected totality, as a system, especially with regard to the possibilities of liberation and oppression. This has been the role of dialectical reason in the modern, critical tradition. Hegel's attempt at a unified vision of the whole, the paradigmatic case of the search for totality denounced by every postmodernist, was itself motivated by a desire to restore integrity and wholeness to modern European society increasingly fragmented and bifurcated by the dichotomies of individual and social, civil society and the state, reason and feeling, religion and secularity. It was also the demand of justice and revolutionary action that originally motivated the young Marx to analyze the historical tendencies of capitalism. The many disasters of the twentieth century, with their appeals to totality, have brought disappointments and humiliations to dialectical reason, but this is no reason to retreat into positivistic empiricism and give up on the need for getting as comprehensive, as systematic, and as dynamic a picture of the historical trends of the world as possible.

The drive toward a unified picture of the whole is not just a product of the will to power, as Foucault, Levinas, Lyotard, and others allege, but also that of the concrete will to justice that seeks to discover liberating possibilities in the historical tendencies of the world. It is also part of the perennial human quest for wisdom, of the contemplative will to know reality as an interconnected totality and to discover the place of human destiny in that totality. The best example of this quest is theology that seeks to know God and all other things in their relation to God as their ultimate end. Today, the developing complexity of different specializations makes it impossible for any one person to command a vision of the whole, even a very rough one; but paradoxically, this is all the more reason to try to do so at least through the collaboration of many. As we see in the case of the debate on the ethics of cloning, which is only one case among many, we need a mechanism—maybe a team of scientists, ethicists, economists, and politicians—whereby we can get a grasp of the human and social consequences of commercialized cloning in their interrelatedness. Increasing fragmentation of human knowledge calls for increasing integration and synthesis if we are to protect human integrity. Postmodernists exaggerate and caricature the classical and modern attempts at a vision of the whole. One may argue, as I do, that such an attempt must be cautious and always subject to the proviso of *differance* and negative theology; one cannot argue that we should simply abandon the quest and retreat each into his or her own ethnocentric cave.

Strategically, I propose three reasons why we have to deemphasize difference and emphasize solidarity in action. First, the reified structures and institutions of injustice in its many forms are impossible for any one group to transform. No group can secure its own liberation through its own, unaided effort. Women need collaboration of men, African Americans need cooperation of Euro-Americans, and Native Americans need participation of many other groups. When we attempt to go our own ways and then realize how impossible it is, we try to do what we can do alone, that is, retreat into our own cultural past and keep its memories and hopes alive; but we also feel impotent and despair as far as present political action is concerned.

Second, the context has changed. The original idea of a special theology for each different group was that each group has its own context and therefore also needs its own theology. In an increasingly interconnected world, however, the boundaries among different contexts are no longer so clear. In fact, the same market tendencies of global capitalism provide a common context for all groups, commercializing the image of woman, creating perpetual poverty for certain ethnic groups, increasing the gap between rich and poor in many developing nations, destroying and violating the environment, confining Native Americans to their reservations, and trivializing human life for all. This is not to deny the differences in the modality and intensity of discrimination for different groups; but such differences, one might say, are submerged in the commodification of our *entire* life. The global context is now *the* context of all contexts, before which fragmentation into different groups is becoming increasingly meaningless and counterproductive.

Third, there are issues that affect us all regardless of our differences, which no group can resolve on its own, and for which we cannot escape responsibility as citizens. A just and prosperous economy, a clean environment, and quality of education will be among such issues. The problems of war and peace on the planet and the imperialist policies of the United States as the sole surviving superpower in the world, should likewise be matters of great common concern, as should be the sheer commercialization of human life in all its aspects. Bloody struggles are going on in so many parts of the world, and the United States is involved in many of them on the side of this or that group. The United States still remains the largest arms seller in the world. Through its multinational corporations and militarism, it plays a major role in the killing of life on the planet and threatening the integrity of life in many nations. Big nations kick around small nations. These are not just feminist issues, African American issues, or Hispanic issues, but compelling issues for all. At stake is not just the lives of a particular group but the integrity of human life in its global and cosmic interdependence. Who, however, among the partisans of different groups today are concerned and agonize over these issues, especially over the organization of civic and human solidarity to respond to them?

Nominalism and Human Solidarity

What we need today, then, is a thoroughgoing reflection on human solidarity, on the interdependence of human beings at many levels. Is human solidarity possible on the postmodern basis of nominalist rejection of essences and natures and a purely sociohistorical, genealogical understanding of values? Is postmodernism capable of providing a sense of human solidarity adequate to the cause of justice and liberation it is committed to promoting?

I can well understand why postmodern thinkers are weary of appealing to any sort of nature or essence. Many such appeals have in fact been used to justify exclusion and marginalization of certain minorities. Yet their alternatives are not very satisfactory either. Iris Young's appeal to certain conditions, such as enforced heterosexuality and the sexual division of labor, fails to cover other nonsexual dimensions of women's lives and cuts them off completely from men, turning women and men into totally different kinds of beings. Linda Nicholson's reference to certain historically constructed patterns of family resemblances rather begs the question of why such patterns persist historically and what there is about women that generates such patterns in the first place. In order to avoid reifying certain characteristics as essential and thereby excluding others, Young, Nicholson, and other postmodern feminists take great pains to deny that there are any determinate characteristics shared by all women.

In their procedure they are all nominalists and empiricists. One would think that at the level of empirical appearances, there are and indeed can be no universally shared characteristics among women nor, for that matter, among any group, except in cases of stipulated membership. This is precisely the level of contingency and particularity. All human beings may have the capacity to know, called the intellect, but how much one actually knows, how well, and in what areas depend on all the contingent conditions of life. This is the level where one should not be looking for similarities. By the same token such a purely empiricist approach regards human beings as merely a series of contingent, external characteristics without asking what there is about the being or reality of human beings that generates such characteristics in their humanness. Both Young and Nicholson operate under the false assumption that "nature" or "essence" means characteristics of an individual simply given in their immutability, necessity, and universality; to which, therefore, the only alternative is the sheer empiricism of contingent appearances that are not deeply rooted anywhere in the intrinsic nature of a human being and that therefore simply vary from person to person and in fact from moment to moment even within the "same" person. If there are family resemblances among them, it is not because they are expressions of common humanity or human nature but because they just *happen* to be similar.

In that case it is quite appropriate to ask whether such an approach could provide a basis for ethical solidarity adequate for the political praxis of justice and liberation; and whether the kind of solidarity provided by the common social conditions such as enforced heterosexuality and the sexual division of labor, family resemblances, and the act of common discussion and struggle would be adequate to the cause of justice and liberation.

I see three problems in this approach. First, these postmodern feminists limit their attention to the question of how to define women as a whole or some groups of women as coalition partners in a nonessentialist way. They are explicitly excluding the entire group of men and in some cases other groups of women as well. Their predominant concern is how to find a common interest among women so as to put together an effective coalition or an activist group. This strategy rejects the politics of identity defined in essentialist terms, but it does remain a politics of identity defined in postmodern nominalist terms insofar as it still limits its inclusive concern to a particular gender or a particular group within the same gender. It fails to consider that the praxis of justice involves not only the internal solidarity of a coalition group but also the work of appealing to, and persuading, as many "others" as possible to enter into mutual solidarity and cooperate in changing oppressive laws and practices. Unless one is under the illusion that one's own coalition is possessed of the sheer political power to make such legal changes on its own, and unless one tries to reduce democratic politics to the politics of brute power, one would have to agree that the praxis of justice involves ethical appeals to others for solidarity in action.

Second, on what basis should all the others—simply different from women as a whole as men are or from some women as other women might be who are not part of the coalition—feel an ethical obligation to enter into solidarity with the group, an obligation that often entails great sacrifices? This leads to a more general question: Why should anyone feel an ethical obligation to enter into political solidarity with others at all who are different in gender, class, religion, culture, nationality, and/or other important aspects?

What does ethical solidarity entail? Negatively, ethical solidarity means respecting the dignity of the other in such a way as not to reduce her to an object of my own arbitrary desire and interest, which in turn entails the readiness to control and discipline my own desires in the presence of the other. It means recognizing the ethical demand of the other, the sovereignty of the other over my desire to kill, rape, rob, or otherwise harm, and appreciating the value of the other as somehow greater than the value of satisfying my desire at the expense of the other (Levinas). Positively, ethical solidarity means actually helping to provide the concrete means—economic, political, and cultural—that will ensure a life worthy of that ethical dignity. These two aspects correspond to negative and positive rights in current ethical discussion, and would require both individual and collective action.

Is there a basis, then, for ethical solidarity of this sort at the purely empirical, contingent level where differences reign? Why should a young, white woman enjoying all the privileges of the ruling class in America feel an ethical solidarity, with all its demands on her desire, for the African-American women in the urban ghettos, Latin American men in refugee camps, or old folks in Africa or Asia waiting for their death? What kind of a common interest can she find with them, when she is not likely to gain anything from them? On the other hand, she can gain much by joining a coalition with other young white women in the struggle against discrimination in the professions. Can the temporary coincidence of interests whose scope and duration are purely contingent be the source of an enduring ethical solidarity with those who are different?

It is perhaps essential here to distinguish between the historically specific *mode* of our humanity and the transcendent *grounds* of our human dignity. A human being always exists in a specific mode in terms of gender, class, ethnicity, culture, religion, nationality, and so on. I am a Euro-American, Episcopalian, middle-class, heterosexual, female, U.S. citizen. Can we say, however, that I have a right to be treated with dignity *because* I am a woman, an Episcopalian, a heterosexual, a Euro-American? Why, then, should those who are other in all these regards feel any obligation or ethical solidarity to honor such a right? If you say you have a human right because you are an American, I can equally say that I am a German or a Brazilian or a Chinese. Any appeal to sheer difference can always be contradicted by a like appeal to sheer difference. It would make sense for me to appeal to you to respect my human dignity *because* I am as human as you are *although* you are oppressing me *because* I am an African American, a woman, a homosexual. It would not make sense for me to make the same appeal because I am an African American, a woman, a homosexual. My *mode* of human existence is always historically particular, and the empirical *ground* of oppression has always been likewise particular. The ethical *ground* of human dignity, however, is always universal: the dignity we share as human beings, although such dignity is always concretized in the particularity of its existential mode in terms of class, gender, ethnicity, culture, religion, nationality. Confusing these modes and grounds has been ethically dangerous: oppressions are based precisely on identifying a particular *mode* of human existence as at the same time the *ground* of human dignity and, therefore, also the *ground* for excluding all those who do not share the same mode from human dignity.

Third, where else can we base this human dignity except on human "nature" or "essence"? Empirical appearances are precisely the realm of particularity and do not provide the ground of ethical obligation. Neither can a purely sociohistorical genealogy of norms and values provide a genuinely ethical sense of obligation. What is only socially constructed can also be socially deconstructed. Social norms themselves need critique. We, therefore, need a source of ethical values more universal and more ethically compelling than either individual contingencies or social constructions, and capable of criticizing and challenging all individual and social norms themselves. Such a source is precisely human nature, which is indeed expressed in empirical appearances and social interpretations, but which is also deeper and more universal than either. The human dignity that can challenge and discipline all arbitrary individual and social desires cannot be itself a product of such desires, nor can it be a convenient product of social construction. It can only be rooted in something more enduring than contingent desires, more universal than individual or group particularities, and more profound than social utility: that is, in human nature, which we all share despite all our differences at a level deeper than individual and historical contingencies, and whose dignity lies precisely in having its basic needs, potentialities, and aspirations honored.

At this level of human nature that we share, we can communicate across all the boundaries of identity politics, understand one another despite all the contingent differences, and expand our perspectives and sympathies despite their limitations. It is human nature that enables middle-class Euro-Americans to join the freedom fighters in the South, an African American to sympathize with the poor Afghan refugees fleeing into Pakistan, a Pearl Buck to write about Chinese life with such sensibility and insight, a Shakespeare and a Mozart to find echoes in the hearts of so many non-English and non-Germans, and a Korean to read *Uncle Tom's Cabin* with tears. Identity politics, whether essentialist or nonessentialist, is necessary as long as identity-based oppression continues; but trying to base such politics on purely contingent grounds not only destroys its own ethical basis; it also reduces human life to contingencies of political coalition and struggle, depriving it of the wealth of possibilities in human solidarity, communication, and sensibility. There are deeper, wider, and more enduring solidarities among humanity based on human nature than some liberation politics can imagine. The fear of excluding some persons and groups through hasty essentialization is well founded and must be addressed by any attempt to retrieve the concept of human nature or essence, as I propose to do shortly; but to dismiss the whole idea of human nature for that reason is also to reduce and cheapen human life to the level of sheer difference and particularity without depth and solidarity. A vision of humanity locked into separate groups of unbridgeable, self-satisfied identity is not a very appealing vision of liberated humanity.

Retrieving Human Solidarity as Solidarity of Human Nature

I think it is quite possible to retrieve the classical concept of nature or essence by combining its insistence on the intrinsic and objective character of nature, with the modern concept of historicity and subjectivity. Without going into a full-blown philosophical discussion of nature or essence, I can begin by saying that nature or essence refers to the basic capacities, needs, and structures intrinsic to a being and definitive of the kind of being it is. Appearances and behavioral characteristics that the empiricist looks for are manifestations of this nature under varying social and individual conditions. In the case of human beings, it is also the very nature or essence of humanity to manifest and even discover itself historically through self-reflection and self-creation. This view can preserve both the enduring stability of human nature and the historical variability of its expression; it can also see concrete human existence precisely as a dialectic of stable human nature and its variable historical expressions, where human nature not only expresses but also discovers itself historically.

This also means that we are still in the process of discovering the full shape of human nature, which leaves human nature open to further determination, without, however, denying the validity of what we have already found. What we already know about human nature may be limited, one-sided, and indeed historically conditioned, but this does not mean it is false. What new historical discoveries compel us to do is to expand the scope of the

fundamental capacities, needs, and structures and recast their mutual relations, not to dismiss the whole idea of nature and revert to sheer empiricist
phenomenalism. Certain capacities, needs, and structures, however expanded,
are deeply rooted within the being of a person; they are not mere contingent,
surface manifestations. When some of these fundamental needs are frus-
trated or some of these capacities and structures are destroyed in some
human beings, the conclusion to draw is not that they are not human beings
and therefore to be excluded from the human community, but that their dignity as human beings has been wounded and that we should, therefore, try to
restore that dignity precisely by satisfying those needs and/or repairing those
capacities and structures.

Among the capacities recognized as part of human nature by classical
Western philosophers are the capacities to know, will, desire, feel, sense,
grow, and reproduce. Among the needs recognized as part of human nature
by modern Western thinkers are material goods and services (economy),
recognition as a person (politics), and search for some ultimate meaning
(culture). Erich Fromm mentions the five basic needs for relatedness, transcendence, rootedness, identity, and a frame of orientation and devotion.[7]
Among the structures recognized as part of human nature by modern Western philosophers are sociality and historicity, or mutual interdependence
under given historical conditions. Human nature is a given fact insofar as
these capacities, needs, and sociohistorical interdependence are already there
prior to our conscious recognition and action; human nature is also a historical task insofar as it is the burden of each individual, in social and historical
interdependence, to actualize the capacities and fulfill the needs in such a
way as to achieve a meaningfully integrated and unified life.

In terms of our present issue, namely, human solidarity and its basis in
human nature, it is relevant to emphasize the fact that the basic capacities
and basic needs require social interdependence or solidarity in history for
their actualization. There are four levels of this interdependence or solidarity:
metaphysical, historical, political, and ethical. Metaphysically, human existence is essentially social and historical. We develop our basic capacities and
satisfy our basic needs only through cooperation with others. What is metaphysically essential to all human beings takes place in history, which is a
process of bringing different individuals, groups, nations, and cultures into
common space and making them more and more interdependent, over the
long run, for the development of their basic capacities and the satisfaction of
their basic needs; we are increasingly compelled to recognize this today at all
levels of life in all parts of the globe. Our fortunes and destinies are today
inseparably intertwined; even imperial nations, or perhaps especially imperial

nations, are dependent on the subject nations, as Hegel's dialectic of master and slave shows. Ethically, we have to recognize that we also depend on one another both for the recognition of our own transcendent dignity as human beings and for procuring the social conditions of life worthy of that dignity, and we ought to accept the obligation to help one another in procuring both this recognition and such social conditions. Politically, it is our common burden to recognize this ethical interdependence as our common destiny and turn our metaphysical and historical interdependence into self-conscious acts of solidarity as fellow citizens and human beings so as to build institutions and structures that will recognize and nurture this solidarity.

Solidarity, therefore, is inherent and intrinsic to human existence as such and needs only to be activated. It is not something we have to artificially invent or add to an existence already constituted as an individual, as nominalist empiricism tends to think. It is something deeper than temporary coalitions, family resemblances, and objective social conditions. The great imperative today is precisely to awaken and develop this sense of human solidarity already there in our metaphysical constitution, historical interdependencies, political interconnections, and ethical obligations. In this regard, it is imperative to go beyond the dichotomy that Richard Rorty constantly sets up between history and nature, between sheer "construction" out of nothing and finding something "already waiting," between "creating" solidarity and "recognizing" solidarity.[8] Human solidarity is something already rooted deep in the sociality of human nature, which alone makes it something human and profound; but it is also in need of disciplined cultivation under concrete historical conditions, which also makes it an ethical task and today a compelling task.[9]

It is true that our solidarity and our perspectives are ordinarily limited to the members and perspectives of the group or culture to which we belong, and in this sense we are, in Rorty's expression, "ethnocentric" in our sympathies and perspectives.[10] It is crucial, however, not to reify either the boundaries of groups and cultures or the perspectives inherent in them. History has been eroding such boundaries by bringing different groups, cultures, and religions into common social space, as it has been bringing ethnocentric perspectives into dialectic with changing realities, thereby modifying them, eliminating them altogether, or incorporating them into an integral part of a new synthesis to come. The alternative to a belief in absolute, universal, unchanging truth is not complacent, frankly relativistic ethnocentrism; instead, it is holding on to one's own belief as true insofar as there are reasonable grounds for it within one's own perspective while also remaining open to its further self-critical expansion as a result of the dialectic of interaction with other groups, cultures, and perspectives in the dialectic of the real world.

No ethnocentric view is self-contained and immune from interaction with other perspectives and with history. The shock of World War I destroyed the internal coherence of bourgeois liberalism and liberal theology. Cultural changes have rendered existentialism, so influential forty years ago, rather quaint today. No cultural identity is fixed and frozen. As different groups and cultures interact in common space, they challenge, modify, broaden, and incorporate one another. People in multicultural metropolitan centers such as New York City and Los Angeles, therefore, practice many different cultures and identities. As Gerd Baumann puts it, "all identities are identifications in context" and "thus situational and flexible, imaginative and innovative."[11] We should not essentialize cultures and cultural identities but take them dialectically. In a world where globalization has been thawing, expanding, and in any event challenging all fixed cultural identities and perspectives, it is essential not to reify such identities and perspectives; instead, we should take them precisely in the context of a world history that transcends and challenges all given perspectives, and therefore see them from the perspective of an emergent totality. Pure ethnocentrism is unaware of the challenge of other cultures in the dialectic of world history and would be simply confined to itself and unable to know itself *as* ethnocentric—which implies awareness of the presence of other cultures.

Postmodernism denies the reality of natures and essences in things and reduces that reality to the reality of "social construction." It is sometimes unclear, however, whether social construction is to be taken only in the sense of "mediation," in the sense that all our access to objective reality is mediated by social interpretation, and that we do not have an unmediated access to objective reality in itself—the error of objectivism and realism—or whether social construction is to be taken in the radical sense of "reduction," in the sense that there is indeed nothing to reality except our interpretations, and that we have to do only with our own ideas, not with objective reality by means of such ideas. The first position is now accepted as true beyond all question; the second is certainly questionable.

The idea of social construction in the radical sense of reduction founders on two things: the difference between social construction or interpretation and social reality, and the difference between social reality and natural reality. Neither social reality nor natural reality is reducible to social interpretation. Consider first the irreducible difference between social construction and social reality. Just as there is a real difference between our idea of death and real death, so there is a real difference between social construction of history and historical reality itself. History—laws, institutions, social trends, crises, wars—is indeed something "interpreted" by us and even "made" by us; but as Hegel and others have pointed out, history has a way of contradicting, unmasking, and even destroying our interpretations, as each age and society can delude itself about itself through its "ideology," by producing consequences unintended and/or unforeseen by the historical agents themselves and transcending their interpretations. There is no war that does not contradict the original intentions of the warmongers. If our interpretations are to remain relevant, they must change and reflect the changing contours of historical reality, which remains the judge of our social construction.

This irreducible difference between social construction and social reality is itself derived from the irreducible difference between social reality and natural reality. The social reality that often contradicts our social construction is more than social construction precisely because as "reality" irreducible to thought, language, and interpretation, social reality presupposes natural reality in the two senses of physical nature and given structure.

First, social reality is itself built upon physical reality. A law, an example of social reality par excellence, is more than social construction; to be real, a law must be physically embodied in law enforcement officers, their physical weapons, office buildings, and public documents that promulgate it. These officers, weapons, buildings, and documents are more than ideas and interpretations; they are the very bases and judges of the latter. Weapons fired kill whether intended or not.

Second, social reality cannot ignore certain "given" structures and tendencies of things, that is, their "natures" and "essences." When social reality ignores such natures, human beings revolt and demand change. Hungry people revolt and demand food. Oppressed people revolt and demand liberation. Isolated people suffer alienation and long for friendship and solidarity. There are certain laws of our nature that we contradict only at great peril to ourselves. These laws and tendencies cannot just be "interpreted" away into nonbeing. In short, we cannot reduce social and natural reality to social construction. Such reductionism is anthropocentrism gone mad. The world is more than a text, although certainly mediated by a text.

Derrida once said that in a world where there is no absolute point of departure, no transcendent truth outside the field of writing, and therefore only a purely strategic justification of discourse—in such a world "the efficacy of the thematic of *differance* may very well, indeed must, one day be superseded, lending itself if not to its own replacement, at least to enmeshing itself in a chain that in truth it never will have governed."[12] I submit that this chain is precisely the chain of history, with its objective demand for the solidarity of others.

Toward a Theology of Solidarity of Others

My contention, then, is that the times call for a change in our paradigm, not for a theology of difference but for a theology of solidarity; not the solidarity of the same but precisely the solidarity of the different, the solidarity of strangers, the solidarity of those who are other to one another. We do not as yet live in a world where the category of the other has become irrelevant; it does remain compelling in a world where oppressive systems of identity still abound in many parts of the world, including the United States. My contention has not been that difference as such is irrelevant but that its absolute accentuation is philosophically incoherent, historically naive, and politically counterstrategic. The new theological paradigm I propose is that of solidarity of others.

Let me begin with some notes on the term: Whenever I use the phrase "solidarity of others," I am always asked, "Why solidarity *of* others, and not solidarity *with* others?" My answer is that solidarity with others implies some privileged vantage point from which I or we look at others as other and choose which others to enter into solidarity with. Furthermore, we tend to look at these others as only victims needing my or our assistance; we tend to be paternalistic. Solidarity of others, somewhat uncolloquial but grammatically perfectly correct, implies that there is no privileged perspective, that all are others to one another, that we as others to one another are equally responsible, and that all are subjects, not objects. I also use the word "other" in two senses: In the ethical, Levinasian sense, it means those whose dignity forbids reduction to a system of identity and totality. In the sociological sense, it means those who have been excluded and marginalized precisely because they have been so reduced to a system of identity. The term includes both senses in one, implying an ethical critique of the sociological phenomenon of marginalization, and demanding that sociological others should be treated as ethical others, which is possible only in and through solidarity of others. Solidarity of others, then, is my way of deconstructing and sublating postmodernism in the Hegelian sense of *Aufhebung:* Otherness is critically *negated* in its absolute claim, *transcended* into the solidarity of others, and *preserved* in its proper meaning in that solidarity.

Are there resources in the Christian tradition for this new paradigm, a theology of the solidarity of others? In my view, Christianity not only has abundant resources for this kind of theology. In fact, solidarity of others has also been of the very essence of Christian faith. I would like to single out three aspects of Christian faith as especially relevant: the Trinitarian conception of God, the model of Jesus Christ, and the dialectic of divine incarnation and divine incomprehensibility, or positive and negative theology. The Trinitarian conception of God, which is the Christian conception of God, is the divine paradigm and source of all created forms of solidarity of the different. Jesus Christ is the decisive embodiment of this solidarity through his life, ministry, passion, crucifixion, and resurrection. Christians are called upon to live the tension between the incarnational dynamic of determinate concretization of faith, hope, and love on one hand; and on the other hand the self-transcending dynamic of the critique and judgment of all determinate achievements under the eschatological reservation.

First, the Trinitarian conception of God as the divine exemplar and source of all created forms of solidarity: According to ancient Christian tradition, God is Father, Son, and the Holy Spirit. In the immanent Trinity there are three persons who share the same divine nature, which is why there are three persons, but not three gods. Each person is a subsistent relation; the whole being of each person lies in its constitutive relationality—or solidarity—to the other two characterized by a relation of difference or "relative opposition," to use a technical term. The Father is not the Son; the begetter is not the begotten. The Father and the Son are not the Holy Spirit; the source of the procession is not the same as the term of the procession. For all these differences the three persons share the numerically identical divine substance. There is perfect equality among the three, as there is perfect mutual indwelling, or perichoresis, of the three in one another. God is a community, a solidarity, of three persons, truly different as persons yet truly united as divine. As there is a real, irreducible difference among the three persons, so there is a complete, total sharing among them. There is a direct, not inverse, proportion between solidarity and otherness in God. It is this triune God who creates finite others and invites them to join her in her eschatological Trinitarian communion by working for solidarity of others in this world. In this economic work the Son, or Word, serves as the divine model and source of communion between God and creation as well as between creatures. The Holy Spirit brings about this communion and solidarity by unifying the divided, reconciling the alienated, and incorporating them into the body of the Son. The Father is the one who sends both the Son and the Holy Spirit for these divine missions of establishing communion among the different and alienated and bringing them into the communion of the immanent Trinity. For all Christians and especially those working for solidarity of others, the triune God should remain a constant source of inspiration as well as an inexhaustible object of profound contemplation.

Second, we know very well today, from all the historical-critical studies, that Jesus had a preferential love for the marginalized others of his society: the poor, sick, hungry, weeping, the impure, the lepers, the blind, lame, and deaf—all of whom were victims of closed systems of identity. Jesus ate and drank with them, preached the good news of the liberating reign of God to come, identified himself with them as the eschatological judge, suffered and was crucified on their behalf, and was vindicated by God by rising from the dead on the third day. Thus he was embodying the demand of justice for them in his life praxis, embodying their sufferings and all the sins of the world that cause suffering in his passion and crucifixion as the Suffering Servant for all, and embodying the hopes of all for liberating salvation in his resurrection. As the new Adam through whom human beings are born again, and as the Word through whom all things were created and re-created, all creatures are called to belong to his body, enjoying communion and solidarity in that body as brothers and sisters and as children of the same Father in the Son in the power of the Holy Spirit. Jesus Christ as the Son of God incarnate is the embodiment of human solidarity in their sinful oppressiveness, their need for liberation, their sufferings as victims, and their eschatological hopes.

Third, Christians are invited to live the tension between the determinacy of the incarnation and the divine transcendence of all determinacy. The Word of God took flesh in the determinate humanity of Jesus of Nazareth at a determinate time and place, doing determinate things. The whole Christian imperative is to recognize this determinate dimension of the divine and its demand for determinate praxis whereby the reign of God becomes concrete in this world. The infinite God does not remain merely infinite but became a determinate flesh, demanding that we too incarnate our faith, hope, and love for God in determinate acts of justice, peace, and love. To actualize and incarnate the demand of the reign of God is to posit determinate acts, establish determinate laws, and critique determinate sources of injustice and oppression. The fact that these determinate acts and laws are not identical with the eschatological perfection of the reign of God is no reason why Christians should not engage in them. Incarnation means immersion in determinate history and determinate society with all its determinate tendencies, pressures, and possibilities. It means "dirtying your hands," sometimes sacrificing purity of intention and making compromises for the second-best outcome.

Derrida's negative theology is afraid of such compromises in the concrete world. Even while saying that justice must be done here and now, he immediately goes on to warn us of the dangers of compromise and the proviso of negative theology, that no determinate religion, messianism, law, or democracy ever measures up to the eschatological, messianic ideal. He is more anxious to tell us what we should *not do*—absolutize the determinate—than to tell us what determinate things we should *do*; he is more interested in subverting, destabilizing, discrediting, and contaminating all claims to identity indiscriminately than in constructing and nurturing a system of identity that would be less oppressive and more liberating. All determinate embodiments are only to be critiqued. In fact, he tends to equate determinacy itself with injustice.[13] In this abhorrence for the determinate and concrete, an essential dimension of the bodily world in which we are meant to live, Derrida brings himself perilously close to being a neognostic as well as close to a postmodern version of Hegel's "unhappy consciousness."

The Christian tradition speaks not only of the incarnate, determinate God but also of the incomprehensible, ever mysterious God, who is always greater, *semper major,* more wholly other, than anything we can say of God. The infinite difference between God and creatures rules out all univocal description or predication of God. The ultimate in our knowledge of God, according to Aquinas, is the humble confession that we do not know what God is.[14] A vision of the divine essence is a possibility only in the eschaton; but even then God does not cease to be incomprehensible, as we do not cease to be finite. According to Karl Rahner, even the idea of analogical predication is not meant to make us complacent about the possibility of predication; it is not simply a hybrid between univocity and equivocity. It is meant to describe the movement of the human spirit caught in the tension of determinate historical existence and stretching toward the incomprehensible God.[15] As Derrida puts it a little more strongly, the fracture between being and knowing "extends its crack into the analogy between God and me, Creator and creature. This time the analogy does not repair, nor reconcile, but aggravates the dissociation."[16]

Christians are meant to live this tension between the determinate and the incomprehensible, not to flee from the determinate in the name of the eschatological proviso of negative theology. Rejection of the determinate is the rejection of the Incarnation. Rejection of divine incomprehensibility is rejection of human finitude. Christians are meant to live the tension between the two with all its ambiguities, despairs, and hopes. With regard to the contemporary task of establishing the solidarity of others, this means full commitment to that solidarity in all its determinacy; it also means the constant discipline of self-criticism and self-negation with regard to any form of determinate identity proposed as a concrete form of solidarity. Always sensitive to the heterological imperative and the proviso of negative theology, one would hesitate to absolutize or reify any determinate form of identity even while fully committing oneself to it. In trying to concretize solidarity in a determinate form, we should also try to avoid any totalizing reduction of the other by absolutizing a particular form of identity; likewise, in trying to avoid such totalizing reduction, we should also try to find a determinate form that would best concretize solidarity, at least for the time being. That is to say, to practice solidarity of others is to live the tension between two poles, without attempting to abolish either, between solidarity and otherness, as well as between the concretizing dynamic of the incarnate God and the transcending dynamic of the incomprehensible God.[17]

I have thus far presented certain resources for a theology of solidarity of others from the Christian perspective. Someone is likely to ask whether what I have done is appropriate in a pluralistic world, where not everyone is a Christian. My brief answer is that pluralism does not entail reducing every distinctive belief to a common denominator or speaking from a neutral, universal perspective—which is precisely the opposite of pluralism. What it does entail is thinking hard through one's own position with what I called the heterological imperative, exploring within the best and deepest of one's own tradition the possibility of making room for the other, and exposing oneself to the dialectic of dialogue and interaction with the other. This is exactly what I have tried to do. I have taken the historical demands of today for some sort of solidarity of others very seriously and examined some of the best and deepest aspects of the Christian tradition as well as some of the philosophical traditions that have something to say about living together in history. What remains to be done is to invite others to a dialogue.

Richard Rorty says that anyone who tries to provide a nonhistoricist and nonnominalist foundation of morality must be either a theologian or a metaphysician at heart.[18] For the reasons I have presented, I am proud to say that I am both, with a difference.

As I said, solidarity of others not only has abundant support in the theological resources of the Christian tradition; it is also of the very essence of the Christian faith. After a philosophical prolegomenon with appropriate critiques of the philosophies, movements, and cultures of postmodernism, I now turn in Part Two to an elaboration of the theology of solidarity, the main burden of this book.

Notes

1. See especially Jacques Derrida, *Of Grammatology* (corrected ed.; Baltimore: Johns Hopkins University Press, 1974), 27–73.

2. The two quotations are from Jacques Derrida, *Margins of Philosophy* (Chicago: University of Chicago Press, 1982), 11 and 10, respectively.

3. See Paul Ricoeur, *Intepretation Theory: Discourse and the Surplus of Meaning* (Fort Worth, Tex.: Texas Christian University Press, 1976), 19–22, 34–37.

4. For a socially critical, materialist approach to the problem of difference, see Nicholson and Seidman's introduction to *Social Postmodernism: Beyond Identity Politics* (ed. Linda Nicholson and Steven Seidman; Cambridge: Cambridge University Press, 1995), 1–35.

5. For a further elaboration of this concept of action, see my *Dialectic of Salvation: Issues in Theology of Liberation* (Albany, N.Y.: SUNY Press, 1989), 166–68.

6. For my critique of Derrida on this point, see Anselm Kyongsuk Min, "The Other without History and Society: A Dialogue with Derrida," in *Philosophy of Religion in the Twenty-First Century* (ed. D. Z. Phillips; New York: Palgrave, 2001), 167–85.

7. Erich Fromm, *The Sane Society* (Greenwich, Conn.: Fawcett Publications, 1955), chap. 3.

8. Richard Rorty, *Contingency, Irony, and Solidarity* (Cambridge: Cambridge University Press, 1989), 94, 196.

9. For an extensive, formal presentation of an anthropology of solidarity, see Anselm Kyongsuk Min, "Praxis and Liberation: Toward a Theology of Concrete Totality" (Ph.D. diss., Vanderbilt University, 1989), 74–178.

10. Richard Rorty, *Objectivity, Relativism, and Truth* (Cambridge: Cambridge University Press, 1991), 23.

11. Gerd Baumann, *The Multicultural Riddle: Rethinking National, Ethnic, and Religious Identities* (New York: Routledge, 1999), 138.

12. Derrida, *Margins of Philosophy*, p. 7.

13. John D. Caputo, *The Prayers and Tears of Jacques Derrida: Religion without Religion* (Bloomington: Indiana University Press, 1997), 128.

14. Thomas Aquinas, *Selected Writings* (ed. and trans. Ralph McInerny; London: Penguin Books, 1998), 316.

15. Karl Rahner, *Foundations of Christian Faith: An Introduction to the Idea of Christianity* (New York: Seabury, 1978), 72–73.

16. Jacques Derrida, *On the Name* (ed. Thomas Dutoit; trans. David Wood, John P. Leavey Jr., and Ian McLeod; Stanford, Calif.: Stanford University Press, 1995), 66.

17. I have discussed different aspects of a theology of solidarity of others in the following articles (all by Anselm Kyongsuk Min): "Toward a Dialectic of Totality and Infinity: Reflections on Emmanuel Levinas," *Journal of Religion* 78, no. 4 (Oct. 1998): 571–92; "Solidarity of Others in the Body of Christ: A New Theological Paradigm," *Toronto Journal of Theology* 12, no. 2 (fall 1998): 239–54; "Dialectical Pluralism and Solidarity of Others: Towards a New Paradigm," *Journal of the American Academy of Religion* 65, no. 3 (fall 1998): 587–604; "From Autobiography to Fellowship of Others: Reflections on Doing Ethnic Theology Today," in *Journeys at the Margin* (ed. Peter Phan; Collegeville, Minn.: Liturgical, 1999), 135–59; "From Tribal Identity to Solidarity of Others: Theological Challenges of a Divided Korea," *Missiology* 27, no. 3 (July 1999): 333–45; "Dialectic of Salvation in Solidarity: Philosophy of Religion after Kant and Kierkegaard," in *Kant and Kierkegaard on Religion* (ed. D. Z. Phillips and

Timothy Tessin; New York: St. Martin's, 2000), 278–94; "Solidarity of Others in the Power of the Holy Spirit: Pneumatology in a Divided World," in *Advents of the Spirit* (ed. Bradford Hinze and Lyle Dabney; Milwaukee: Marquette University Press, 2001), 416–43; "The Other without History and Society," in *Philosophy of Religion* (ed. Phillips), 167–85.

18. Rorty, *Contingency, Irony, and Solidarity,* xv.

PART TWO

SOLIDARITY OF OTHERS: TOWARD A POSTMODERN THEOLOGY

FIVE

RENEWING THE DOCTRINE OF THE HOLY SPIRIT IN AN OPPRESSIVE WORLD
*Prolegomena to a Pneumatology of Liberating Solidarity**

Under the impact of contemporary history, theological revision has been going on at an increasingly faster pace in recent decades. The rise of new intellectual horizons in practically all areas of human knowledge; the perception of outraged justice and oppressed humanity in too many parts of the world; the impact of economic, political, and cultural changes in general; the lessons of historical criticism in biblical studies—all these, and many other factors, have led to revisionary attempts, often quite radical (e.g., pluralism in theology of non-Christian religions), in all areas of traditional dogmatics. Theologies of the last two centuries have been essentially "revisionary" (Tracy) theologies. In this regard it is safe to say that some areas have been touched more than others by the revisionary spirit. Christology, ecclesiology, theology of religions, theological ethics, theology of ministry, and theology of secularity, among others, have undergone more intense and more systematic revisionary scrutiny than has, say, the doctrine of the Trinity.

In this chapter I propose to deal with the preliminary, systematic issues involved in renewing the doctrine of the Holy Spirit for our time, focusing in particular on three questions: (1) What is the historical context that demands such renewal and to which such renewal seeks to respond? (2) What is the scriptural basis for such renewal? (3) What sort of shift is required in the categories that control the systematic reconstruction of the

---

* This chapter was originally presented as a paper at the Euro-American Studies Seminar during the annual meeting of the American Academy of Religion, Kansas City, November 23–26, 1991. I thank the Faculty Development Committee of Belmont Abbey College for funding the research and writing of this paper during the summer of 1991.

doctrine? As should be clear, I am not here trying to elaborate even an outline of a doctrine of the Spirit, which I do try to provide in the next chapter,
but only to discuss the necessary presuppositions, the prolegomenon, of such
a doctrine.

Dialectic of Contexts

The most frequently mentioned contexts of theology today are the global,
the regional, the ecclesial, and the academic, each with its own "public"
(Tracy) and its own set of problems to be addressed in its own way. The
global context consists of the pressing problems of economic, racial, sexual,
and ecological liberation affecting all the countries of the world, and the
daunting challenges of establishing a minimum of political solidarity essential for just and peaceful coexistence, domestic and international, in an
increasingly multicultural and pluralistic world. The regional context refers
to the set of needs and problems peculiar to a particular region of the world
with its own history and culture, such as North America as an imperialist,
capitalist power, Latin America with its legacy of colonialism and dependent
economy, East Asia with its non-Christian culture caught in the grip of mod-
ernizing development and cultural revival. Thus we have been speaking of
"North American theology," "Asian theology," Western "feminist theology,"
African-American "womanist theology," and the like in an increasingly self-
conscious way. The ecclesial context consists of problems and needs internal
to a particular Christian communion or Christianity as a whole, ranging
from the problem of ecclesial identity to declining membership to the issue
of women's ordination and the relationship between laity and clergy. The
academic context consists of the problems facing theology such as criteria of
meaning and truth, rules of interpretation and verification, and other marks
that lend scientific status and intellectual credibility to a discipline that
must defend the intelligibility and salvific relevance of Christian faith and
must do so as one discipline among other disciplines within the contemporary university.[1]

Although these four contexts are mutually distinct and irreducible, I would
like to argue that their distinctiveness and autonomy are at best relative and
that they are not four "coequal" contexts either in theological significance or
in conditioning or contextualizing power. Among the four contexts the
global context of the struggle for liberation and coexistence in a pluralistic
world is *the* overriding and unifying context of *all* theologies, contextualizing
the regional, the academic, and the ecclesial contexts themselves. The global
situation—the world—that generates the cry for liberation and the need for
solidarity that makes it possible for "strangers" or "others" to live together in

a multicultural context—is not something external to either the particular regions or the academe or the church; these three contexts are "in" that world and "of" that world. The global demand of liberation and solidarity should not be the sole concern of "socioethical" theology, as though it were only marginally important to scientific theology and church dogmatics.

The global condition today is defined by the conflict between imperialist forces trying to impose their respective economic and political interests on the rest of the world in the name of a "new world order" and the indigenous forces trying to secure even a minimum of autonomy and dignity against the pressures of global imperialism. This conflict is a product of the increasing interdependence of nations and regions brought about by the dynamics of trade and technology unleashed by the imperialist nations themselves. The result is the globalization of the internal contradictions of capitalism, with its ideology of freedom, commercialization of all aspects of life, and underlying class struggle between rich and poor. All this generates local and regional strifes and revolutions, incalculable ecological disaster, and the ever-present threat of military dictatorship over populations demanding liberation, as well as the threat of military and nuclear interventions by imperialist nations in regions seeking autonomy. The collapse of Soviet Communism may mean the end of the anticommunist ideology as a potent capitalist political tool in the suppression of internal dissent as well as in the justification of overseas adventurism; but it does *not* mean the end of the problems and contradictions inherent in the capitalist order itself.

These dynamics and conflicts of global capitalism also bring together different peoples of the world, along with their different cultures and religions, into common political space, subjecting them to the dialectic of capitalism that both represses and homogenizes, often pitting one group against another. But the dynamics of global capitalism also expose the dominant majority to the challenge of the other in its many forms—economic, cultural, and religious—and sensitizes them to the reality of an increasingly multicultural, pluralistic world. There is not a single metropolis in the world today that has not been touched by multiculturalism. If no indigenous, non-Western culture is safe from contamination by Western, especially American, culture, there is also no Western enclave free from the presence of non-Western cultures. For opposite reasons both Western and non-Western nations are undergoing the trauma of multiculturalism; the former because they have brought different peoples into their midst as cheap laborers, nurses, doctors, mine workers, and maids, often as "illegal aliens"; the latter because they are thoroughly dependent on Western nationals for capital, managerial know-how, and consumption of what they produce.

This global condition also contains an internal demand to resolve those contradictions and inhumanities, a demand expressed in the cry of the masses (*ochlos*) for the basic needs of life, equality, and justice, literally a matter of life and death for the absolute majority; and in the growing sensitivity of the middle classes to ecological issues, likewise a matter of life and death, indeed, for all humanity. The increasing restlessness in the former Communist nations such as Russia, the People's Republic of China, the eastern part of Germany, and the many nations of Eastern Europe now making the transition from bureaucratic communism to capitalism, testify not only to the problems of transition but also to the inherent contradictions of capitalism itself. Perhaps the most common and profound challenge is to devise a system in which those who are different in race, culture, and religion can still live together with a modicum of justice, equality, and sense of solidarity as human beings, to promote a culture of "solidarity of others."

The regions, the academe, and the church are subject to this global condition and challenged by this global demand. They are subject to the idolatry of economic and technological power, conditioned by the ideological horizon created by that idolatry, immersed in the ambiguities and contradictions inherent in the global condition, and certainly always exposed, whether they like it or not, to the challenge of the other.

In such a world the concerns of a regional theology cannot be abstracted from the conflicts introduced into the region precisely by the global forces. The colonial legacy and continuing economic and political dependence of Latin America are simply inseparable from the imperialist forces of the North on which they depend, although the problems created by such interdependence are relatively different in Latin America and North America. Likewise, in such a world, theology's academic pursuit of "truth" must be sensitive to the question of "justice" if it is not to serve the oppressive status quo; it must attempt to discern ways of making theological sense of the immense, concrete suffering and evil imposed by that status quo and to provide transcendent yet historically effective hope for the many struggles to overcome that suffering against the "powers and principalities" of the world. It must be a socially "critical" pursuit of "truth" that also "liberates" humans from all dehumanizing oppressions while also reconciling them with a modicum of mutual solidarity. A fortiori, a church preoccupied with its own internal matters—be they preaching, the liturgy, management, or spirituality—would not be a church faithful to its own evangelical identity and mission, that of first exemplifying through its own *Lebenspraxis* and then proclaiming in its prophetic words the messianic *basileia* of God inaugurated by Jesus, its inspiring vision of the whole of creation and humanity reconciled with the triune God in a solidarity of others, and its demand for concrete and effective *metanoia* toward that solidarity. The church does not exist for its own sake; it exists for the other, for the liberating redemption of the world in solidarity.

In short, *prior* to the distinction among regional, scientific, ecclesial, and socioethical theologies, *all* theologies—including dogmatic, moral, liturgical, sacramental, spiritual, and historical theologies—must be sensitive to, and guided directly or indirectly by, this global *Sitz im Leben* and its demand for liberation in solidarity, which constitute, as it were, the "ontological" (Heidegger) condition or horizon for all "ontic" theologies.

The Bible on the Spirit

Without going into the specifics of pneumatology, let me now go on to summarize briefly the various biblical teachings concerning the Spirit (ignoring the differences of traditions within the Bible), before going on to ask, in the next section, what such teachings demand of constructive pneumatology in light of the contemporary context and its screaming needs.

The Hebrew Bible pictures the Spirit (*ruakh*) as the divine power that creates, sustains, and renews the life of all creation (Gen 1:2, Ps 33:6; 104: 29–30; Job 33:4; 34:14–15). At crucial junctures of the nation's history, the Spirit commissions political leaders (e.g., Moses, Gideon, Saul, David) on behalf of the people and inspires prophets (e.g., Isaiah, Jeremiah, Ezekiel) to proclaim justice and repentance (Ezek 11:5). The Spirit transforms personal and national life into a new people of God, changing a "heart of stone" into a "heart of flesh" and guaranteeing God's fidelity to the new covenant (Ezek 11:19–20; 36:26–28; Ps 51:10–12; Isa 59:21). The outpouring of the Spirit will be a sign of the last day, the "day of the Lord" (Joel 2:28). The Spirit will empower the future messiah to inaugurate a reign of justice and peace and create a community of liberated life in which the alienation among different human groups, between humanity and nature, and between humanity and God is definitively overcome (Isa 11, 32, 61). In short, the Spirit is the creative, vitalizing, activating, liberating, empowering, eschatological presence of God in humanity and creation.[2]

New Testament images of the Spirit are thoroughly christological, as its Christology is thoroughly Trinitarian (not yet, of course, in the technical sense of later conciliar definitions). The Spirit, "the Spirit of God," is also "the Spirit of Jesus" (Acts 16:7), "the Spirit of Christ" (Rom 8:9; 1 Pet 1:11), "the Spirit of the Lord" (2 Cor 3:17; Acts 5:9), "the Spirit of Jesus Christ"

(Phil 1:19), and "the Spirit of his Son" (Gal 4:6). The Spirit is "the promise of my Father" (Luke 24:49; cf. Acts 2:38–39), the Counselor "whom I shall send to you from the Father, even the Spirit of truth, who proceeds from the Father," who "will bear witness to me" (John 15:26). We are "sanctified by the Spirit for obedience to Jesus Christ" (1 Pet 1:2). The function of the Spirit is to be understood only in relation to Jesus Christ, as the function of Jesus Christ is to be understood only in relation to God the Father.[3]

As the eternal Son and *eikōn* of God, Christ is the divine principle *in, through,* and *for* whom the world is both created and re-created (2 Cor 4:4; Col 1:15–16). He is the "first-born of all creation" (Col 1:15), "the first-born among many brethren" (Rom 8:29). All humans are "called into the *koinōnia* of his Son" (1 Cor 1:9), "to be conformed to the image of his Son" (Rom 8:29), destined "to be his sons through Jesus Christ" (Eph 1:5). In Christ there is a primordial, divine solidarity of all humanity and indeed of all creation both with God and among themselves. Through their solidarity in sin and death, "in Adam all die" (1 Cor 15:22), and the whole of creation was subjected to futility and the bondage of decay (Rom 8:20–21). Hence, it was the mission of the Son, "the first-born from the dead" (Col. 1:18), to re-create and reestablish the original solidarity of all creation by justifying, sanctifying, reconciling, and uniting all things, "renewing" humanity "after the *eikōn* of its creator" (Col. 3:10). The Son is making us "all one in Christ Jesus" beyond all invidious and oppressive distinctions—religious, ethnic, sexual, political, and economic (Gal 3:28; Col 3:11; Eph 2)—and liberating all creation from the power of sin and death, "the last enemy" (1 Cor 15:26), so that "as in Adam all die, so also in Christ shall all be made alive" (1 Cor 15:22).

Jesus of Nazareth showed his sonship by proclaiming not himself but the approaching *basileia* of God his Father and its eschatological demand for conversion and new life. He preached God's unconditional love; total trust in God's caring providence; freedom from the bondage of law, wealth, and power; a discipleship of self-sacrificing service for the other; a preferential love for the wretched of the earth; and a preferential warning to the rich and mighty of this world regarding the ultimate eschatological reversal of human fortunes in God's kingdom of justice. Jesus not only preached but also lived in his praxis the good news, the warning, and the demand of the kingdom, in the kind of company he kept, the many exorcisms liberating the oppressed from the power of evil, and his daring prophetic critique of the ruling classes of the day. He did all these to the point of being executed, as a political criminal, by the mightiest empire of the ancient world. God, however, did not abandon him to death and futility, but vindicated the divine validity of his life by raising him from the dead and exalting him as Lord, the Messiah, the Son of God.

The vocation of the Christian, then, is to enter into the discipleship of identification and solidarity with this crucified yet risen Lord, to live "in" Christ, to "put on" Christ, to "live no longer for themselves but for him who for their sake died and was raised" (2 Cor 5:15). To be baptized is to be crucified, buried, and raised with Christ (Rom 6:3–11; Col 2:12). Under the reign of sin, "it is no longer I that do it, but sin which dwells within me" (Rom 7:17); but in the reign of grace, "it is no longer I who live, but Christ who lives in me" (Gal 2:20). Entering into a solidarity of life and death with Christ entails "walking in newness of life" (Rom. 6:4), crucifying the "old," sinful nature and the "world" in us, and putting on "new" humanity (Col 3:5–10). Thus we are in the primordial solidarity of destiny with Christ, the original *eikōn* and Son of God, through the concrete discipleship of crucifixion and resurrection; we are called to be "renewed" according to the Creator's *eikōn* (Col 3:10) and live as God's free children, not as frightened slaves (Gal 4:7). As God's own *eikōn* and children in Christ, we are also called upon to enter into a solidarity of unity and equality with one another, beyond all destructive divisions, for we "are all one in Christ Jesus," "the first-born among many brethren," to whose *eikōn* we are meant to be "conformed" (Gal 3:28; Col 3:11; Rom 8:29).

The mission of the Son is to overcome alienating divisions and hostilities and reconcile and unite all humanity and all creation with God and among themselves by rendering them truly the images and children of God in him, the primordial image and Son of God, so that God will reign over all her creation and "will be all in all" (1 Cor 15:28, author's translation). Hence, the mission of the Spirit, the Spirit of the Son, is to promote the Christification of the world by promoting God's *basileia* in the world and by unifying and reconciling the world with God in Christ. As Leonardo Boff puts it, "The mission of the Spirit consists in permanently actualizing the significance of the incarnation as a process through which God the Son takes on history with all its changes and makes it holy history, the history of the blessed Trinity."[4]

Thus, various New Testament traditions portray the Spirit as the empowering divine presence intimately involved in the mission of Jesus, the development of the Christian community, and the incorporation of all humanity and creation into the sonship of Christ and their reconciliation with the Father and among themselves. The Lukan tradition presents the Spirit as the inner divine power of Jesus of Nazareth, inspiring and empowering him in his *entire* messianic career, from conception to resurrection. Through the Spirit, Jesus was conceived (Luke 1:35) and revealed to Simeon as the Messiah (Luke

2:26, 30). Through the descent of the Spirit, Jesus inaugurated the new messianic age and his own ministry as the messiah (Luke 3:22; Acts 10:38), conquering the forces of evil in the wilderness of temptations (Luke 4:1). He returned to Galilee "in the power of the Spirit" (Luke 4:14), and was anointed and commissioned by the Spirit to preach the good news to the poor (Luke 4:18), "rejoicing in the Holy Spirit" (Luke 10:21), and empowered to conquer demonic forces of evil (Luke 11:20; Matt 12:28). Finally, Jesus, who "through the eternal Spirit offered himself without blemish to God" (Heb 9:14) on the cross, was also raised from the dead by the same Spirit (Rom 8:11).

Just as the Spirit permeated the messianic life of Jesus of Nazareth and empowered him to live and proclaim the kingdom of his Father on earth, rendering him the fitting embodiment of the eternal Image and Son of the Father, so also the Spirit acts in the world to "incorporate" all humanity and creation into the sonship of Christ and reconcile them with God the Father so that "God will be all in all." The Spirit, as the Spirit of the risen Lord, seeks to actualize *universally,* making effective for all, what Jesus of Nazareth accomplished in the *particularity* of his historical life.

The mission of the Spirit is first of all to incorporate humanity into the body of Christ and enable them to live "in Christ," whose Spirit she is. The Spirit does this by bearing witness to, and revealing, the "mystery" of Christ, especially Christ crucified (1 Cor 2:2, 7, 10), and enabling us to confess that "Jesus is Lord" (1 Cor 12:3). It is only through the Spirit that we belong to Christ: "Anyone who does not have the Spirit of Christ does not belong to him" (Rom. 8:9 NRSV). The Spirit is precisely the Spirit of "life in Christ Jesus" (Rom 8:2). To live in Christ is to live in the Spirit; to be a member of Christ's body is to be (part of) the temple of the Spirit, who dwells in us (1 Cor 3:16).

Just as Christ is the primordial Son of God, so the Spirit as "the Spirit of his [God's] Son" is "the spirit of adoption" (Rom 8:15), through whom we become "sons [and daughters] in the Son [filii in Filio]." "God has sent the Spirit of his Son into our hearts, crying 'Abba! Father!'" (Gal 4:6), and "it is the Spirit herself bearing witness with our spirit that we are children of God" (Rom. 8:16). "All who are led by the Spirit of God are children of God" (Rom 8:14). Through the Spirit we "are being changed into his *eikōn* from one degree of glory to another" (2 Cor 3:18).

The Spirit effects this adoption of God's children by liberating, transforming, reconciling, empowering, and assuring. The Spirit that "gives life" (2 Cor 3:6) liberates us from the power of sin, death, and the law (Rom 8:2) by justifying and sanctifying us and enabling us to "put to death the deeds of the body" (Rom 8:13 NRSV). "Where the Spirit of the Lord is, there is freedom" (2 Cor 3:17 NRSV). We received "the spirit of sonship," not "the spirit of slavery to fall back into fear" (Rom 8:15). This liberation also entails transformation of the old life of the "flesh" into "the new life of the Spirit" (Rom 7:6), living and walking by the Spirit, whose fruits are love, joy, peace, patience, kindness, goodness, faithfulness, gentleness, and self-control (Gal 5:22–25), whereby we become "servants of one another" (Gal 5:13). It means being "crucified to the world" and rising as "a new creation" (Gal 6:14–15).

This transformation in turn entails overcoming of all alienating and oppressive distinctions and reconciliation of all humanity in Christ. What counts is neither circumcision nor uncircumcision but "faith working through love" (Gal 5:6). Liberation from the law also means liberation from, and transcendence over, our slavish obsession with oppressive divisions such as distinctions based on gender, class, religion, ethnicity, even *charismata*. What is truly important is that, by virtue of the Spirit of adoption as children dwelling in us, *all* of us are children of God and baptized "into" Christ so that we "are *all one* in Christ Jesus" (Gal 3:26–28, emphasis added), "the first-born among many *brothers [and sisters]*" (Rom 8:29, emphasis added). "By one Spirit we were all baptized into one body—Jews or Greeks, slaves or free—and all were made to drink of one Spirit" (1 Cor 12:13). What counts is the renewal of our nature according to the *eikōn* of the Creator so that "Christ is all, and in all," beyond all invidious distinctions (Col 3:10–11).

As Christ "is our peace, who has made us [Jews and Gentiles] both one, and has broken down the dividing wall of hostility" (Eph 2:14), so the Spirit of Christ is essentially a unifying and reconciling Spirit. The "mystery" of Christ revealed by the Spirit is precisely that "the Gentiles are fellow heirs, members of the same body, and partakers of the promise in Christ Jesus through the gospel" (Eph 3:6). It is also "in one Spirit" that both Jews and Gentiles have access to the Father (Eph 2:18). In the final analysis, "there is one body and one Spirit, just as you were called to the one hope that belongs to your call, one Lord, one faith, one baptism, one God and Father of us all, who is above all and through all and in all" (Eph 4:4–6). In short, the Spirit of divine sonship is also and always the Spirit of universal human solidarity as sisters and brothers in the *one* family of God the Father.

The Spirit also empowers us precisely for the task of the liberating and reconciling transformation of the world, of responding to the demands of the kingdom of God, which "is not food and drink but righteousness and peace and joy in the Holy Spirit" (Rom 14:17 NRSV). There are varieties of gifts (*charismata*), service (*diakonia*), and workings (*energēmata*) in the church, but "all these are inspired by one and the same Spirit, who apportions to each one individually as he wills" and does so "for the common good" (1 Cor 12:4–11), "to equip the saints for the work of diakonia, for building up the body of Christ," the church in the world (Eph 4:12). The Spirit empowers us to bear witness to the death and resurrection of Jesus (Acts 5:32), to the ends of the earth (Acts 1:8), with boldness (Acts 4:31), and without fear of persecution (Acts 7:55). She enables us to achieve the *koinōnia* of "one heart and soul," of apostolic teaching, the breaking of bread, prayer, and even shared material possessions in the interest of justice (Acts 2:42–47; 4:32–37), to universalize the mission of the church to include the Gentiles, and to discern God's will at important junctures in the life of the church (Acts 10:19; 13:2; 15:28).[5]

Finally, as the "guarantee" of eternal life (2 Cor 5:5; Eph. 1:14), the Spirit assures us of our ultimate salvation. As the Spirit raised Jesus from the dead, so the Spirit "will give life to your mortal bodies" (Rom. 8:11 NRSV). "He who sows to the Spirit" by responding to her demand for liberation, transformation, and reconciliation as children of God in Christ "will from the Spirit reap eternal life" (Gal 6:8). Those who are "washed," "sanctified," and "justified" in the Spirit will "inherit the kingdom of God" (1 Cor 6:10–11). The Spirit of adoption makes us "heirs of God and fellow heirs with Christ" (Rom 8:17). Those who hear and believe in the gospel are "sealed" with the promised Holy Spirit, "the guarantee of our inheritance" (Eph 1:13–14), in whom we are "sealed for the day of redemption" (Eph 4:30).

Concrete Totality as a Theological Category

The biblical images of the Spirit are rich in content and soaring in vision. Theologically, these images tell of how "in Christ God was reconciling the world to himself" (2 Cor. 5:19), of "the mystery of his will, according to his purpose which he set forth in Christ as a plan for the fullness of time, to unite all things in him, things in heaven and things on earth" (Eph 1:9–10). It is the story of how God creates and re-creates the world so as to unite all things with himself in the intimacy of his own divine life, so that "God may be all in all [ta panta en pasin, omnia in omnibus]" (1 Cor. 15:28, author's translation), "to the praise of his glory" (Eph. 1:14). It is not simply the doctrine of God's immanence in the world as opposed to her transcendence or that of the "economic" Trinity as opposed to the "immanent" Trinity. It is more precisely the doctrine of how God "sublates" (*aufhebt*) the very "dividing wall of hostility" (Eph 2:14) between transcendence and immanence, Creator and creature, as perpetrated by fallen creation, into the living union of all creation in God and with God by renewing and reconciling them, with

Jesus Christ, the primordial *eikōn* and Son of God, as the universal originating and teleological norm and model. The doctrine of the Spirit, therefore, is as comprehensive as the Trinitarian doctrine of God, of which it is an integral aspect. As such, it has not only personal (interior, spiritual) and ecclesial dimensions, but also sociohistorical and cosmic dimensions, *all* of which are called to unification and reconciliation in God's own life through Christ in the Spirit.

Historically speaking, however, constructive theology and popular spirituality have not always respected the concrete, unified totality of these dimensions. Instead, they have tended to restrict the locus and activity of the Spirit to the spiritual, intellectual interiority of the individual,[6] no doubt due to the influence of certain selected traditions emphasizing the dwelling of the Spirit "in" us, especially in our "hearts"; or the "spirit" in a dualistically misunderstood opposition to the "flesh"; or the intellectual virtue of wisdom as the chief grace of the Johannine "Spirit of truth" intellectualistically understood; or as in recent years, the particular *charismata* of healing and speaking in tongues in their miraculous aspects. When the sociohistorical dimension of the Spirit was recognized, it was recognized only in its ecclesial form, that is, its guiding presence in the church, often only in the form of the presence of the Spirit in the sacraments of baptism and confirmation and in the special guidance of the institutionalized "magisterium" of the (Catholic) church, which then could monopolize the charisms in the name of "infallible" guidance by the Spirit of truth.[7]

The corollary of this selective restriction and clerical monopoly—significantly softened in the aftermath of the Second Vatican Council in the Catholic Church—has been the neglect of the sociohistorical and cosmic locus and activity of the Spirit and the oppressive stifling of the Spirit and the creative diversity and dynamism of the gifts she distributes "as she chooses" (1 Cor. 12:11). With the clear exceptions of Jürgen Moltmann, Jose Comblin, Peter Hodgson, and some others, many contemporary discussions of the Spirit still limit the work of the Spirit to her presence in Jesus of Nazareth, the church, and individual Christians, saying virtually nothing about the liberating and transforming activity of the Spirit in "secular" history or in the cosmos.[8] In short, the tendency has been, and still largely is, to "reify" and "stifle" the Spirit in the "personal" dimensions of spiritual and intellectual inwardness, in the "institutional" dimensions of the clerical magisterium of the church, and at best in the "ecclesial" dimensions of the church understood more democratically as the whole "people of God," in which the Holy Spirit distributes her gifts and responsibilities among all, not only to the officers of the church. The historical, political, and cosmic role of the Holy Spirit is yet to be taken seriously.

Given the contemporary global context of theology, with its screaming demand for economic, sexual, racial, ethnic, cultural, and ecological liberation, the task of a theology of the Spirit today should be to mediate the rich biblical tradition on the Spirit and the contemporary urgencies of liberation by recapturing the sociohistorical and cosmic dimensions of the Spirit already there in the tradition and integrating them into a broader conceptual framework. What is most urgent in this regard, I submit, is to "de-reify" the diverse dimensions of the Spirit, integrate the interior, spiritual, personal, and institutional dimensions into the sociohistorical and cosmic contexts, where alone they really belong as *human* dimensions—angels may or may not be historical, but humans certainly are—and to introduce among such dimensions and contexts a dialectic proper to *human* existence—again, angelic existence may or may not be dialectical, but human existence certainly is.

We also recognize the inevitable although often hidden intrusion of anthropological assumptions into the content of theology itself, as the history of theology, especially Trinitarian theology since Augustine, clearly testifies.[9] This entails a radical shift in anthropology, the locus of the activity of the Spirit, *from* the dualism—underlying many traditional pneumatologies—of the internal and the external, the personal and the social, the spiritual and the material; and *to* the "dialectical" conception of human existence—in the Hegelian, not Kierkegaardian, sense—as a "concrete totality" of personal, social, and cosmic existence. The first task of a renewed pneumatology, in short, is a renewed anthropology, the anthropology of concrete totality, the human subjects whom the Spirit seeks to penetrate and con*form* to the primordial form and image of the Son by liberating, transforming, and reconciling; and who in turn are empowered to respond to such overtures of the Spirit only as concrete totalities.

Let me now sketch an outline of an anthropology of concrete totality.[10] The being of a human person is not primarily that of an isolated soul, an individual subject, or an existential self who subsequently and accidentally enters into relations with others. It is primarily—ontologically speaking— that of a being who finds oneself "always and already" existing "in" the world. This world is, first of all, the cosmos, the heavens and the earth, and all they contain in their often majestic, frequently terrifying, and always mysterious relationships. This is the ultimate and *internal* context and condition of human existence in *all* its dimensions, into which we are born and perish as dust and ashes. Souls, individuals, communities, nations, cultures—all these must respect the ecological imperative of the cosmos or else they perish.

Second, and only as a moment of the cosmos, the world is also constituted by social relations among groups differentiated along the lines of sex, race, and nation; these groups interact in the spheres of economics, politics, and culture. Third, and only as a moment of these social relations, the world is also constituted by family relations. These cosmic, social, and familial relations are not mutually reducible, but they are not mutually external or separable either. As moments of a concrete totality, they are mutually internal.

The human person is indeed a self but not a "worldless" self. It is a self intrinsically constituted and permanently conditioned—both a priori and a posteriori—by this network of cosmic, social, and familial relations. These relations are essentially historical, always in process of changing and developing—by virtue of tensions, conflicts, and contradictions peculiar to particular social conditions—between humans and the cosmos, among different groups in society, and among the different spheres of social relations. The human being is a "concrete totality" of these constitutive relations: a "totality" because it is an internally united whole, not an external collection, of such relations; and "concrete" because it is a whole internally differentiated and historically developing by virtue of the internal tensions and contradictions among the differentiated elements. A dialectic is inherent in human existence; the tension among the different elements is everywhere, and so is the internal demand and *telos* to "sublate" (*Aufheben*) oppressive and alienating differences into the creative contrasts of liberating solidarity. To speak of a human being, then, is to speak of a human being never as an isolated, static entity but always as a being already "thrown" into, and constituted by, these concrete relations, *and* as such now struggling for authenticity and integrity of these relations in liberation and solidarity in concrete history and society.

An individual sufficient unto himself or herself—either as a subject of self-interest (capitalism), as a constitutive source of the world (idealism and phenomenology), or as a self-determining freedom (existentialism)—is a metaphysical fiction, at best a half-truth invented by Western modernity for its own historical reasons. The freedom of an individual is not the creative freedom of God but the responsive or reactive freedom of a creature who does not "create" but only receives the conditions of one's own freedom. The ability of the individual to interpret and "constitute" the world is at best partial and is itself constituted and conditioned by the world of concrete social relations. The very conditions of self-interest—the object of self-interest, the means of pursuing such self-interest, and above all the very desire for promoting self-interest—are all socially and historically given. For the freedom, knowledge, and self-interest of an individual are precisely those of a concrete totality of the countless social and cosmic relations that constitute the being of the individual.

In this world of the many historically mediated and conflictual relations, the human being is called upon to fulfill his or her existence. This call is not a demand from outside but an internal demand of human existence, precisely as a concrete totality, to "sublate" the many contradictions inherent in that totality—existential, historical, and personal—into forms of liberating solidarity. Humans must make a living (economics) as *the* most fundamental condition of all else, establish humane relations of power with one's fellows (politics), and create a world of transcendent meaning (culture). The means of living, modes of humane relations, the world of meaning—these are not already given as forms of liberating solidarity but must constantly be liberated from the oppressive and alienating otherness in which they are found so as to serve the cause of solidarity of others. Humans must sublate the raw otherness of nature into meaningful embodiments of human fulfillment without violating either the integrity of creation or of other humans; transform the oppressive otherness of classes, sexes, nations, religions, and cultures into the constructive, dynamic, and enriching diversity essential to human koinonia, and convert the despairing otherness of existential meaninglessness into signs of transcendent hope. The concrete totality which is human existence is not a perfected or fulfilled totality but always a more or less broken totality with an internal demand for healing, reconciliation, and relative totalization.

It is the task of human freedom to meet this demand of human existence, but it is the freedom of a human being not as an individual but as a concrete totality and therefore as a sociohistorical being in solidarity with others. The isolated individual does not and cannot produce the economic, political, and cultural forms of liberating solidarity; just as oppression and alienation are not results of isolated individual actions. Only the collective praxis of a community can produce those forms of liberating solidarity. The meaning of human freedom is fulfilled only in the collective praxis of a community aware of its common responsibility for the situation of oppression and alienation, committed to a common action against the oppressive status quo, and united in a common hope in the possibility of a shared liberating future; human freedom comes only in the praxis of a community whose members share a concrete sense of *solidarity of destiny*. It is the glory of human freedom to serve this—essentially political—praxis of liberating solidarity.

One of the central tasks of an anthropology has been to specify the unifying principle or center of human existence in all its internal diversity and dialectic. Traditionally, intellect, will, heart, "existence," "dialogue," and inter-subjectivity have been suggested as such unifying centers. These are basically categories of individual existence separated from the concrete dialectic of socio-historical existence altogether, or of social existence in the sense of abstract intersubjectivity divorced from the concrete and often bloody clashes of a conflictual history. They fail to take human existence as a concrete totality, they "reify" a certain dimension by separating it from the concrete totality, and thus they ultimately reduce human existence to an ahistorical abstraction in theory and contribute to such reduction in practice by serving as ideologies of the status quo.

In the perspective of concrete totality, on the other hand, it is praxis—that is, social action of liberating solidarity—that constitutes the unifying center of human being. To act is to involve and mobilize all the dimensions of human existence; the subjectivity of intellect, will, feeling, and body; and the objectivity of the concrete social world, with its pressures and its resources. To act is also to actualize the various powers and dimensions of human being that otherwise would remain merely potential, over against the oppressive and alienating facticity of social conditions; and thus also to realize the *telos* of human being, the concrete transcendence of the many historically mediated dichotomies in liberating solidarity. That is, praxis alone can bring together all the dimensions and relations of human being in all their historicity and concrete dialectic, and bring the teleological burden of that totality to a self-conscious focus for whatever degree of concrete solution it is capable of achieving in history.

It is *this* human being as a concrete totality with liberating praxis of solidarity as its unifying center—not a soul, a spirit, a "heart," or an isolated individual—that is called to God's transcendent salvation. The subject of sin and grace, of damnation and salvation, is not some isolated, individual interiority but the human being as a concrete totality. It is the *whole* of our existence with *all* its relations and its historical dialectic that is enslaved by the power of sin and death and that therefore also calls for justification, sanctification, and glorification. Likewise, it is in the *whole* of our existence and by the praxis of concrete totality that we must respond to that call by concretizing in a conflictual world and in historically effective ways the signs and fruits of our salvation. Our relation to transcendence and our relations to immanence are not mutually reducible, but they are not mutually separable or external either. The concrete totality of our immanent relations is itself under the lordship of God and is possible only as a moment of God's own Trinitarian plan to unite all things on the eternal model of the union of the Father and the Son through the reconciling activity of the Spirit, the bond of love.

Transcendent salvation, therefore, cannot mean simply transcendence *of* all history but the salvation of all history *through* the many concrete, liberating transcendences of historical oppressions and alienations, that is, through the liberation, transformation, and reconciliation of our existence *in* history. The temptation to the dualism of transcendence and immanence, sacred and pro-fane—so endemic to theology, including the most liberal—must radically be resisted. The anthropology of concrete totality as an inner moment of theol-ogy itself requires systematic translation and integration of traditional theo-logical categories into terms of concrete totality in order to render theology historically concrete and effective. Theology, in turn, provides anthropology with the transcendent horizon and symbols of meaning and hope for histori-cal existence.

It is likewise essential for a renewed contemporary theology of the Spirit to keep its anthropological horizon firmly centered on this concrete totality of human being as its addressee. Today, perhaps more than ever, this totality has been divided, broken, and wounded. The creation has been "subjected to futility" (Rom 8:20) on a global scale by ruthless exploitation and pollution of nature. In practically every society, class struggles are going on, sometimes violently, often beneath the facade of normality, between rich and poor, mighty and lowly, privileged and unprivileged, under the hegemony of global imperialist powers and their local cronies. The result has been massive, need-less destruction of nature and human lives, by war, oppression, discrimina-tion, starvation, torture, imprisonment, and often genocide. The struggles have become infinitely more complicated by the increasingly multicultural, multiethnic, and multireligious contexts in which they occur.

It is *this* sort of world that the theology of the Spirit is called upon to address today. In *this* world, what does it concretely mean to say that the Spirit gives life, liberates from the power of sin and death, reconciles beyond all invidious distinctions, and guarantees eternal life? What does "the Spirit of adoption" (Rom 8:15)" or "the new life of the Spirit" (Rom 7:6) mean and demand of us as concrete totalities? What does it demand of the wealthy? Of the poor? Of the privileged, indifferent white middle classes? Of the ethnic minorities? How do the oppressors show the "fruits" of the Spirit? How do the oppressed? What does the messianic kingdom that Jesus was empowered to proclaim by the Spirit, mean and demand in a world of rampant injustice, massive starvation, ethnic alienation, and cosmic violence? What does it mean to be empowered by the Spirit to proclaim Jesus as Lord in a world divided by hubris, greed, struggle to life, and death? Do the churches today have the ear to "hear what the Spirit says to the churches" (Rev 2:11)?

Given the present global context and its screaming demand for sexual, racial, economic, and ecological liberation in a solidarity of others, the task of a renewed theology of the Spirit would be to answer and elaborate on three questions: (1) What do the biblical teachings about the Spirit mean for wounded creation and the wretched of the earth today? (2) How and where do we discern the "signs" of the vitalizing, liberating, transforming, and reconciling activity of the Spirit in the present world? (3) How or by what sort of praxis do we respond to such signs? In each case, what is required would be to concretize the biblical categories into terms of concrete totality while keeping that totality open to the horizon of the Spirit.[11] I'll attempt to elaborate on some of these questions in the next chapter.

Notes

1. For a general discussion of "context" as a constitutive element of all constructive theology, see David Tracy, *The Analogical Imagination: Christian Theology and the Culture of Pluralism* (New York: Crossroad, 1981), 3–46; Anselm Kyongsuk Min, *Dialectic of Salvation: Issues in Theology of Liberation* (Albany, N.Y.: SUNY Press, 1989), 44–52. For a recent example of a contextual theology, see Susan Brooks Thistlethwaite and Mary Potter Engel, eds., *Lift Every Voice: Constructing Christian Theologies from the Underside* (San Francisco: Harper & Row, 1990). Eilert Herms discusses the issues of church dogmatics or theology in the ecclesial context in his "Die Lehre im Leben der Kirche," *Zeitschrift für Theologie und Kirche* 82 (1985): 192–230. For a distinction among "ecclesial theology," "scientific theology," and "social-ethical theology," each addressing the issues of the church, the academe, and the world, respectively, see Ingolf U. Dalferth, "Wissenschaftliche Theologie und kirchliche Lehre," *Zeitschrift für Theologie und Kirche* 85 (1988): 98–128.

2. On the role of the divine Spirit in the Hebrew Bible, see Hans Walter Wolff, *Anthropology of the Old Testament* (trans. Margaret Kohl; Philadelphia: Fortress, 1974; paper, 1981), 32–39; Eduard Schweizer, "Spirit of God," in *Bible Key Words* (ed. Gerhard Kittel; trans. Dorothea M. Barton, P. R. Ackroyd, and A. E. Harvey; New York: Harper & Brothers, 1961), 3:1–7.

3. For a detailed overview of the concept of the Spirit in the New Testament, see Eduard Schweizer, "Spirit of God," 24–108; James D. G. Dunn, *Jesus and the Spirit* (Philadelphia: Westminster, 1970).

4. Leonardo Boff, *Trinity and Society* (trans. Paul Burns; Maryknoll, N.Y.: Orbis, 1988), 193.

5. On the role of the Spirit in the Acts, see Howard Clark Kee, *Good News to the Ends of the Earth: The Theology of Acts* (Philadelphia: Trinity Press International, 1990), 28–41: "The Spirit as God's Instrument in the Present Age." On the relation between the Spirit and the church in the New Testament, see Rudolf Schnackenburg, *The Church in the New Testament* (trans. W. J. O'Hara; New York: Seabury, 1965), 123–26, 158–64. For an excellent study of the gifts of the Spirit in the whole New Testament, see James D. G. Dunn, *Baptism in the Holy Spirit* (Philadelphia: Westminster, 1970).

6. In his *Message and Existence: An Introduction to Christian Theology* (New York: Seabury, 1979), even such a contemporary theologian as Langdon Gilkey assumes the basically Augustinian dualistic anthropology of "inner and outer, personal and social" (227), and restricts the work of the Spirit to "the inward, the personal," leaving "objective" history to the work of the kingdom (219); of course, he sees a dialectic between inner and outer, but such a dialectic comes *after,* not *before,* the split into inner and outer.

7. For a trenchant critique of the monopolization of charisms by the hierarchy in Roman Catholicism, see Karl Rahner, *The Spirit in the Church* (New York: Seabury, 1979), 33–74: "The Charismatic Element in the Church"; Leonardo Boff, *Church, Charism and Power: Liberation Theology and the Institutional Church* (trans. John W. Diercksmeier; New York: Crossroad, 1985), 154–64: "An Alternative Structure: Charism as the Organizing Principle."

8. For examples of this limited approach, see the three-volume work on the Spirit by Yves Congar, *I Believe in the Holy Spirit* (trans. David Smith; 3 vols. New York: Seabury, 1983); Walter Kasper, *The God of Jesus Christ* (trans. Matthew J. O'Connell; New York: Crossroad, 1984), 198–232: "The Holy Spirit, Lord and Giver of Life"; John J. O'Donnell, *The Mystery of the Triune God* (Mahwah, N.J.: Paulist, 1989), 75–99. For Moltmann's ecological doctrine of the Spirit, see his Gifford Lectures 1984–85, *God in Creation: A New Theology of Creation and the Spirit of God* (trans. Margaret Kohl; San Francisco: HarperCollins, 1985). For a liberation-oriented doctrine of the Spirit, see Jose Comblin, *The Holy Spirit and Liberation* (trans. Paul Burns; Theology and Liberation; Maryknoll, N.Y.: Orbis, 1989); and Peter C. Hodgson, *God in History: Shapes of Freedom* (Nashville: Abingdon, 1989); and idem, *Winds of the Spirit: A Constructive Christian Theology* (Louisville, Ky.: Westminster John Knox, 1994). It is significant that in his later work, *The Word and the Spirit* (trans. David Smith; San Francisco: Harper & Row, 1986), Congar, in response to Moltmann's criticism, added a short chapter on "The Holy Spirit in the Cosmos" (122–29).

9. On the presence and importance of anthropological assumptions in theology, see my *Dialectic of Salvation,* 163–69.

10. I have elaborated in some detail an anthropology of concrete totality in Anselm Kyongsuk Min, "Praxis and Liberation: Toward a Theology of Concrete Totality" (Ph.D. diss., Vanderbilt University, 1989), 74–178.

11. For convenience I summarize basic categories of the anthropology of concrete totality for elaboration and development: concreteness, totality, differentiation, internal relations of varying degrees, cosmicity, sociality (sexuality, familiality, nationality, class), economics, politics, culture, conflict, ideology, historical particularity, praxis, actualization, reification, liberation and oppression, solidarity and alienation, hope in the ultimate salvation of the whole.

Basic categories of biblical theology are the following: God's sovereignty and kingship, the primordial solidarity of all creation with God in the Son, the cosmic presence of the Spirit as "giver of life," solidarity of all humanity in Adam as communion of sinners, slavery to the power of sin and death, the saving solidarity of all humanity in Christ, the "Spirit of sonship" liberating and transforming and reconciling and empowering for saving solidarity and new creation, the dialectic of crucifixion and resurrection, discipleship of prophetic witness and praxis, the preferential option for the oppressed.

SIX

SOLIDARITY OF OTHERS IN
THE MOVEMENT OF THE HOLY SPIRIT
Pneumatology in a Divided World*

The Oddity of the Holy Spirit

Trinitarian theologians have always recognized something odd about the Holy Spirit in comparison with the Father and the Son. The Father is the source of all divinity and all reality, to whom we owe all honor and glory. He is a distinct center or subject of action who "generates" the Son and "spirates" the Spirit. The Son is the Word of the Father and his perfect image (*eikōn*), the model of all creation. As a distinct center of action, the Word became flesh and revealed the Father to us. All creation is to be "incorporated" into his body. Both the Father and the Son are distinctive or substantive entities, each in his own right. Both are also relational realities. The being of the Holy Spirit, on the other hand, appears to be only relational, without a distinctive reality of her own. The Holy Spirit proceeds from the Father and the Son or from the Father of the Son, and exists as their mutual love. The Spirit neither becomes incarnate nor reveals the Father but rather makes it possible for the incarnate Son to become incarnate and reveal the Father. The Spirit is neither the lover nor the beloved but is their reciprocal love, which makes the Spirit rather odd. Both the lover and the beloved are entities in their own right and related to each other. Mutual love indicates at best mutual relation or activity but hardly a distinct subject of being and action. In the absence of readily intelligible personhood, the Holy Spirit seems always in danger of being reduced to a relation between the Father and the Son, turning the Trinity itself into a binity.[1]

* An original version of this paper was presented at an international conference on the theology of the Holy Spirit held at Marquette University, Milwaukee, April 17–19, 1998.

Is it not perhaps possible, however, to say that the distinctiveness of the Holy Spirit lies precisely in its apparent lack of distinctive substantiality, in being wholly relational and as such the divine source of all relations, communions, and solidarities, just as the distinctiveness of the Father lies in his being the *principium sine principio,* and that of the Son in his being the *principium de principio?* The idea of the Holy Spirit as an entity whose essence lies totally in being relational and creating relations seems corroborated in many passages of the New Testament. In each case, the role of the Spirit is never to call attention to herself but to relate and bring together diverse parties into communion and fellowship. The Spirit comes from the Father and testifies not about herself but about the Son in his work for the Father (John 15:26; 16:13–14). As the Spirit of the Son, the Spirit brings together people of diverse races, religions, genders, and classes; incorporates them into the one body of Christ, the Son; and renders them all children of the Father in the Son (Gal 4:6; 1 Cor 12:13; Rom 8:14–17). It is in "one Spirit" that we, Jews and Gentiles, have access to the Father through Christ (Eph. 2:18). Like the mutual love of the Father and the Son that she is, the Spirit does not bear witness about herself or seek to glorify herself. The Spirit is the self-forgetting God whose sole role seems to create fellowship between the Son and human beings, and in the Son, among human beings themselves as well as between them and the Father, and ultimately to introduce all creation into the fellowship of the Father and the Son.

Perhaps our age, with all its divisions and hostilities, has a special need to appreciate the Holy Spirit precisely as the Spirit of fellowship and solidarity. Today we are living in an increasingly divided, fragmented, and alienating world. The middle classes of the advanced industrial societies may be materially well off, but they suffer alienation and meaninglessness on a massive scale: their families are broken, their neighborhoods have become armed fortresses, and human relationships have been reduced to impersonal, commercial, and often mechanical exchanges. The clashes between classes, genders, ethnic groups, cultures, and religions have become more acute all over the world. We have become others to one another in the most alienating ways. The fear of the other, the stranger—xenophobia—is eating away at the very fabric of our common life so deeply and so pervasively that we are increasingly reduced to our own individual resources in utter helplessness and loneliness. Perhaps there is a strong but suppressed yearning for the return of the Spirit of fellowship, who will turn *xenophobia* into *philoxenia,* the love of the stranger, and turn hostility and suspicion into solidarity and trust, empowering us to live as human beings with dignity and meaning. We cannot remain isolated, hostile, and suspicious others to one another. Deep down, we need fellowship and solidarity of others to sustain our existence, our very dignity and meaning. The cry of oppression, alienation, and loneliness we hear everywhere today is a silent invocation of the Holy Spirit, an *epiklēsis* to the Spirit of fellowship to come and connect us once more. *Veni, Sancte Spiritus! Veni, pater pauperum! Veni, dator munerum! Veni, lumen cordium!* Come, Holy Spirit! Come, Father of the Poor, Come, Giver of Gifts, Come, Light of [Our] Hearts!

In this chapter I propose to highlight the person and role of the Holy Spirit as the Spirit of solidarity of others. In the next part, I provide a brief analysis of the contemporary world in its fragmentation and alienation as the *Sitz im Leben* for contemporary theology. In the third part, I present the self-forgetting, reconciling role of the Holy Spirit in the Bible. In the fourth, I retrieve the classical notion—from Augustine and Aquinas—of person as relation, and of the Holy Spirit as impetus and movement of love. My thesis is that as the Spirit proceeds from the Father and the Son as their mutual love, so it is the function of the Spirit to create, empower, inspire, and liberate finite beings precisely for solidarity and communion with God and with one another through the exemplary mediation of the Son, whose life is the definitive embodiment of solidarity of others. The personhood of the Spirit lies precisely in the power and activity of relating, reconciling, and in general creating connection, solidarity, and communion in the life of both the immanent and economic Trinity. In the last part, I indicate some of the areas of contemporary life in which we can especially locate signs of the movement of the Holy Spirit, as well as some of the ways of our pneumatological praxis responsive to those signs.

Solidarity of Others: Demand of a New Kairos

There are many ways of analyzing and characterizing the dominant needs and urgencies of the times in which we live and in which we also have to carry on our theological reflection. Looking at the world from the perspective of North America, I can see several overriding needs. There is, first of all, the need for liberation of certain oppressed groups throughout the world, be they women, ethnic minorities such as Native Americans and African Americans, the economically marginalized and socially excluded. For all the progress that has been made, the need for liberation from imposed suffering remains urgent. There is, second, the need for liberation of nature from human exploitation and destruction, which is ultimately our self-destruction. The status of the ecology is getting steadily worse. Third, there is the urgency of interreligious and intercultural dialogue and understanding. This need too is becoming more and more compelling as intercultural contacts become more intimate and extensive. These three needs have been recognized by theologians for some time, as their respective theologies—various liberation theologies, ecological theology, and religious pluralism—seem to testify. There is a fourth need, the need of the middle class for community and meaning, which has largely been ignored by theologians, especially liberal ones, and addressed instead by the growing movements of pentecostalism, spirituality, and mysticism.

These needs are not mutually reducible, and still less are they mutually separable. They are products of a global process that has been going on for centuries, whose pace has been accelerating in recent decades, and whose impacts are especially felt and recognized today. I am referring to the process of growing global interdependence brought about by trade, transportation, and now increasingly information technology. Interdependence is an ambivalent process and has many sides to it. On the one hand, it brings diverse peoples ever closer together, often by sheer colonialism, imperialism, and economically motivated migration. This forces peoples to face one another as masters and slaves, employers and employees, oppressors and oppressed, majorities and minorities, as mutual competitors, as colleagues and neighbors, and in any case heightens their sensitivity to the other as other. Interdependence ironically intensifies the struggle for liberation and competition, often pitting the oppressed against one another.

On the other hand, interdependence also throws the challenge of living *together* with others by creating together common conditions of living with dignity and meaning. Interdependence does not simply juxtapose or place diverse peoples side by side in blissful indifference to one another. It brings them into common political space where, like it or not, they have to find a mode of living together with a modicum of justice and peace. They have to agree on a minimum system of identity—laws, policies, regulations—that will guarantee basic economic needs, political rights, and meaningful culture for all groups. Interdependence, which intensifies the pluralistic consciousness of otherness, also intensifies the political challenge and responsibility of creating a common res publica. Pluralism itself is possible only in a political community that supports the value of pluralism and thus only insofar as it is compatible with the demands of common life. By the same token, the political community remains legitimate only insofar as it protects the just demands of pluralism and viable only to the extent that it proves acceptable to the different groups.

Global trade also leads to increasingly massive exploitation and waste of natural resources and degradation of the natural environment, creating incalculable, often irreversible ecological disasters for all. Liberation and ecology are not two separate problems. It is the self-expanding dynamic of the free market with all its irrationalities that creates rich and poor, masters and slaves, generating the need for liberation of the oppressed; and creating in the same process the unrestrained, competitive exploitation and degradation of nature, which in turn stimulates the ecological movement. By the same token, both need a political solution that will restrain at once the exploitation of the poor and the degradation of nature. "Poverty and environmental decline are both embedded deeply in today's economic systems."[2] The free market as such will not liberate either the oppressed or nature from its own dynamic of exploitation. It is short-sighted and misleading to pit the demands of liberation and those of ecology against each other. Our ecological relation to nature is always mediated by our political relation to one another in society, just as our social relations are always mediated by our natural relations. Problems of liberation and ecology are two products of the same economic process that embodies both our social and natural relations.

The problem of interreligious dialogue and understanding is not a separate problem either. Religions as such do not encounter one another. Only concrete human beings with their religions do. It is the globalizing process that brings together people of diverse origins, languages, religions, and cultures and in the process also generates the need for mutual understanding in the matter of religions, cultures, and languages. It is not primarily their religions or cultures but the global economic process that brings them into common political space, that brings together Muslims, Buddhists, Hindus, Confucians, Jews, and Christians into the metropolitan centers of the world such as Los Angeles, Chicago, New York, London, Birmingham, and Frankfurt. By the same token, it is the dynamics of the concrete context of coexistence that determines the success or failure of interreligious dialogue. Human beings do not enter into a dialogue as pure, disembodied intellects; they do so only with their concrete needs, interests, and perspectives. Encountering the religious other as other, without prejudice, and with the willingness to learn from the other—conditions stipulated by theorists of interreligious dialogue—will be possible only when others perceive a minimum of justice and equality in the socially imposed conditions of life. No authentic dialogue is possible between oppressors and oppressed. The problem of interreligious dialogue and understanding is not reducible to the economics and politics of justice, but neither is it separable from, or independent of, the latter. Furthermore, the globalization process tends to erode all traditions, homogenize all lifestyles, and trivialize all ultimate values—which should concern all religions in their respective struggle to maintain their own identities, especially through the transmission of their tradition to the young—which in turn should be a compelling theme of interreligious dialogue as well.

One of the serious problems neglected by mainline religions and their theologians is the problem of the middle class, the majority in advanced industrial societies. They are materially well off and politically free, better off and freer than human beings have ever been; yet they also suffer, in silence, broken families, loneliness, alienation, and lack of transcendent meaning in their lives. Their wealth depends on their fortunes in the free market, which makes their lives always anxious, while the reigning impersonality and commercialism of the market reduce *all* aspects of life to the trivial, superficial, and meaningless. There is a silent cry for authenticity, depth, communion, and transcendence, which they seek to find in spirituality, mysticism, and new religions. This problem of the middle class, however, is inseparable from the global economic process, which in the same process makes them wealthy while depriving and marginalizing others, exploiting nature, and bringing diverse religions together into common space. The sheer number of the middle class as a majority in society makes their problem an urgent concern of pastoral care. Their position in the network of the global process also renders their situation a compelling theological problem. As human beings, they too suffer from the problem of existential meaning in their lives. As beneficiaries and agents of the global economic process, they also bear political responsibility for the oppression of the poor, exploitation of nature, and the general consequences of the globalizing process. They cannot just separate their problems from their responsibilities; somehow, their personal search for transcendent meaning must be related to their social responsibility for what their own governments and corporations do both at home and abroad, and must be integrated in particular with their self-transcendence in political solidarity with the countless suffering others of the world.

What is common to the preceding problems both formally and materially is the challenge of others, those who are other and different in class, gender, ethnicity, religion, and culture. The problem of liberation is the problem of creating economic, political, and cultural conditions for living with dignity and meaning. Insofar as no one group today can achieve its liberation by its own unaided effort, since every group requires the collaboration of other groups, the problem of liberation becomes the problem of collaboration and solidarity of others in mutual liberation. Insofar as some groups are more oppressed than others, it also means preferential option for those who suffer more, and transcendence of collective selfishness and obsession with one's own group in the struggle for liberation. The ecological problem is doing this precisely in such a way as to also respect the rhythm and integrity of nature, of which human beings are a part without being its master. Nature remains an other that cannot be reduced to human self-identity. The precondition for interreligious dialogue is the establishment of justice and equality in the very conditions of living together as and with others so as to make genuine mutual trust possible. The problem of the middle class is in part how to find self-transcendence not only in spiritual immersion in the Transcendent but also in concrete, political solidarity with the suffering others of this world.

In short, the compelling problems of the contemporary world can be summed up as the problem of solidarity of others; of how to transcend ourselves in solidarity with others so as to learn to "live together with others," those who are different in class, gender, ethnicity, religion, and culture, including nature; of how *together* to create the common social conditions of life that will guarantee basic needs, justice, and meaningful culture to everyone. The problem is not how to leave one another alone in all their differences; it is learning to live together with others, both suffering and enjoying the dialectic of otherness and togetherness.

The context of theology has been changing over the last few decades. We have come a long way from the 1970s, when various identity theologies, ecological theology, religious pluralism, and the new-age movement came into existence, each with its own compelling vision and power. Much has been achieved in the meantime, yet much also remains to be done today. The difference is that the complexity of interdependence among different groups as well as among different problems has so grown as simply to make it impossible for each group or issue to liberate or resolve itself by its own unaided effort. We can only liberate our own groups by pooling our activities and resources together, or we have no liberation at all. Finding a way of living together for all our differences is the compelling goal of our time, as it is a compelling task of our time to learn to work together precisely for that goal. Solidarity of others as both the goal and means is the demand of the new kairos in which we live today. We cannot continue to do theology in the twenty-first century as we did in the twentieth. We need a different direction and a different paradigm. Solidarity of others provides that direction and paradigm.

The Holy Spirit as the Spirit of Solidarity of Others

Is it possible to interpret the Holy Spirit as the Spirit of this solidarity of others that we so desperately need? I would like to begin with a discussion of the biblical presentation and early Christian experience of the Holy Spirit for a clue to its function and activity before going on to a conceptualization of its personhood.[3]

The Hebrew Bible presents the divine Spirit, the *ruakh* of God, in a variety of roles. The Spirit is pictured as creating, sustaining, and renewing the life of all creation (Gen 1:2; Ps 33:6; 104:29–30; Job 34:14; Isa 32:15); empowering leaders such as Moses, Joshua, Gideon, Saul, and David for political leadership at critical points in the history of the nation; inspiring the prophets to proclaim God's justice and peace to idolatrous and oppressive kings (Amos, Isaiah, Ezekiel); transforming the nation's "heart of stone" into "a heart of flesh" in a new covenant (Ezek 11:19–20; 36:26–28; Ps 51:10–12; Isa 59:21); and above all inaugurating the messianic, eschatological age of social justice, harmony with nature, and reconciliation of all creation with God (Isa 11, 32, 42, 61).[4]

In the specifically Christian context of the New Testament, the role of the Spirit becomes more distinct, more christological, and more ecclesial. The Holy Spirit empowers Jesus in his salvific work from his conception through his ministry of proclamation and healing on behalf of the kingdom to his resurrection from the dead (Matt 1:20; Luke 4:1, 18; Matt 12:28; Acts 10:38; Rom 8:11). The Spirit bears witness to Jesus, proclaiming his divine sonship (Luke 3:22; John 1:33), testifying to his coming in the flesh (1 John 4:2), enlightening individuals to recognize his soteriological significance (Luke 1:67–68; 2:26, 30) and his lordship (1 Cor 12:3), inspiring people to believe in him and his gospel of salvation (Eph 1:13–14). First and foremost, the Spirit is God's eschatological presence and power: inaugurating the end time by raising Jesus from the dead and in principle all human beings in him as the new Adam (Rom 8; 1 Cor 15); manifesting its eschatological presence by granting the gift of prophecy equally to men and women, young and old, masters and servants (Acts 2); eliminating the division between Jew and Gentile (Acts 10, 15); liberating us from the bondage of law, sin, and death (Romans, Galatians); and empowering us to live as new creation (Gal 5–7). The Spirit guides the church, the body of Christ, the eschatological community of those born again through faith in Christ: speaking to the churches in times of crises (Rev 2–3), guiding the churches and their leaders in their pastoral and doctrinal decisions (Acts 8, 10, 13, 15, 16), enabling them to preach the word of God with joy and courage in times of persecution (Luke 12:12; Acts 4:31; Rom 15:18–19; 1 Cor 2:4; 1 Pet 1:12), and building up the church by empowering members to maintain their unity (Acts 4) and serve the common good with their diverse gifts of ministry (1 Cor 12; Eph 4).

Both the Hebrew Bible and the New Testament speak of the Spirit as God's creative, vitalizing, empowering, liberating, guiding, and directing eschatological presence in the universe, human history, and in the case of the New Testament, especially in the church. It is crucial, however, to note a peculiarity of the Holy Spirit in comparison with God (the Father) and Christ (the Son). Both God the Father and Christ are distinctive persons, each with his own subjectivity as agent and demanding a distinctive response from us. God creates the world and sends his Son to redeem the world. God sends rain on the just and the unjust. We are to give thanks and glory to God. The Son is born as a definite human individual, engages in specific ministries for his Father's reign, dies on the cross, and is raised from the dead by God. We are "to be conformed [*summorphous*] to the image of his Son, in order that he might be the first-born among many brethren" (Rom 8:29)— so that we would follow him, bear witness to his resurrection, and hope to share in his fellowship with the Father.

There is something odd, however, both about the identity of the Holy Spirit and our response to her. It is generally acknowledged that the person-hood of the Spirit as God's *ruakh* is ambiguous in the Hebrew Bible. The Spirit is more a personification of God's breath, power, or wisdom than a dis-tinctive agent in her own right. In the New Testament, the ambiguity may be considerably reduced but not altogether eliminated. Insofar as the Spirit is the subject of verbs such as searching (1 Cor 2:10), knowing (1 Cor 2:11), teaching (1 Cor 2:13), giving life (2 Cor 3:6), dwelling (Rom 8:11), crying out (Gal 4:6), having desires (Gal 5:17), leading (Gal 5:18), bearing witness (Rom 8:16), interceding (Rom 8:26–27), strengthening (Eph 3:16), inspir-ing, apportioning, and willing (1 Cor 12:11), speaking and sending (Acts 13:2, 4), and being grieved (Eph 4:30); and insofar as the fruits of the Spirit are personal attributes such as love, joy, peace, patience, and so on (Gal 5:22–23), it is arguable that the Spirit is a person.[5] Because of the peculiarity of the ontology of spirit, however, even these references can be interpreted as the metaphorical personifications of God's presence, power, and activity in the world, not as a spiritual subject of action in her own right, distinct from God. A person's spirit, soul, or mind is normally part of the person, who remains the subject of that spirit, soul, or mind, not a distinct entity apart from the person. Likewise, the actions of a person's spirit, soul, or mind belong to the person as their subject. Furthermore, if the Spirit stands for God's presence, power, and actions in the world, either such presence, power, and actions belong to the category of accidents, not substance, which alone can subsist and be persons in case of rational substances, or become identical with God's own being by virtue of divine simplicity. In any event, the ontol-ogy of the Holy Spirit, one might say, remains at least odd.

There is likewise something odd about the action of the Holy Spirit and our response to that action. We usually pray to the Father in the name of the Son, but not to the Holy Spirit. We give thanks and glory to the Father for what he has done through the Son, but not to the Spirit. (I recognize that the *Gloria Patri* is a late development in Christian history.) We follow the Son in his pursuit of the Father's will in the world, but not the Spirit. We bear witness to the Son, but not to the Spirit as such. This oddity of our response to the Spirit follows from the oddity of her action in the world, which is not so much to call attention to herself, either to her own sovereignty or to her own action in the world, as to empower us to follow the Son in his fellowship with the Father. The Spirit inspires us to pray to the Father in the name of the Son without herself being the object of our prayer, to give thanks and glory to the Father without herself being the object of our glorification, and to bear witness to the Son without herself being the object of our witnessing. The Father wants us to do his will in the world and become his children. The Son wants us to confess and follow him in his life, death, and resurrection. The Holy Spirit wants us to do neither regarding herself, instead only empowering us to do the Father's will and to confess the Son in word and deed. The Son becomes incarnate in Jesus and reveals the Father. The Spirit neither becomes incarnate nor reveals the Father; instead, she makes such incarnation and revelation possible.

The Holy Spirit is self-effacing, selfless God whose selfhood or personhood seems to lie precisely in transcending herself to empower others likewise to transcend themselves in communion with others, to urge the Father to give himself to the Son and the Son to give himself to the Father and to the world for the sake of the Father, and to liberate humanity and creation from their self-isolation and empower them to transcend themselves toward one another and toward God in union and solidarity.[6] The Holy Spirit remains the transcendental horizon of our knowledge of God, that power by which (*principium quo*) we get to know God, without the Spirit herself being a direct object of our knowledge; the Spirit remains also the transcendental power of our praxis, that power by which we are empowered to act and live as children of the Father and brothers and sisters of the Son, without herself being either the Father or the Son. This does not mean that we cannot also thematize the Holy Spirit as object of our prayer, glorification, witnessing, and knowledge; but it does mean that we can only do so precisely in the transcendental horizon and power of the Holy Spirit herself, which is not true of the other two persons.[7]

Scripture confirms this role of the Holy Spirit as the transcendent and transcendental power of self-transcendence and Creator of relations. In the Hebrew Bible the Spirit empowers the future messiah not to seek himself or even the Spirit but to fear the Lord, to establish a relationship of justice and equity among the people, and to restore the original harmony between beings in nature, between nature and humanity, and between God and all creation ("the wolf shall dwell with the lamb, . . . and a little child shall lead them," Isa 11: 1–9). The eschatological outpouring of the Spirit is not intended to call attention to herself through wonders and signs but to establish the prophetic equality between women and men, young and old, servants and masters (Joel 2:28–29; Acts 2:16–21), as well as to eliminate linguistic barriers among different ethnic groups (Acts 2:1–12) as signs of the end time. The role of the Spirit in Jesus' conception, ministry, death, and resurrection is not to establish Jesus' own identity in himself but to empower him to bear witness to his Father's reign by bringing human beings closer to God and one another through repentance, forgiveness, and hope. The testimony of the Spirit at Jesus' baptism is not intended to either call attention to the Spirit herself or show Jesus' divinity in himself but to proclaim the fellowship between the Father and the Son ("Thou art my beloved Son; with thee I am well pleased," Luke 3:22).

The work of the Spirit with the church and individual Christians is likewise to empower them to bear witness not to themselves or even to the Spirit but to Christ in praxis and preaching, and to bring them to the Father through him. The purpose of the diverse gifts of the Spirit is not to celebrate diversity as such but to serve the common good, which is to build up the body of Christ (1 Cor 12). The fruits of the new life in the Spirit are precisely love, joy, peace, patience, kindness, goodness, faithfulness, gentleness, and self-control—which are thoroughly self-forgetting and relational because they come from becoming "servants of one another" (Gal 5:13, 22–23) and "bearing one another's burdens" so as to "fulfill the law of Christ" (Gal 6:2). We "grieve the Holy Spirit" not in our self-isolation but in our alienating relations such as bitterness, anger, slander, and malice; we please the Spirit by being kind to one another and "forgiving one another, as God in Christ forgave you" (Eph 4:30–32).

As an eschatological power, the ultimate goal of the Holy Spirit is to create a relation of unity and reconciliation among all the alienated parties, among human beings themselves, between human beings and nature, and between God and all creation. Human beings have been alienated from one another because of oppressive differences in class, gender, ethnicity, religion, and culture. Human sinfulness has also brought about alienation between humanity and nature, which likewise groans for liberation from decay and futility (Rom 8:20–21). These social and natural alienations, however, are derived from the basic alienation between God and humanity. This basic alienation, as well as the other alienations, can be overcome only when human beings are regenerated as children of the same Father and thus become sisters and brothers of one another in the one divine family.

Such regeneration itself becomes possible only through the mediation of the Son. The Son is the primordial image of the Father, "the first-born of all creation," in whom, through whom, and for whom all things were created (Col 1:15–16). He is the model or archetype of all creation. In his incarnate existence as a human being, Jesus the Son showed his communion with the Father by dedicating himself to his kingdom, in which his unconditional, universal love for humanity, especially for the oppressed, became concrete. In preaching, healing, and table fellowship, Jesus identified himself with the outcast others of society, the marginalized "nobodies" excluded from the dominant social systems of identity. For this solidarity with suffering others, Jesus was murdered by crucifixion as a political criminal. The Father, however, raised him from the dead, vindicating Jesus in his life and death, and accepting all humanity in solidarity with him. As Suffering Servant, he lived and died for solidarity of others, bearing our sins and sufferings in his body, a universal person representing all humanity in its brokenness and alienation. As "the first-born from the dead" (Col 1:18), he is the new Adam in whose resurrection we too will share, a universal person modeling and embodying all humanity re-created onto authentic solidarity of others in God. For in him we are "one" beyond all oppressive and invidious distinctions based on class, gender, power, ethnicity, religion, and culture (Gal 3:28; Col 3:11; Eph 2:14–19). We are all "called into the *koinōnia* of his Son" (1 Cor 1:9) and to be "conformed to the image of his Son" (Rom 8:29). As the eternal image of the Father, the Son is the model for the creation and re-creation of all things, including humanity, and it is precisely the salvific "mystery" of God's will to "unite all things in him [the Son], things in heaven and things on earth" (Eph 1:10).

Overcoming human alienations, then, takes being born again as children of the same Father and experiencing solidarity of others as sisters and brothers of the Son who embodies that solidarity in his life and resurrection. It is precisely in this work of divine filiation of humanity and achieving reconciliation of all in the Son that the Holy Spirit shows her most appropriate identity. As the Spirit of Christ, it is the Holy Spirit in us who cries "Abba! Father!" (Gal 4:6) and makes us "children of God, and if children, then heirs, heirs of God and fellow heirs with Christ, provided we suffer with him in order that we may also be glorified with him" (Rom 8:15–17). "All who are led by the Spirit of God are sons [and daughters] of God" (Rom 8:14). It is the Spirit who incorporates us into the "one body" of Christ through baptism and empowers us to transcend oppressive distinctions (1 Cor 12:13). It is also "in one Spirit" that both Jews and Gentiles have access to the Father through Christ (Eph 2:18). By liberating us from the law, sin, and death, and empowering us to transcend ourselves in solidarity with those who are different, the Spirit unites and introduces us into the communion of the Son with the Father, accomplishing the "mystery" of God's salvific will. In this sense the Spirit is "the principle of the communion of the saints,"[8] "the animating power of the economy,"[9] and "the universal contact point between God and history."[10] If Christ is the corporate person embodying the solidarity of all in God, it is precisely the Spirit who, in the words of John Zizioulas, "realizes in history that which we call Christ, this absolutely relational reality, our Savior."[11]

As the Son, Christ also creates relationships between humanity and God as well as among human beings, but does so as the *exemplary* model in which we participate and to which we are to conform. It is the Spirit who *actualizes* the full potentialities of the model in all its relationships by bringing about our participation and conformity, and does so not by calling attention to herself but by making us members of the body of the Son. As the Spirit of the Son, the Holy Spirit effects solidarity of others by introducing them into the communion of the Father and the Son.[12] As Alasdair Heron well points out, "The Spirit is God, but God acting within, directing us, not to himself as Holy Spirit, but to the incarnate Son, and in him, to the Father."[13]

The Person as Movement of Relation and Solidarity

How, then, should we conceptualize the role and personhood of this self-effacing, other-directed, relation-creating God in the immanent Trinity? Perhaps the economic role of the Holy Spirit as the power of self-transcendence for communion and solidarity gives us a clue to its being in the immanent Trinity, where it has been recognized, since Augustine, as the mutual love of the Father and the Son. Whether Eastern or Western, it seems that all theologians (have to) recognize a certain primacy or "monarchy" of the Father as the unoriginate origin of all things, including the divinity of the Son and the Spirit and all finite reality. The Father is the originating principle in the Trinity from whom both the Son and the Spirit proceed. He eternally "generates" the Son by sharing the totality of his numerically identical divine substance with him. The Son is the Father's Other in whom the Father's divine substance is totally shared and externalized, the Word and Image in which the Father knows himself and all reality. As the Other, Word, and Image of the Father, the Son is the othering and pluralizing principle in God and all reality. The Word is the archetype for the creation of all finite others and models in himself all finite reality in its structure and plurality. It is only appropriate, therefore, that the Word alone should become incarnate, not the Father who remains the *unoriginate* origin of all things, not the Holy Spirit whose role is precisely to make the incarnation, the personal union of the divine and the human possible, not to become herself incarnate.[14]

It is out of the Father's love for the Son that the Father generates him by giving and sharing his whole divine being with the Son. The Son returns the Father's love by an equally total self-giving to the Father. Out of this mutual love between the Father and the Son, there proceeds the Holy Spirit, which the Father "spirates" by way of will and love, as he "generates" the Son by way of intellect and word. It is, then, in the Spirit of this mutual love that the Father generates the Son and in the process distinguishes himself as Father and unites himself to the Son, just as the Son distinguishes himself as Son and unites himself with the Father by accepting and returning the Father's gift of self. The Spirit is the uniting and reconciling principle for the communion and solidarity of Others in God and in the world. Proceeding from the Father of the Son (or from the Father and the Son), the Spirit unites the Father and the Son in their mutual otherness in a communion of Others, and reconciles finite others with the Father by uniting them to the Son in his fellowship with the Father.[15]

Without the Father as the originating principle, nothing would exist, not even the Son or the Spirit. Without the Son as the pluralizing, othering principle, the Father alone would exist, and there would be neither the Trinity nor any finite creature. Without the Holy Spirit as the uniting, reconciling principle, however, there would be neither the Son nor finite creatures because there would be no love to generate the Son and create finite realities in the Son; and even if these others did exist, they would remain completely separate in sheer otherness and isolation. In the absence of the reconciling and connecting Spirit, the world would tend to fragmentation and nothingness. The Spirit gives being and life precisely by relating, uniting, reconciling, and bonding.

Now, according to Aquinas, the difference between the Son and the Spirit is analogous to the difference between intellect and will. The procession of the intellect is by way of likeness of the object; the procession of the will is by way of love, impulse, movement, and inclination to the object.[16] It is the nature of love to move and impel the will of the lover toward the object loved. There is here, however, a peculiarity to note. The procession of the intellect terminates in a concept or idea of the object understood, and there exists a word, that is, Word, to describe the relation between the subject and object of understanding and speaking. The procession of love terminates in a certain impression of the loved object in the affection of the lover, but there is no appropriate word other than love to express the relation between lover and beloved. As we do with "Word" for the Son, so we have to do with "Love" for the Spirit. Although understanding and loving are actions, they remain in the agent; and in the divine agent, they are identical with the divine essence and thus subsistent Word and subsistent Love respectively. The Holy Spirit is the subsisting "unitive love"[17] or bond between the Father and the Son, proceeding as "the love of primal goodness [amor primae boni-tatis] whereby the Father loves himself and every creature,"[18] and also as the gift of the Father, as the eternal "aptitude to be given,"[19] insofar as love is the most primordial of all gifts.

The three divine persons are not all equal in every respect. As engendering love, the Father is the source of the Son and, in him, also of the Spirit. As receptive love, the Son is derivative from, and subordinate to, the Father. The Spirit too is derivative, from the Father of the Song, or more precisely, from their self-relating to the other. The point of the Trinitarian doctrine, how-ever, might be precisely that these differences need not be degrading and oppressive differences. In the eternal simultaneity and perichoresis of the tri-une God, such differences are sublated into positive modes of mutual love. The Father's love for the Son sublates his ontological superiority to the Son into an expression of love; the Father does not take glory in his ontological superiority but uses it precisely by sharing and emptying his total divinity with the Son; for the capacity to share one's total self with an Other and still remain oneself or rather be more authentically oneself for doing so, is the prerogative of an infinite being. The Son does not feel degraded but feels more himself in deriving and receiving his total being from the Father, giving himself back totally to him, and returning his love. The Spirit does not feel humiliated but rejoices in deriving her existence not from one but from two persons, sublating that dependence into a celebration of love between the Father and the Son. The Spirit finds her true identity not in asserting her equality as a distinct person in her own right but in effacing herself in order to inspire the union of the Father and the Son in their eternal communion. The unequal relations of origination, the only source of differentiation in God according to classical Trinitarianism, is sublated into modes of love beyond equality, into engendering, receptive, and uniting love.

It is the uniting love of the Holy Spirit that also sublates the primordial inequality of the divine persons into the primordial equality of love. The Father remains indeed the source of both the Son and the Spirit. There is inequality between the begetter and the begotten, between the source of pro-cession and that which proceeds. This inequality of origination, however, is canceled by the equality of the content that is communicated in the process of origination. What occurs in the process of generation and procession is not only the Son and the Spirit but also the communication of the numerically identical divine substance of the Father. Relationally unequal, the three persons are totally equal in their divine nature. The Father is neither the Son nor the Spirit, but the Son and the Spirit are precisely what the Father is, namely, divine. Because of the sharing of the numerically one divine substance among the three persons, they also exist *in* one another (perichoresis).[20] The role of the Spirit as uniting love in this communication and perichoresis is crucial. It is precisely this uniting love that eternally inspires the Father to share the totality of his divine substance with the Son; and inspires the Son to receive, return, and share that totality with the Father; and makes it possible for the Father and the Son to exist *in* each other in a communion of a "we."[21] It is the uniting and equalizing function of the Holy Spirit that keeps the Father's ontological originality from becoming monarchy/patriarchy and turns it into creative, sharing love, as it also keeps the Son's ontological dependence from becoming impotent masochism and turns it into responsive, sharing love.

This brings us to the question about the personhood of the Holy Spirit. Is it not forcing it to turn mutual love, normally an activity or relation among human beings, into a person by making it subsistent on the ground that in God there are no accidents? On the other hand, unless we do so, how can we avoid falling into binity?[22] Here I would like to argue that we should recognize that the divine persons are not persons univocally but analogically, that each person is a "person" in a different way, and that we should stretch our notion of person to fit the theological data rather than trying to adapt the theological data to our own fixed notion of person.

According to the classical tradition, persons in God are "constituted" by relations, which in relating also distinguish the persons from one another.[23] The identity or person of the Father lies precisely in relating himself to the Son by way of total sharing. As the originating principle in the Godhead, the Father's personhood lies in engendering, creative love. As the pluralizing principle, the Son's personhood lies in the relation of derived, receptive, responsive love to the Father. The Father and the Son are not persons in the same way. The relationality of the Holy Spirit is much more complex. As the mutual love of the Father and the Son, the Spirit is related to both in their mutual relation. It is not simply from the Father or simply from the Son but precisely from their reciprocal love that the Spirit proceeds; and as such, the Spirit not only is related by way of origin to both but also relates them to each other in the eternal simultaneity of perichoresis. Generation and filiation mediate and are mediated by (passive) spiration.[24]

The peculiarity of the Spirit here is that her personhood lies precisely in relating and uniting the Father and the Son to each other, not to herself, in transcending herself in order to inspire the relation of love between the two from which she proceeds. The Father's relation to the Son is direct in that to be a father is to generate a son; his relation to the Spirit is indirect in that his love for the Son accompanies his generation of the Son as its enabling horizon. The same is true, conversely, of the Son's relation to the Father and the Spirit. His relation to the Father is the direct object of his filiation; his relation to the Spirit is an indirect accompaniment of that filiation as its enabling horizon. The relation of the Spirit to the Father and the Son, on the other hand, is both direct and doubly relational in contrast to the respective relation of the Father and the Son, which is singly relational. If we are not to reduce the Trinity to a bland community of three abstractly equal persons, it is imperative to consider each person precisely in the difference from the others and introduce the dialectic of such differences into the community of the triune God.

In taking relations as constitutive of divine persons, the classical tradition was quite aware that human categories do break down when they are applied to God. In the Boethian definition person means "an individual substance of rational nature." A person means a substance or subsistent being, not an accident such as relation; a rational rather than an irrational being; and an individual entity rather than a generic nature. In God, however, relations are subsistent, a rational being contains the possibilities of nonrational beings as their Creator, and a subsistent relation is at the same time his or her own essence. In the divine persons as subsistent relations, traditional dichotomies break down: substance and accidents, rational and irrational, individual and nature. At the heart of the classical tradition is this relational definition of the divine person. Here we are invited to revolutionize our concept of person: instead of a fixed, individual substance of rational nature, we are to conceive of the person in terms of relations, processes, and movements. It is also important to realize that in God this relationality is itself a mode of being of divine persons in whom essence and existence coincide, and therefore a modality of the *Ipsum esse per se subsistens,* of the fullness, actuality, and movement of the divine *esse.* This is especially true of the person of the Holy Spirit who, as the will of the Father, connotes love, impulse, movement, and inclination. The Holy Spirit—as a subsistent relation of the mutual love of the Father and the Son, whose function lies precisely in creating relations and relating the relations to the mutual love of the Father and the Son—moves and relates all things to their ultimate end as the grace of divine motion that executes the plan of divine providence.[25]

In relation to the economy of salvation, we can say that the Holy Spirit is the divine energy that creates, redeems, and re-creates all reality. She is a cosmological power—the divine breath, wind, power, and force—that creates nature, liberates it from futility and transience, prepares it for human solidarity, and transforms it for its ultimate, eschatological re-creation.[26] She is an interpersonal power that creates relations, communions, and solidarities by producing the "fruits" of the Spirit such as "love, joy, peace, patience, kindness, goodness, faithfulness, gentleness, self-control" (Gal 5:22–23). She is an ecclesial power, the "soul" and "heart" of the church as the body of Christ, which vivifies, renews, and unifies the church in its proclamation, liturgy, and witness to the kingdom in the world.[27] The Spirit is also a historical power inspiring social events and movements in history that embody greater possibilities of liberation from oppression into solidarity of others.

As the vitalizing, liberating, and transforming power for solidarity, the Spirit is active wherever there is a movement of self-transcendence toward communion and solidarity at all levels, cosmic, interpersonal, ecclesial, historical. She is present not only in the church and in the "hearts" of individuals, not only in pentecostal gatherings and interpersonal relations, but also in all areas of our social life and our relations with nature. Perhaps the point of the classical pneumatology that turns the movement of love itself into a subsistent or personalized love is to revise our static, substantive conception of the person and to see the Holy Spirit precisely in the movements and events of the world, or as "the force field of God's mighty presence,"[28] where relations are created and solidarities formed for liberation and communion. It is not possible to confine the role of the Spirit to any one level, interpersonal, ecclesial, historical, or cosmic. The great imperative today is precisely to overcome all such dualisms: matter and spirit, inner and outer, individual and social, church and world, humanity and nature, finite and infinite. As a relating, integrating, and reconciling power and activity, the Spirit promotes solidarity of others precisely by sublating such dualisms.

Winds of the Holy Spirit Today

Where are the winds of the Holy Spirit blowing today? Where should we be especially attentive to the signs of its movement? We are living in a divided, oppressive, and alienating world, with daunting challenges to the fellowship of the Holy Spirit. The Spirit of Jesus crucified on behalf of all and still being crucified in the members of his body (cf. Col 1:24), continues to struggle and cry not only "Abba! Father!" but also "my God, my God, why have you forsaken me?"[29]

One of the places where we can look for the signs of the Spirit today might be precisely where we should look for them at all times, in situations of natural inequality in which the weaker always remain vulnerable to manipulation and domination by the stronger. There are many such situations today, as there always have been: the relation between parents and children, teachers and pupils, the healthy and the sick, legitimate authority and those subject to that authority, violent nature and human victims. These are relations that are essentially unequal yet also "natural" in the sense of being inherent in the human condition as such, not artificially caused by oppressive social arrangements. The possibilities of manipulation, violence, and suffering here remain huge. How could the stronger in the relation show the active, self-giving love of the Father? How could the weaker show the receptive, responsive love of the Son? And how does the Holy Spirit mediate and reconcile the two by inspiring the two loves respectively? How does she sublate these natural inequalities into the equality and friendship of mutual love and sharing? Despite appearances to the contrary, there are today countless ministers of the Holy Spirit actively involved in the praxis of uniting, reconciling love all over the world: self-sacrificing parents, dedicated teachers, caregivers for the ill, family and pastoral counselors, conscientious public servants, relief workers, and contributors for victims of violent nature.

The most distinctive and most frightful crisis today, however, has been the artificial, structural creation of oppressive, alienating inequalities based on class, gender, ethnicity, culture, religion, and technology, which also mediate and intensify the negative potentialities inherent in natural inequality. Today we suffer immeasurably more from one another because of structural, institutional, and organized inequalities than from the hands of nature or inherent natural inequality. Artificial suffering caused by exploitation of the poor, discrimination against women, marginalization of ethnic minorities, oppression of homosexuals, suppression of dissent, exclusion of the religious other, imperial domination of other nations, and the grand, full-scale technological assault on nature restrained by nothing—such perpetrated suffering is the central fact of our time and our world. As discussed earlier in the chapter, our challenge is not to leave others alone in their otherness but to forge a solidarity of others in which others *together* can achieve the minimum conditions of common life, such as basic needs, basic justice, and basic culture, as a condition for the flourishing of constructive, enriching otherness in the realm of freedom (Marx). The struggle involves resistance to, and overcoming of, the powers and principalities of this world, the vested interests and the entrenched powers. It involves sweat, blood, and unlimited patience and hope. The struggle is infinitely multifaceted: it may be local, national, or global; on the gender front as well as on the classist and racist fronts; on the level of politics and culture as well as on that of economics.

The winds of the Holy Spirit have been blowing in this area for some time. The very heightened sensitivity to classism, sexism, racism, ethnocentrism; the rise of pluralist cultural and religious sensibility and the ecological movement; the formation of active grassroots movements and organizations—these also are facts of our time and our world, and signs of the movement of the Spirit who unites and reconciles into solidarity of others. The Spirit sometimes works vociferously, as in revolutionary movements and mass protests; more often quietly, as in routine organizational work for social change as well as in works of mercy by unsung heroes and prayers for peace by unknown contemplatives. The breach of the Berlin Wall, the collapse of Soviet Communism, the dismantling of apartheid in South Africa, the displacement of military dictators in many parts of Latin America, the achievement of democracy after three decades of repressive dictatorship in South Korea—these and more stand as signs of hope. All too often—as in Palestine, Iraq, Ethiopia, Angola, Afghanistan, Kashmir, Ruanda, Kosovo, Colombia, Sri Lanka, North Korea, and Ecuador—the Spirit also moans and sighs on the verge of despair, interceding for us to the almighty Father in the name of his crucified Son.

The human praxis of the Holy Spirit, then, is to discern the authentic presence of her movement in the world and respond to her challenge and call. The Spirit is where the action is, the action of self-transcendence and liberation in and for solidarity of others. In this regard our response must fully respect the irony of the Holy Spirit as the self-effacing God: the point of the praxis and spirituality of the Spirit is not to call attention to, or cultivate, the Spirit for her own sake but to attend to that to which the Spirit calls us: the solidarity of others in the solidarity of the Son. This praxis of the Spirit requires certain adjustments in our theories and attitudes.

The first necessary adjustment is in our basic metaphysics. A substantialist metaphysics is not capable of appreciating the larger historical relations and movements because of its primary focus on individual substances and its relegation of relation and movement to the secondary categories of accidents, not to speak of its ahistorical orientation. The metaphysics of I-Thou, interpersonal relations may be an improvement on substantialist metaphysics as far as relations among persons are concerned; but it is just as inadequate in comprehending historical movements and challenges because it abstracts from the concrete dialectic of social relations. Persons are not taken as the concrete totality of constitutive social, historical relations but only as subjects of consciousness and intentionality. They are taken in isolation from the concrete challenges and pressures of our sociohistorical existence that exercise a profound impact on the very content of such consciousness and intentionality.

We need a concrete social metaphysics that sees a society as a totality of economic, political, and cultural relations at a particular time in history—relations that do not merely exist side by side but enter into a dialectic of negation and transcendence among themselves, necessarily generating transformations of structures and institutions, so that they see human individuals precisely as dynamic networks of personal, social, and natural relations within the conditions set by society. A concrete social metaphysics will see the work of the Spirit precisely in the qualities and transformations of social relations in their dialectic and in their impact on individuals. Traditional pneumatology limited itself to the role of the Spirit in the sanctification of individuals and at most in the guidance of the ecclesiastical magisterium, not also in history and the universe, in concrete social struggles, and in our violent relations to often violent nature; that traditional doctrine has not a little to do with its lack of a concrete social horizon.

Second, the praxis of the Holy Spirit requires a political sense of history in order to discern the most relevant signs of her work. Human suffering today is more a result of artificial social structures, institutions, and habits of thought than that of merely natural disasters. In short, it is politically caused and can be only politically redeemed in the broad sense of collective human action for the creation of the common conditions of life. Genuine politics requires a sense of solidarity with regard to the very alienating conditions in which we live, the collective responsibility for transforming the conditions, and the ends and values we pursue. As collective praxis for the improvement of the res publica, politics involves the horizon of totality and identity. We cannot live as others in common space while doing our own things. We have to establish minimum totalities or systems of identity such as laws, institutions, and policies that apply to all and that will provide basic needs, justice, and culture for all. Like it or not, we have to think in terms of totalities, often global, even if we have to act locally. It is indispensable to analyze the impact of global economic totalities on the welfare of the nation and its citizens, and to arrange measures for such an impact. Apolitical attitudes, often in the name of a postmodernist critique of totality, fail to take this political dimension seriously. A politically conscious pneumatology will discern the signs of the Spirit in the political implications of social change and political responses to them rather than abdicate the whole realm of politics in the name of human impotence.[30]

Third, it is imperative to maintain openness and flexibility with regard to where the signs of the Spirit are to be found. A tendency of postmodernist and eschatologically oriented pneumatologies is to see signs of the Spirit only in the new, the unpredictable, the surprising, the unusual—only in what negates and contradicts human expectations and labors. It is true that the Spirit as the eschatological dynamism of transformation is especially experienced in the emergence of the new and unexpected. It is equally true that the new and unexpected, if these are to bear concrete fruits in terms of enduring impact on our historical existence, must become *institutionalized* and become the basis of a new order that is also stable and dependable. Human beings cannot live in a Humean universe of pure succession of unrelated novelties. We should be able to experience the Spirit not only in the extraordinary and exciting but also in the ordinary and quotidian, where most people live. A pneumatology of difference underestimates the existential significance of order and stability, the ordinary and quotidian, the institutional and affirmative.

Finally, how is this theology of the Holy Spirit as the Spirit of solidarity relevant to the situation of religious pluralism? Is not such a thoroughly Christian, quite traditional theology an obstacle to interreligious dialogue? Several things can be said in response:

1. The interreligious situation does not require that religions give up their particular beliefs; but it does require that each religion penetrate its own tradition deeper and retrieve its own grounds for relating to, and appreciating, other religions. This is precisely what I have done in this chapter and will do more in the next.

2. A dynamic theology of the Holy Spirit as the Spirit of solidarity of others in God makes it possible for Christians to believe, as Vatican II recognizes, that the Holy Spirit is also active in the world, in other religions and cultures, "offering to every human being the possibility of being associated with this paschal mystery [of the death and resurrection of Christ]," but that we do not yet know how she is present there; this "how" remains "known only to God."[31] There is no danger that a pneumatology of solidarity will deny the solidarity it affirms is precisely the solidarity of others in God including *religious* others.

3. The actual perceived difference between Christianity and other religions is not itself an argument for the absence of the Spirit in the latter. The Holy Spirit is the Spirit of Christ, and there cannot be any contradiction between them in principle. However, even though the historical Jesus as the Word incarnate does remain the decisive, normative Savior of all humanity, this decisive universal significance is derived, as the classical tradition fully

recognizes, not from his humanity as such, which is an "instrument" of God's salvific work, but from his hypostatic union with the Word. Insofar as there is not only identity of person between the human Jesus and the divine Word but also difference of nature, it is legitimate to say that the Word cannot be exhaustively identified with all that has been revealed through Jesus. It is possible to think that the Holy Spirit as the Spirit of Christ may be actualizing different aspects of the Word in other religions. The difference between Christianity and other religions, then, is not a contradiction between the Word and the Spirit as such but a difference between the Word incarnated in the particularity of the human Jesus and other manifestations of the Word brought about by the Spirit in non-Christian religions. Even though we do not yet know how different religions may be mutually compatible, the fellowship of the Word and the Spirit in the immanent Trinity also gives us hope that they may be compatible and complementary, and that in and through those religions the uniting and reconciling Spirit is nonetheless working to bring different religions together into a solidarity of others in her own mysterious way.[32]

Before we go on, however, to discuss the relation among religions in a pluralistic world in chapters 8 and 9, it is also imperative first to discuss the place of Jesus Christ in the new paradigm of solidarity, to which I now turn.

Notes

1. See Jürgen Moltmann, *The Trinity and the Kingdom* (San Francisco: HarperSanFrancisco, 1991), 168–69.

2. Christopher Flavin, "Rich Planet, Poor Planet," in *State of the World 2001: A Worldwatch Institute Report on Progress Toward a Sustainable Society* (ed. Worldwatch Institute; New York: W. W. Norton, 2001), 5.

3. On the history of pneumatology, see Yves Congar, *I Believe in the Holy Spirit* (trans. David Smith; 3 vols. in one-volume ed.; New York: Crossroad, 1997).

4. On the role of the Spirit in the Hebrew Bible, see Hans Walter Wolff, *Anthropology of the Old Testament* (trans. Margaret Kohl; Philadelphia: Fortress, 1974; paper, 1981), 32–39; Eduard Schweizer, "Spirit of God," in *Bible Key Words* (ed. Gerhard Kittel; trans. Dorothea M. Barton, P. R. Ackroyd, and A. E. Harvey; New York: Harper & Brothers, 1961), 3:1–7; Gordon D. Fee, *God's Empowering Presence: The Holy Spirit in the Letters of Paul* (Peabody, Mass.: Hendrickson, 1994), 904–10.

5. Fee, *Holy Spirit*, 829–31.

6. See further Bernd Jochen Hilberath, "Identity through Self-Transcendence: The Holy Spirit and the Fellowship of Free Persons," in *Advents of the Spirit* (ed. Bradford E. Hinze and D. Lyle Dabney; Milwaukee: Marquette University Press, 2001), 263–92.

7. On the Holy Spirit as the transcendental horizon of our knowledge of God, see Killian McDonnell, "The Determinative Doctrine of the Holy Spirit," *Theology Today* 39 (1982): 142–61; idem, "A Trinitarian Theology of the Holy Spirit," Theological Studies 46 (1985): 191–227.

8. Congar, *I Believe in the Holy Spirit,* 2:18.

9. Catherine LaCugna, *God for Us: The Trinity and Christian Life* (San Francisco: Harper, 1991), 296.

10. McDonnell, "Trinitarian Theology of the Holy Spirit," 211.

11. John D. Zizioulas, *Being as Communion: Studies in Personhood and the Church* (Crestwood, N.Y.: St. Vladimir's Seminary Press, 1985), 110–11.

12. For a detailed overview of the concept of the Spirit in the New Testament, see Schweizer, "Spirit of God," 24–108; James D. G. Dunn, *Jesus and the Spirit* (Philadelphia: Westminster, 1970); Fee, *God's Empowering Presence*; my essay, Anselm Kyongsuk Min, "Renewing the Doctrine of the Spirit: A Prolegomenon," *Perspectives in Religious Studies* 19, no. 2 (summer 1992): 183–98.

13. Alasdair I. C. Heron, *The Holy Spirit* (Philadelphia: Westminster, 1983), 176.

14. Karl Rahner, *The Trinity* (New York; Crossroad, 1974), 24–33; idem, *Foundations of Christian Faith: An Introduction to the Idea of Christianity* (New York: Seabury, 1978), 212–28: "What Does It Mean to Say: 'God Became Man'?"

15. For a thorough historical, biblical, and theological discussion of the concept of the Holy Spirit as the mutual love of the Father and the Son, see Patrick Coffee, "The Holy Spirit as the Mutual Love of the Father and the Son," *Theological Studies* 51, no. 2 (June 1990): 193–229.

16. Thomas Aquinas, *Summa Theologiae* (ST), (4 vols; Matriti, Italy: Biblioteca de Autores Cristianos, 1955–58), I.27.4; I.36.1. All translations are the author's. Aquinas' *Summa Theologiae* has been translated as *Summa Theologica* by the Fathers of the English Dominican Province (5 vols; New York: Benziger Brothers, 1948; reprinted by Christian Classics, 1981).

17. *ST,* I.36.4.

18. *ST,* I.37.2.

19. *ST,* I.38.1.

20. *ST,* I.42.5.

21. Hans Urs von Balthasar, *Creator Spirit* (vol. 3 of *Explorations in Theology;* San Francisco: Ignatius, 1993), 127; idem, *Spirit and Institution* (vol. 4 of *Explorations in Theology*; San Francisco: Ignatius, 1995), 232–35.

22. Moltmann, *Trinity and the Kingdom,* 168–69.

23. *ST,* I.40.2.

24. The statement that "the Father and the Son love each other by the Holy Spirit" does not mean, for Aquinas, that the Spirit is either the efficient cause, a sign, or a formal cause of the mutual love of the Father and the Son; rather, it is the "formal effect" of that mutual love (see *ST,* I.37.2). It is reasonable, however, to believe that in the eternal simultaneity of perichoresis such a formal effect also exercises an impact, however derivative, on the agents themselves, the impact of reinforcing their mutual love, just as the relations and acts of human love reinforce and mediate the mutual love of the human agents, although only analogically.

25. *ST,* I.45.6; I–II.109.1.

26. On the presence of the Holy Spirit in nature, see further chapter 10, below, and Jürgen Moltmann, *God in Creation: A New Theology of Creation and the Spirit of God* (trans. Margaret Kohl; London: SCM, 1985; HarperCollins paperback ed., 1991), 98–103.

27. *ST,* III.8.1.

28. Wolfhart Pannenberg, *Systematic Theology* (trans. Geoffrey W. Bromiley; 3 vols.; Grand Rapids: Eerdmans, 1991–98), 1:382.

29. Jürgen Moltmann, *The Spirit of Life: A Universal Affirmation* (Minneapolis: Fortress, 1992), 73–77.

30. An example of an apolitical or even antipolitical pneumatology, otherwise brilliant, is Michael Welker, *God the Spirit* (Minneapolis: Fortress, 1994); see my review, Anselm Kyong-suk Min, "Liberation, the Other, and Hegel in Recent Pneumatologies," *Religious Studies Review* 22, no. 1 (Jan. 1996): 29–30; and my essay, idem, "Toward a Dialectic of Totality and Infinity: Reflections on Emmanuel Levinas," *Journal of Religion* 78, no. 4 (Oct. 1998): 571–92.

31. Second Vatican Council, *The Pastoral Constitution on the Church in the Modern World* (*Gaudium et Spes*; Dec. 7, 1965), § 22.

32. See Jacques Dupuis, *Toward a Christian Theology of Religious Pluralism* (Maryknoll, N.Y.: Orbis, 1997), 385–90.

SEVEN

SOLIDARITY OF OTHERS
IN THE BODY OF CHRIST
Christology in a Divided World

Beyond Identity Theologies

For various historical reasons, recent theologies have been deliberately
regional rather than comprehensive, insofar as each of them has tried to find
its theological locus in the experience of a particular group and concentrated
its concern on the liberation of one kind of others. These theologies often
proceeded with indifference to other kinds of people, sometimes even at
their expense, and at best in solidarity with others where the agenda of one's
own group still remains the center and norm. The Latin American theology
of liberation has been aimed at the challenge of the economic other; feminism (black, Hispanic, and white) at the challenge of the sexual other; ethnic
theologies at the challenge of the ethnic and racial other; and pluralist theologies at the challenge of the religious other. Although there has been a
growing concern over what appears to be theological fragmentation, the
prevailing emphasis has been on irreducible difference and otherness, not
only from the oppressors but also from fellow victims: "I am a woman, not
a man," "a black, not a white," "a Hispanic American, not an Anglo," and
so on.

As a theologian in the liberationist tradition, I appreciate the historical
necessity and contribution of each of these regional theologies. As the self-
assertive reaction of historically oppressed groups to the false, imperialist
universalism of male Western theology and colonialism, they have contributed not only to the liberation of their own groups but also to the critical
awakening of Western Christianity as a whole from its own imperialist slum-
ber. However, I also believe that the time has come for oppressed groups to
enter into a more self-conscious, systematic solidarity with one another and

to work out a new theological paradigm that does not deny the importance of particularity but indeed sublates it into solidarity of others.

In this chapter I argue for a new paradigm for North American theology: solidarity of others in the body of Christ. I do this in three steps. First, I present six reasons for moving beyond the current situation of identity theology and theological regionalism. Second, I provide further elaboration of the basis and concept of solidarity of others as the central, ruling category of a new paradigm. Third, I try to retrieve the metaphor of "the body of Christ" as a metaphor that is most authentically Christian, most comprehensive, yet also most relevant to the compelling contemporary task of building solidarity of others. Needless to say, I am presenting only an outline of the new paradigm, not its full elaboration.

There are a number of reasons why the present situation of theological fragmentation and regionalism has to be transcended. First of all, the contexts, whose particularity used to justify the particularity of theologies, have become so interdependent that it is no longer possible to sharply separate one context from another in its particularity. Regionalism is quickly becoming a thing of the past. The dynamics of global capitalism have been involving all groups alike, blacks and whites, women and men, Asians and Latin Americans, Buddhists and Muslims, in an interdependent destiny of economic exploitation, political instability, cultural homogeneity, spiritual alienation, and totalitarian commercialism that reduces all of life to commodity.[1] It is the same dynamics that produces the extravagant wealth of the corporate elite, the instability of the middle classes, the discrimination and denigration of women, the chronic unemployment of blacks, and the exploitation of the poor and women in the non-Western world. The same dynamics brings diverse groups, cultures, and religions into common political space to compete and struggle, often against one another and under uncommon and unequal conditions. The subjects of suffering are different and particular in gender, region, culture, and religion, but they are increasingly subject to the same universalizing, homogenizing, and conflictive pressures of global capitalism as *the* context of contexts. The globalizing context has been making the different groups interdependent in their very particularity. As Cornel West put it, "If we go down, we go down together."[2]

Second, the increasingly interdependent context makes it impossible for any particular group to liberate itself by its own isolated effort, without the cooperation of other groups. Neither Asian Americans nor black Americans nor black women nor Hispanic men nor Hispanic women nor, for that matter, white women can win their own liberation by themselves. Sometimes these groups are tempted to do so, and in the process they are often manipulated and pitted against one another by the establishment, each seeking its own liberation *against* others. It is difficult enough to change unjust laws and institutions even when united, and almost impossible to do so when disunited and pitted against one another. Different groups are not allowed simply to exist side by side and each to pursue its own liberation. They will either seek liberation *together* or be forced to seek it *against* one another. The interdependence of the very contexts of oppression requires solidarity of praxis even for the sake of one's own liberation. Again, as West put it well, paraphrasing Benjamin Franklin at the signing of the Declaration of Independence in 1776, "We are at a crucial crossroad in the history of this nation—and we either hang together by combating these forces that divide and degrade us or hang separately."[3]

Third, we must consider the intrinsic pluralism of concrete subjectivity. The concrete subject is not reducible to a single category, whether that of gender, region, class, or religion. In a way appropriate to the essential sociality of human existence and the intrinsic pluralism of that sociality, the human subject is constituted by a plurality of social relations such as gender, race, region, class, religion, and more. I am not only a male but also a Korean, not only a Korean but also a member of the middle class, not only a member of the middle class but also a Christian. I am not reducible to a single category or a collection of separable categories. As embodied in concrete subjects, the categories are intrinsically interdependent. I cannot concentrate exclusively on my class, gender, ethnicity, or religion, without suffering the worst kind of schizophrenia. As Jeffrey Escoffier aptly points out in his critique of a rigid and reified multicultural politics of identity, "we are all born within a web of overlapping identities and group affiliations," and a relevant multicultural project requires that "we give up some of the rigid boundaries that differentiate social identities and become permeable selves."[4] The interdependence of the categories must be explicitly acknowledged and acted on. The demand of the kairos is to turn this objective interdependence of categories into self-conscious solidarity of subjects precisely in their categorical diversity.

Fourth, there is the increasing interdependence of approaches to consider. Thus far, each regional theology has tended to concentrate on one aspect of the human totality. Black theology has tended to concentrate on race, feminism on gender and psychology, Latin American liberation theology on class, third-world theologies on culture, pluralist theologies on religion. One may argue, with good reason, for the analytic priority of one over others, as I will later in this paper, since not all aspects are equally significant and relevant; but it is not arguable that they are separable from one another or from the human totality. There is a thorough interdependence among them precisely because they are aspects of the one and same human totality. Feminism cannot be indifferent to the impact of class, race, and religion on the status of women and sexism as such; likewise, black theology cannot be indifferent to the impact of class, patriarchy, and religion on racism. It is sheer formalism and particularism to absolutize any one approach to the exclusion of, or indifference to, other approaches. Again, we need to transform this interdependence of approaches into a self-conscious solidarity among groups.

Fifth, we must also consider the ethical solidarity of all humanity. The demand for liberation is legitimate only as an ethical demand, and ethical demands are justifiable only as appeals to common, universal humanity, not as appeals to particularity as such. It is not ethically justifiable to demand that others treat me as an equal *because* I am a man, a Korean, or a Christian; this would deprive women, non-Koreans, or non-Christians of their right to equality and subordinate them to my difference and particularity. It is ethically justifiable to demand that others treat me as an equal because I— *although* a man, a Korean, and a Christian—am a human being and as such worthy of the same human dignity to which all are entitled on the ground of common humanity. My difference and particularity cannot be the *grounds* of my ethical claim, although they are necessary *modes* in which my humanity exists concretely. Particular modes of existence can be liberating when they serve as concrete *signs* of a common humanity that deserves equal respect and yet has been violated. They become oppressive when they are asserted as grounds of ethical claims to the sacrifice of universal humanity.

No one group, therefore, has the moral right to win liberation at the expense of the oppression of another. Ultimately, ethics requires groups to work together to create the common social conditions of economics, politics, and culture that would protect and nurture our common humanity. It is a call not only to recognize the common humanity of all in all our particularities but also to work together with one another to produce those social conditions without which we cannot be human and which we can only create together, not separately. The goal of all liberation struggles has to be the liberation of all groups precisely in their solidarity as human beings, not in their isolation. No one is indeed free unless all are free, and all are also called upon to share in the work of liberation of one another.

Finally and perhaps most importantly, there is the theological reason for overcoming particularism in theology. Everything in the tradition of Christology and Trinitarian theology tells us that sheer particularism is simply not Christian. Christian theology has always stressed the common collective destiny of all humanity and indeed all creatures in creation, sin, and redemption, their call to unity and solidarity in Christ through the reconciling work of the Holy Spirit to the glory of God, the Father and Mother of us all. A sense of ourselves, for and in all our differences, as common children of the same Father and as sisters and brothers of Christ, the primordial image of God, along with the sensitivity to the Holy Spirit, who gives life precisely by creating fellowship and solidarity, must be an essential characteristic of all authentically Christian theology. Even when, for necessary historical reasons, a particular theology is aimed at the liberation of a particular group of the oppressed and based on the experiences of that group, it is crucial not to forget this dimension of the solidarity of all humanity in their diversity. A God in whom only a particular group can find itself to the exclusion of other groups, even when that group is an oppressed group, is only a tribal God, not the Christian God; a discourse about such a God may be tribal lore but not Christian theology.

Solidarity of Others: A New Paradigm

I have stated several reasons—historical, political, anthropological, methodological, ethical, and theological—for sublating theological regionalism. Let me now move on to a brief, further elaboration of the concept of solidarity of others into which that regionalism, I think, should be sublated. First of all, I am not arguing for another abstractly universal theology to be imposed on all of us; such a theology may be universal insofar as it is imposed on the rest of us but remains abstract because it does not reflect everyone's needs and experiences.[5] Rather, my plea is for each regional theology, while rooted in its particularity, to extend its loci to include needs and experiences other than its own and to cooperate in the construction of a more concretely universal theology by contributing its own theological vision, not only of its own particularity, but also of human solidarity. The plea is for a theology of solidarity of others, a theology of *others* insofar as it must be rooted in particularity, a theology of *solidarity* of others insofar as it seeks to reach out, in its sense of context, concern, and goal, to others as fellow creatures, humans, and sisters and brothers in Christ.

My proposal, therefore, is for a theology of tension, tension between particularity and universality. A self-complacent theology of universality is an imperialist theology insensitive to the particular. A self-complacent theology of particularity may be a good political tract or a good sociological analysis, but it is not Christian theology, which is necessarily concerned with God, the absolutely comprehensive horizon, and with all things *sub ratione Dei*.[6] What we need is a theology of tension between otherness and solidarity, a theology of solidarity of others in the triune God. Insofar as class, race, and gender continue to be significant sources of oppression and insight, each regional theology need not abandon itself and strive for a universal theology unrooted in the particular; it should, rather, without forgetting itself, strive to reach out to others in self-conscious, systematic solidarity and contribute to a theology of solidarity of others that will emerge as a result of each theology trying to broaden its sense of context, concern, and goal beyond itself. In the process regional theologies will become more universal, while solidarity will become more concrete.[7]

The alternative to the abstract imperialist universalism of Western theology is not the sheer pluralism of theology that absolutizes particularity as such. Neither the globalizing context nor the need for cooperative praxis nor the interdependence of categories allows such pluralism any more than such pluralism is ethically justifiable or theologically acceptable. The issue is not whether we should or can leave one another alone in their respective otherness. As long as we are increasingly compelled to inhabit common social space in the same national community, it is simply not possible to leave one another alone, although it is what the establishment would devoutly wish for. We are rather compelled to agree on, and produce, common conditions of living *together,* laws, policies, and structures that will, on the one hand, promote authentic otherness that enriches and reconciles; while protecting us, on the other hand, from destructive otherness that isolates and divides. The real issue is not only how each group is going to preserve its otherness and integrity against the ever-present encroachment and domination of an hegemonic group, but also whether and how we as others can and should yet live *together* by jointly producing those conditions of solidarity that rule out such domination and concretize some sense of the common good.

Without some measure of a sense of community and its concretization in laws and structures, we are compelled to fight and struggle *against* one another rather than to leave one another alone in mutual isolation—which might be quite desirable under certain circumstances, as witness the Los Angeles uprising of April 29, 1992, in which blacks, Latinos, and Korean Americans were tragically involved in mutual destruction. "The insistence on *difference* can produce an *indifference* (or worse) toward Others."[8] The political problem of the one and the many remains unavoidable.[9] The politics of difference is not possible or justifiable except as part of a politics of solidarity. Secular movements of identity politics are becoming increasingly aware of their own inadequacy and turning toward some sort of politics of solidarity.[10] The only alternative to sheer pluralism is solidarity of others that indeed affirms otherness but also sublates it into solidarity. Without this solidarity, the postmodern turn to the other will be no different from the modern turn to the subject: it will lead to individualism, relativism, and nihilism, as surely as did subjectivism.[11]

The problem of solidarity applies not only to domestic but also to international problems. This is especially compelling to those living in the privileged nations of North America and Western Europe and trying to do theology there. Our theological locus is not just our ethnicity, gender, or class but also the political entity that acts in "our" name. All the citizens of a nation are collectively responsible—regardless of their differences in gender, ethnicity, and class—for what their government does overseas for good or evil; for or against global peace; for or against oppression of certain peoples, cultures, and religions; as well as for what it does for or against the ecological integrity of nature. This responsibility grows as the nation is the more powerful. As the only surviving superpower in the twenty-first century, the responsibility of the United States in particular for both global justice and integrity of creation remains preeminent, and theologians with loci in that superpower cannot remain indifferent to that exceptional responsibility and accountability in the name of difference and otherness. In any event, it is imperative to find a mode of discourse and praxis that enables us to conceive and practice our *collective* responsibility for all our differences and preoccupations, and to develop a sense of national and international solidarity of those who are other in ethnicity, class, and gender—people who are also mindful of the responsibility and consequences of their collective action on others in the world and in nature.

In line with postmodern discourse in general, I am using the term "other" as a critical concept. In its first, ethical sense, it refers to human beings in their dignity that transcends and thus resists reduction to identity, subjective or collective: hence, the ethical sense refers to human beings in their resistance to theoretical and practical totalization. It intends a critique of domination perpetrated in the name of a closed system of identity. In its second, sociological sense it refers to those excluded from social systems of identity precisely as victims of such totalizing reduction: the economically exploited, politically oppressed, culturally deprived, the socially marginalized in general. It is precisely the denial of otherness in the ethical sense that produces others in the sociological sense. In this sense, the postmodern turn is a turn to the "face" of the other (Levinas), away from the subject with its reductionist compulsion to unity and totality.[12]

Like the concept of the other, solidarity is also a critical concept, with a set of rich, interrelated meanings. It is, first of all, an ontological category referring to the constitutive interdependence of all reality, both the fundamental sociality of human existence and the metaphysical interconnectedness of all things, including human beings, in nature. Second, it refers to the historical process in which all nations and all aspects of life are becoming interdependent, spectacularly and painfully so in our day. Third, it is also an ethical concept, the challenge to recognize our metaphysical and historical interdependence as an intrinsic definition of our own being, as our common destiny, and to transform such interdependence into self-conscious *acts* of ethical, political solidarity. Fourth, solidarity is a theological concept referring to koinonia, "the communion of saints," the fellowship of those reborn in Christ by the power of the Holy Spirit as children of God, the Father and Mother of us all, an eschatological vocation and destiny to which all are called. Thus, solidarity is a concept rich in associations in that it is both metaphysical and ethical, a category of both theoretical and practical reason, with both philosophical and theological depth of meaning. It also allows for varying degrees of intimacy from communion to community to association and alliance to (generally unconscious) metaphysical interdependence with remote creatures.

I prefer "solidarity" to the more theologically popular term "communion." Communion implies a state of union already achieved and an interpersonal, face-to-face relationship. Insofar as all historical relations are always in the dialectical process of change and transcend by far the intimate, interpersonal relations, communion is inadequate and misleading as a historical, social category. It abstracts from the concrete dialectic of change, contradiction, and the struggles for power, and fails to attend to the larger historical consequences of social phenomena. I preserve "communion," however, as the fourth, theological meaning of "solidarity," as the eschatological goal and significance of all historical solidarities. I take solidarity as the larger, more inclusive category.

In all these meanings, solidarity connotes double resistance: resistance to individualism and resistance to totalitarianism. As a mode of interdependence of those who are *other,* solidarity is neither another abstract universality nor an undifferentiated totality, the reduction of all to the same; it is a form of concrete universality or togetherness of others without totalization. As *interdependence* of others, however, solidarity is not a pluralism of self-absolutizing individuals either; it is otherness precisely in togetherness, not in isolation or competition. The concrete form of (political) solidarity cannot be predicted because it depends precisely on the concrete sociohistorical forms of interdependence that emerge among different groups in concrete societies; but past experience can tell us what it should *not* be. It should not be "assimilation" of minorities to the single standard of the dominant group; or "amalgamation" typical of the melting pot, in which no group preserves its identity; or sheer pluralism, in which assertion of group identities is purchased at the expense of a minimum of togetherness. Over and beyond these forms, we can only struggle together in a way appropriate to the nature of the concrete dialectic of interdependence obtaining at a particular time, while leaving the concrete form of solidarity to emerge as a result of that struggle and dialectic.[13]

I am also advocating solidarity *of* others, not merely solidarity *with* others. Solidarity *with* others still implies a privileged center or a normative perspective that regards the liberation of one's own group as the overriding concern and selects the relevant others with whom to enter into solidarity, precisely for the sake of, and around, one's own agenda and goal. Others are not recognized as truly other, and solidarity becomes a tool of one's own liberation, one's own identity. Solidarity *of* others, on the other hand, rejects the centrality of any one group, requires *decentering* concerns from one's own group and *recentering* them on solidarity, considering even one's own needs not from a privileged perspective but in the context of solidarity, the solidarity of all in their needs, praxis, and goal. All others are recognized as other to one another and as worthy of respect and attention from one another.[14]

It is only within this context of solidarity, not outside it, that I also introduce a differentiating principle, the preferential option for the more oppressed. Not all the oppressed are equally oppressed; some are more oppressed and deserve more attention than others. If the oppressed are justified in claiming affirmative action from their oppressors, the more oppressed are likewise justified in claiming preferential concern from their less oppressed sisters and brothers. Solidarity means attention to difference in suffering and preferential solidarity with those who suffer more, not reduction of all to abstract equality. This also introduces certain complexity into the praxis of solidarity. As ethnic minorities, Koreans suffer more than white women as white, but they do not suffer as much as do blacks. White women suffer more than white men, but less than black men. As a minority, I am a victim; but as a male, I am also a victimizer. A sense of relativity in suffering and a preferential option for those who suffer more should lead all to accept legitimate differentiation as well as concrete justice in a situation often characterized by either claims of abstract equality or collective selfishness. Genuine solidarity means overcoming the propensity among oppressed groups to argue and fight among themselves over which group suffers more and therefore deserves more; it means the honesty of the less oppressed to recognize that they are less oppressed than some others; and it means their generosity to identify themselves with those who are more oppressed.

Without being an economic reductionist, I would also like to claim that the poor in the economic sense deserve the preferential option more than any other group; that is, economic oppression enjoys a certain primacy among different types of oppression. This is because the materially poor suffer not only material poverty, which is painful enough, such as hunger, sickness, and homelessness; they also suffer political oppression and cultural deprivation. The category of economy is, in this sense, a universal category; it determines not only who shall live in abundance and splendor and who shall die or live in scarcity and misery, but also the distribution of political power and cultural opportunities. The economic category is not only economic but also political and cultural in its consequences. This is why oppressions based on gender, race, region, and religion are the more painful and more reprehensible when they take economic forms. There may still be discrimination on the basis of gender, race, region, or religion even among economic equals, but as long as they are economic equals and thus also possessed of equal political and cultural power, such "discrimination" will never amount to "oppression." Genuine economic equality deprives would-be oppressors of their most potent tool of oppression and radically reduces the severity of suffering inherent in noneconomic types of oppression.[15]

The preferential option for the more oppressed means that each group, in elaborating its own theology and setting forth its practical agenda, will not only consider its own experiences and needs but also show appropriate sensitivity to the experiences and greater needs of the more oppressed. At a minimum, this means not pressing for the needs of one's own group at the expense of, or against, those of the more oppressed. At a maximum, it means pressing for the needs of the more oppressed even at the expense of one's own group when there is a conflict between the two. In most instances, it means not pressing for the cause of one's own group alone in simple indifference to the cause of the more oppressed, but exploring the greatest common denominator among the oppressed groups and working for a cause common to all. In any event, the preferential option for the more oppressed should serve as a permanent check against collective selfishness in the struggle for liberation.[16]

Solidarity of Others in the Body of Christ

In the depth of the Christian tradition, is there any symbol or metaphor that is most authentically Christian and yet also most compelling in conveying this concept and challenge of solidarity of others in its many aspects? Is there a metaphor that expresses the many sufferings of exclusion and oppression, the preferential concern for the more oppressed, the hope of liberation and inclusion, solidarity of all humanity in their diversity, their suffering and victory in the struggle for solidarity, the courage to open up to the other? I think there is, and it is the classical metaphor of the body of Christ.

There are four dimensions to the body of Christ: the bodily, the christological, the ecclesiological, and the Trinitarian. First of all, there is the dimension of the physical body or *sōma* (*sarx*). It represents the fundamental materiality of human existence, its concreteness and lowliness, its creatureliness, frailty, transience, and mortality. As such, the body is also the basis of the totality of human existence, its naturality, sexuality, sociality, historicity, and even spirituality and transcendence. In this sense of the totality of life, Paul exhorts Christians "to present your bodies as a living sacrifice, holy and acceptable to God, which is your spiritual worship" (Rom 12:1). The body is not something we *have* but something we *are*. The body is the most concrete sign of solidarity in all that is human, with nature as a whole, with sexual and social others in history, with the traditions of our ancestors, with God the totally Other, whom we can only worship in our bodies and only think in bodily images. All human contradictions—our joys and sorrows, hopes and despairs, triumphs and sufferings, especially those of oppression and rejection—are felt most concretely in the body. The body is not an independent, atomistic entity that can be considered in separation from other things; instead, it designates the concrete totality of human existence as being-in-the-world.[17] It is no wonder that in ages when poverty, sickness, and short life were the rule for the absolute majority of human beings, they also wanted to escape from the body as a sign and source of all that was undesirable in this world. In the Christian tradition, the body, in the form of the "flesh," is also the sign of human sinfulness, human resistance to the Spirit in all its aspects, the tendencies of unredeemed human nature to dominate, exploit, divide, and destroy. The body stands as a permanent preventive of all spiritualism, idealism, intellectualism, and solipsism. The human being is neither an angel nor an island.[18]

This sense of the physical body is subsumed, not eliminated, in the christological meaning of the body as the body of Christ. In the christological sense, it means first of all the concrete, historical body of Jesus Christ, in which he ministered, suffered, and was killed by crucifixion. The Word became flesh. During his ministry, he proclaimed the coming kingdom by audibly preaching to the people, healing their sick bodies, eating and drinking with them, sharing their quarters, and encouraging them with the material signs of the messianic age: the good news to the poor, freedom to the captives, restoration of sight to the blind, liberation of the oppressed, the resurrection of the dead. Christ's ministering body was a sign of the solidarity of praxis and hope. In siding with those excluded from society, he too was excluded from the political, religious, and legal systems of identity, dying as the Suffering Servant in whose suffering and cry from the cross we hear the sufferings and cries of all the victims of history. In his suffering as the ultimate Outsider, we see the suffering of all the outcasts of history. His suffering body was a sign of the solidarity of suffering. His crucifixion as the ultimate Other was also a critique of all systems of identity, theoretical and practical, a condemnation of all historical reductionisms. His crucified body was a sign of the solidarity of resistance and critique.[19]

That the body of Jesus could have a universal significance for all humanity as a sign of such solidarity, is not due to the mere fact that it was the body of the historical Jesus, but to the fact that it was the most concrete form of the humanity of Jesus, who became, through the hypostatic union, the self-expression and "real symbol" of the Word, itself the self-expression and symbol of the Father.[20] Through that body the Son proclaimed the Father's will for the salvation of humanity and obeyed the Father to the point of dying on the cross, bearing the "sin of the world," sharing in the tragic depth of human existence on the one hand, and revealing the Father's profound love for humanity on the other. If the salvific work of the Word become flesh reached its height in his death on the cross, the most moving symbol of that height was Jesus' "opened heart [apertum Cor]," pierced by the Roman soldier's lance and pouring out blood and water (John 19:34). The Preface of the Sacred Heart of the Roman Liturgy thanks and praises the Father, "who didst decree that thy only begotten Son, hanging upon the Cross, should be pierced by a soldier's lance, so that his Heart, that storehouse of divine bounty [divinae largitatis sacrarium], being thus opened, might pour out upon us streams of compassion and grace; and that the Heart which has never ceased to burn with love of us might be a haven of rest for the devout, and for the penitent an open doorway to salvation."

In this sense there is profound truth to Rahner's statement that

> if properly understood, the devotion to the Sacred Heart of Jesus belongs to the very essence of Christianity. . . . The only reason we are saved is because the heart of the incarnate Word was pierced through and streams of living water flowed from it. The pierced heart of Jesus Christ is the center of the world in which all the powers and currents of world history are, as it were, bound together into one.[21]

It is this crucifixion of Jesus, containing all the sufferings of history, its "depths and abysses," that constitutes, for Balthasar and Moltmann, the locus for the theology of the Trinity. As Moltmann put it, "The material principle of the doctrine of the Trinity is the cross of Christ. The formal principle of knowledge of the cross is the doctrine of the Trinity. . . . The theology of the cross must be the doctrine of the Trinity, and the doctrine of the Trinity must be the theology of the cross.[22]

There is, then, the risen body of Christ, eschatologically transformed and possessed of a universal meaning no longer confined to the here and now. It is a sign of the fullness of redemption and re-creation, the eschatological victory over sin, death, and suffering. As the risen body of the Son, it is also the exemplary source of the coming fullness of redemption and re-creation of all humanity and indeed of all creation. It is the body of the new Adam, in whose suffering and resurrection we are called upon to share through baptism (Rom 6:3–11; Col 2:12), as it is the body of the Son, to whose image we are to conform (Rom 8:29). The body of the risen Christ is a sign of solidarity of all humanity in Christ and with Christ, in suffering and the victory over suffering. It is a sign of our common eschatological hope.

Finally, we cannot overlook the cosmic body of Christ. The entire cosmos, of which humanity is only a part, is the material expression, image, or sign of the eternal Word, through whom and for whom it has been created (1 Cor 8:6; Col 1:16; Heb 1:2). According to Paul, the whole creation also longs for liberation from futility and transience and a share in the fullness of redemption brought about by the risen Christ (Rom 8:19–22). Sallie McFague speaks of the cosmos as the body of God.[23] From an explicitly Trinitarian perspective, I prefer to speak of the cosmos as the body of Christ. It is Christ through whom and in whose image the cosmos has been created (Col 1:15), Christ who took flesh in that cosmos, Christ in whose suffering the cosmos also participates when violated and raped in the many human crimes against nature, and Christ in whose resurrection the cosmos also longs to participate in a new heaven and a new earth.[24]

The ecclesiological sense of the body of Christ, perhaps the only sense in which the metaphor has been used in the tradition, has four dimensions to consider: the ecclesiastical, eschatological, solidaristic, and eucharistic.[25] The ecclesiastical dimension refers to the church as the body of Christ. Those who belong to the church constitute the body of Christ the head by sharing in his ministry, suffering, crucifixion, and resurrection. They live "in" Christ and "from" Christ. They form "one mystical person" [*una persona mystica*] with him in the solidarity and communion of grace and life.[26] Christians are "always carrying in the body the death of Jesus, so that the life of Jesus may also be made visible in our bodies" (2 Cor 4:10 NRSV), while also trying to "complete" in their flesh "what is lacking in Christ's afflictions for the sake of his body, that is, the church" (Col 1:24 NRSV).

The fact that the church is the body of Christ also means that Christ remains the absolute sovereign over the church. It is essential here to remember the words of Ernst Käsemann:

> We become members of the church because we have a part in Christ and not the reverse: we do not partake in Christ because we are members of the church. Here the irreversibility of the order is of vital importance. Christ is there before the church and he is not absorbed into that church.[27]

This also means that we cannot simply identify Christ and the church—the church as the mystical body of Christ, and the church as a visible organization—something the Reformers insisted on and postconciliar Catholicism began to recognize. As Emile Mersch put it more than half a century ago,

> A person can be a member of the visible society of the Church without actually living the life of Christ as a perfect member of the mystical body; this is the case with a Catholic hardened in sin. Likewise, one can truly live the life of Christ without being actually attached to the visible society that is His Church; an example is a pagan who would have received grace and charity without being aware of the Church, or a fervent catechumen.[28]

As Moltmann well pointed out, however, the church is not limited to those who follow Christ with an explicit faith. As the body of Christ, the church is wherever Christ is. *Ubi Christus, ibi ecclesia.* According to Matthew 25, Christ as the eschatological judge is present in the hungry, thirsty, strange, naked, sick, and imprisoned—something all contemporary ecclesiologies simply must take seriously, given so much oppression and suffering in the world today. Care for the suffering others of this world is not merely a matter of Christian ethics; it is also at the heart of ecclesiology. The church is constantly called upon, and challenged by, its own christological essence to expand its boundary and enter into the solidarity of all the excluded others of history. A church content with a secure identity is not a true church. Its identity must always remain vulnerable to the transforming challenge of otherness.[29]

The well-known metaphor of the body has been effectively used to manifest the nature of solidarity in which each person enjoys a distinctive function, but in which such distinctiveness also serves the common good of the whole. As Paul so eloquently put it,

Just as the body is one and has many members, and all the members of the body, though many, are one body, so it is with Christ. For in the one Spirit we were all baptized into one body—Jews or Greeks, slaves or free—and we were all made to drink of one Spirit. (1 Cor 12:12–13 NRSV)

There are varieties of gifts, ministry, and working in the body of Christ, but there is also the unity of the same Spirit, Lord, and God who inspires them all for the common good (1 Cor 12:4–7). Otherness is preserved, not reduced, yet not by absolutizing itself and excluding others but precisely by serving the common good of the body. The body does not allow either totalitarian uniformity or hierarchical absolutism, which suppresses the legitimate diversity of charisms. What matters the most is the sovereignty of Christ the head and the Holy Spirit that gives life, and the universal priesthood of the faithful in the service of that sovereignty. The members of Christ constitute a community of life sustained and nourished by the life of the same Christ and the same Spirit, and as such they enjoy the most profound and intimate kind of mutual union and fellowship among themselves, which transcends any empirical tie in the world. Without rejecting or looking down upon anyone, therefore, they share in one another's sufferings and joys in full consciousness of mutual dependence and solidarity. "If one member suffers, all suffer together [*sumpaschei*]; if one member is honored, all rejoice together [*sunchairei*]" (1 Cor 12:26). As a master metaphor of solidarity, the body preserves otherness but also transcends it in the togetherness of life, suffering, and joy.

This is true not only for the internal organization of the church in its variety of gifts and ministries, but also for the social composition of the church with its variety of ethnic, religious, gender, and economic groups. Baptism means incorporation into the body of Christ, in whom "there is no longer Jew or Greek, there is no longer slave or free, there is no longer male and female; for all of you are one [*heis*] in Christ Jesus" (Gal 3:28 NRSV; cf. 1 Cor 12:13; Col 3:11). Baptism renders all one in Christ beyond all distinctions. Paul's point here is not so much equality of those baptized, although we today take inequality as incompatible with baptism, as the more demanding "oneness" in Christ. Baptism does not erase the otherness of Jew and Greek, woman and man, although I think it does erase the otherness of free and slave; but baptism affirms not only the equality of those baptized in their otherness but also their oneness or solidarity in Christ in and despite their otherness. The body of Christ is not the formal unity of those reduced to the same but the solidarity of others, the oneness of those who are different.[30]

There is also the eucharistic body of Christ, the body of Christ rendered present to us through sacramental symbols. Through the Eucharist, all the dimensions of Christ's body mentioned thus far become visibly present to us in all their meanings, invitations, and challenges. Through it we enjoy the koinonia of "the body of Christ" and "the blood of Christ." "Because there is one bread, we who are many are one body, for we all partake of the one bread" (1 Cor 10:17 NRSV). In the Eucharist, itself a potent symbol of solidarity of others, we encounter the ministering, suffering, crucified, and risen Christ; renew the memory of his praxis, suffering, and victory; hear the challenge to the human solidarity of suffering, praxis, and hope; and look forward to the new heaven and new earth. The Eucharist is a celebration of the last eschatological table fellowship the historical Jesus shared with the outcast others of his society, and a sign of the reign of God we long for "until he comes." It is also both a thanksgiving of the entire people of God to the Father for the grace of salvation brought to us through the Son and an invocation, an *epiklēsis,* of the Holy Spirit, who makes such grace, remembrance, fellowship, and eschatological hope possible. In this sense the eucharistic body of Christ is the liturgical concretization and summary of the entire mystery of salvation. The Second Vatican Council accordingly calls the Eucharist "the source and summit" of the whole Christian life.[31]

Finally and most important, there is the Trinitarian dimension of the body of Christ. The body of Christ is essentially a Trinitarian event. The creation of the material universe, the cosmic body of Christ, the redemption of humanity as the wounded and suffering body of Christ, the re-creation of both history and nature as participation in the risen body of Christ—all these are rooted in the eternal solidarity or perichoresis of the immanent Trinity, three distinct persons yet sharing in the unity of the divine substance, and take place in time through the economic activities of the triune God, God in Christ through the power of the Holy Spirit. The Holy Spirit creates, redeems, and re-creates all things precisely by bringing things together in Christ as the primordial model of the creature created in the image of God. It is the Holy Spirit, the Spirit of both the Father and the Son, who gives life by establishing the unity in diversity and solidarity of others in the manifold body of Christ. All purely christocentric or christomonistic discussion of the body of Christ that excludes an essential role of the Holy Spirit tends to fall into monism, mechanism, hierarchical thinking, and totalitarianism without internal differentiation and vitality. The Trinity, especially pneumatology, remains an essential context for all theological reflection on the body of Christ.[32] Furthermore, the body of Christ in all these senses is both the "cosmotheandric" reality and the most fitting symbol of that reality that embodies the unity, harmony, and solidarity among God, humanity, and the cosmos—what Raimundo Panikkar has been trying to retrieve for our time.[33]

The Body of Christ as a Metaphor

To sum up, the metaphor of the body of Christ is most appropriate as the ruling metaphor of a theology of solidarity of others. As a metaphor, the body as the body of Christ is something concrete and visible. In its content, it is also most comprehensive in that it sums up all the essential theological dimensions of human existence, which renders it appropriate to serve as a central idea of Christian theology.[34] In its dynamics, it is dialectical in that it speaks not only of suffering but also of the overcoming of suffering, not only of praxis but also of praxis of solidarity and solidarity of praxis. Above all, it is an effective symbol of solidarity of others in all its theological aspects and historical dialectic. As such, it is a most appropriate metaphor for a theology of solidarity in the North American context, with its many divisions demanding healing through solidarity. Those who belong to the body of Christ are compelled to find the crucified Christ in all the others who are excluded and marginalized by the tyranny of identity, whether economic, sexual, racial, cultural, or religious; and to enter into the praxis of solidarity of others with hope in the risen Christ. For all our otherness, we are all one—in the most fundamental and most profound sense—in Christ Jesus in the fellowship of the Holy Spirit.

Perhaps the greatest obstacle to the metaphor is that it is too Christian and not open to the challenge of pluralism. Some may object that it is an effective symbol of *solidarity* all right, but perhaps not of the solidarity of *others*. Does it adequately accommodate the otherness of those who are not Christians? I reserve a full discussion of religious pluralism for the next two chapters. Here I confine myself to a twofold response. First, like all doctrines, the doctrine of the body of Christ is intelligible only within the horizon of a particular faith and its presuppositions, of Christian faith in this case. It is meant, therefore, primarily for the community of Christian faith, and for others only as a "graceful" challenge to consider in a dialogue conducted with mutual respect and pluralist sensibility. It is not meant to be imposed on all, across all the differences of basic horizon and ultimate concern. Second, I do not agree that the challenge of the pluralistic situation requires the simple renunciation of all distinctive beliefs of ours, which would only reduce all religions to the same and deny the validity and reality of pluralism. What the situation does require is returning to the depth of our own tradition and retrieving there the possibility of responding to pluralism. Both rooted in our own identity and responsive to the otherness of the new situation, this possibility may even force us to rethink our own position, including our fundamental, defining beliefs. However, whether we are to renounce any of our fundamental beliefs should be left to the outcome of dialogue, not demanded as dialogue's precondition.

There is no doubt that the metaphor of the body of Christ has often been used in the past to separate those who belong to Christ and his church and those who do not.[35] My point is that as a Trinitarian event, the metaphor contains a self-expanding dynamic of solidarity to include not only all humanity but also all creation, and that it is time for us to develop that dynamic. Obviously, it should not be used to further divide and separate humanity already mortally divided. It also has the resources to bring humanity together in the self-expanding fellowship of suffering, praxis, and hope.

Likewise, the metaphor of the body of Christ contains, among other things, the organic, biological dimension, which can easily lend itself, as it sometimes did in the past, to the justification of a totalitarian, hierarchical subordination of the members of the body to their presumed (human) "head," in the name of unity, harmony, and communion.[36] This danger is not to be denied or forgotten. The metaphor, however, is not just that of the body but also that of the body of *Christ,* which contains the historical, eschatological, and Trinitarian dimensions. Inherent in the metaphor, then, is not only the self-expanding dynamic of solidarity, but also the self-critical dialectic of liberation for solidarity *of others.* The self-expanding dynamic of fellowship of suffering, praxis, and hope to which the metaphor invites all, is simultaneously a dialectic of liberation that condemns all oppression of otherness in the name of the historical Jesus, who exemplified the solidarity of others in his own body even to the point of crucifixion; in the name of the eschatological Jesus, whose resurrection signals both critique of our fallen, oppressive existence and victory over oppression; and in the name of the Trinitarian God, who creates and liberates precisely for the communion of others in God, through Christ as the model of such communion and the Holy Spirit as the agent of that communion. As discussed, the body of Christ is inseparable from the Holy Spirit, who is the "soul" or the "heart" (Aquinas) of the body and the source of the unity and communion in diversity.

The metaphor of the body of Christ has also been criticized for the danger of unduly divinizing the church as an extension of the incarnation in time.[37] Such a danger need not be denied insofar as the metaphor is used in its ecclesiological sense alone. The metaphor, however, contains not only the ecclesiological but also the bodily, christological, and Trinitarian dimensions, which together provide critical and countervailing resources against any temptation the church may feel to glorify itself. The church is indeed the body of Christ, but it is so only by participation empowered by the Holy Spirit. In itself, the church consists of human beings in all their bodily lowliness and fleshly weakness, and always remains subject to the judgment of the crucified body of Jesus as well as in need of the eschatological hope made possible by his risen body. The metaphor is multifaceted enough to provide the necessary checks and balances.

Deep down, all metaphors are bodily images. As such, they are always in danger of being reified and absolutized. A particular dimension of the image is isolated from the rest and then made central to all, lending justification to particular claims and ideologies. The fruitfulness of a metaphor thus depends on the multiplicity of dimensions it evokes and on the dialectic among that multiplicity that provides balance, expansion, and critique. The multiplicity lends richness to the metaphor; the dialectic provides depth, intensity, and defense against reification. My claim is that the metaphor of the body of Christ is a most fruitful theological metaphor because it is a rich association of so many dimensions from the bodily to the christological, and from the ecclesiological to the Trinitarian, and because it contains an inherent dialectic of mutual expansion and critique among the dimensions so as to prevent reification. Besides, it is a most biblical, most authentically Christian metaphor that is at the same time most appropriate to the desperate need of the times in which we live, the need for solidarity of others.

Notes

1. For analyses of the global situation and trends set off by global capitalism, I have found the following works helpful: Richard J. Barnet and John Cavanagh, *Global Dreams: Imperial Corporations and the New World Order* (New York: Simon & Schuster, 1995); Robert N. Bellah, "Changing Themes in Society: Implications for Human Services: Social Change and the Fate of Human Services" (speech to Lutheran Social Services, San Francisco, Apr. 28, 1995); Robert Gilpin, *The Political Economy of International Relations* (Princeton, N.J.: Princeton University Press, 1987), 364–408; Paul Kennedy, *Preparing for the Twenty-First Century* (New York: Random House, 1993), 329–49; the whole issue of *The Nation* 263, no. 3 (July 15/22, 1996) is devoted to an analysis of globalization; William Pfaff, *The Wrath of Nations: Civilization and the Furies of Nationalism* (New York: Simon & Schuster, 1993); Robert Wuthnow, *Christianity in the Twenty-First Century: Reflections on the Challenges Ahead* (New York: Oxford University Press, 1993).

2. Cornel West, *Race Matters* (New York: Random House, 1993; Vintage Books, 1994), 8.

3. Ibid., 159. I am indepted to my copyeditor, David Garber, for information about the source of the expression "hang together or hang separately."

4. Jeffrey Escoffier, "The Limits of Multiculturalism," *Socialist Review* 21, nos. 3–4 (July-Dec. 1991): 64 and 70, respectively.

5. For a trenchant critique of abstract universality unrooted in the particular, see Iris Marion Young, "Polity and Group Difference: A Critique of the Ideal of Universal Citizenship," in *Feminism and Political Theory* (ed. Cass R. Sunstein; Chicago: University of Chicago Press, 1990), 117–41.

6. Thomas Aquinas, *Summa Theologiae* (*ST*), (4 vols; Matriti, Italy: Biblioteca de Autores Cristianos, 1955–58), I.1.7: "All things are dealt with in sacred doctrine under the logic of God [*sub ratione Dei*] either because they are God himself or because they have an orientation to God as to their principle and end."

7. In his *A Radical Jew: Paul and the Politics of Identity* (Berkeley: University of California Press, 1994), 228–60, Daniel Boyarin encourages this sort of tension between universality and particularity from the Jewish perspective. He advocates a "diasporic" consciousness and tension whereby Jews dissociate ethnicities and political hegemonies and learn to share space with others while also holding on to their own Jewish cultural identity. I must say, however, that his emphasis on solidarity still remains inadequate.

8. Ibid., 235.

9. For insightful recent discussions of the problem of the one and the many in U.S. politics, see Martin E. Marty, *The One and the Many: America's Struggle for the Common Good* (Cambridge, Mass.: Harvard University Press, 1997); and National Endowment for the Humanities, ed., *A National Conversation on American Pluralism and Identity: Scholars' Essays* (Washington, D.C.: National Endowment for the Humanities, 1994).

10. See Jodi Dean, *Solidarity of Strangers: Feminism after Identity Politics* (Berkeley: University of California Press, 1996).

11. For a trenchant critique of Jean-François Lyotard's postmodernism in this regard, see Seyla Benhabib, "Epistemologies of Postmodernism: A Rejoinder to Jean-François Lyotard," *New German Critique* 33 (fall 1984): 103–26; and Peter Murphy, "Postmodern Perspectives and Justice," *Thesis Eleven* 30 (1991): 117–32.

12. For this dialectic of same and other, and the concept of the solidarity of Others, I am especially indebted to Emmanuel Levinas, *Totality and Infinity: An Essay on Exteriority* (Pittsburgh: Duquesne University Press, 1969). For my critical appreciation of Levinas, see Anselm Kyongsuk Min, "Toward a Dialectic of Totality and Infinity: Reflections on Emmanuel Levinas," *The Journal of Religion* 78, no. 4 (Oct. 1998): 571–92.

13. In this respect, my view perhaps comes close to that of Andrew Sung Park, *Racial Conflict and Healing: An Asian-American Theological Perspective* (Maryknoll, N.Y.: Orbis, 1996), especially 85–106.

14. For a recent feminist approach to the solidarity of others, see Dean, *Solidarity of Strangers*. For other aspects of this solidarity, see my essay, Anselm Kyongsuk Min, "From Autobiography to Fellowship of Others: Reflections on Doing Ethnic Theology Today," in *Journeys at the Margin: Toward an Autobiographical Theology in American-Asian Perspective* (ed. Peter C. Phan and Jung Young Lee; Collegeville, Minn.: Liturgical, 1999), 135–59.

15. On the primacy of political economy among the sources of marginalization, see my work: Anselm Kyongsuk Min, *Dialectic of Salvation: Issues in Theology of Liberation* (Albany, N.Y.: SUNY Press, 1989), 22–28, 70–72; idem, "The Political Economy of Marginality," *Journal of Asian and Asian American Theology* 1, no. 1 (summer 1996), 82–94; The United States Conference of Catholic Bishops, *Economic Justice for All: Pastoral Letter on Catholic Social Teaching and the U.S. Economy* (Washington, D.C.: U.S. Catholic Conference, 1986), § 86.

16. As an example of this preferential option for the more oppressed in theology, I mention Susan Thistlethwaite's *Sex, Race, and God: Christian Feminism in Black and White* (New York: Crossroad, 1989), in which she, a white feminist, incorporates black women's experiences into her own methodology.

17. Ernst Käsemann, *Perspectives on Paul* (trans. Margaret Kohl; Mifflintown, Pa.: Sigler, 1996; SCM, 1971), 114.

18. For the Hebrew and Christian conceptions of the body, see Hans Walter Wolff, *Anthropology of the Old Testament* (Philadelphia: Fortress, 1974), 10–80; and Eduard Schweizer, *The Church as the Body of Christ* (Richmond: John Knox, 1964), 9–40. For a brief general treatment of the significance of the body, see Elisabeth Moltmann-Wendel, *I Am My Body: New Ways of Embodiment* (London: SCM, 1994); Sarah Coakley, ed., *Religion and the Body* (Cambridge: Cambridge University Press, 1997). For a brief discussion of the many different dimensions of the body (personal, social, cosmic, theological, ecclesiological, and so on), see Karl Rahner, *Jesus, Man, and the Church* (trans. Margaret Kohl; vol. 17 of *Theological Investigations*; London: Darton, Longman & Todd, 1981), 71–89: "The Body in the Order of Salvation."

19. Jürgen Moltmann, *The Crucified God* (London: SCM, 1974), 65–75.

20. For the concept of "real symbol" as the self-expression of the symbolized, see Karl Rahner, *More Recent Writings* (trans. Kevin Smyth; vol. 4 of *Theological Investigations*; London: Darton, Longman & Todd, 1966), 221–52: "The Theology of the Symbol."

21. Karl Rahner, *The Content of Faith: The Best of Karl Rahner's Theological Writings* (New York: Crossroad, 1992), 306.

22. Moltmann, *Crucified God*, 241; for Balthasar's Trinitarian interpretation of the cross, see Hans Urs von Balthasar, *Mysterium Paschale* (Grand Rapids: Eerdmans, 1993), 136–40.

23. See Sallie McFague, *The Body of God: An Ecological Theology* (Minneapolis: Augsburg Fortress, 1993).

24. On the cosmic Christ, see Jürgen Moltmann, *The Way of Jesus Christ: Christology in Messianic Dimensions* (San Francisco: HarperSanFrancisco, 1990), 274–312; Schweizer, *Church as the Body*, 57–74; Teilhard de Chardin, *The Phenomenon of Man* (New York: Harper, 1959); Karl Rahner, *Foundations of Christian Faith* (New York: Crossroad, 1978), 178–203; Matthew Fox, *The Coming of the Cosmic Christ* (San Francisco: Harper, 1988).

25. For a classical discussion of the church as the body of Christ, see Emile Mersch, *The Whole Christ* (Milwaukee: Bruce, 1938); idem, *The Theology of the Mystical Body* (St. Louis: Herder, 1951); Paul S. Minear, *Images of the Church in the New Testament* (Philadelphia: Westminster, 1960), 173–220.

26. Aquinas, *ST,* III.19.4.

27. Käsemann, *Perspectives on Paul,* 116.

28. Mersch, *Theology of the Mystical Body,* 480. For a critical, dialectical conception of the relation between Christ and the church as his body from the Protestant perspective, see Peter C. Hodgson, *Revisioning the Church: Ecclesial Freedom in the New Paradigm* (Philadelphia: Fortress, 1988), 44–47.

29. See Jürgen Moltmann, *The Church in the Power of the Spirit* (San Francisco: HarperSanFrancisco, 1991), 126–29.

30. Daniel Boyarin proposes an opposite view of Gal 3:28 in *A Radical Jew,* 9, 208, 257, interpreting Paul as completely suppressing particularity ("neither Jew nor Greek") in the name of abstract universality ("all one in Christ Jesus"). Boyarin's interesting thesis is that, caught between the particularism of the Jewish religion and the universalism of Greek culture, Paul was concerned over the salvation of the Gentiles, and found a way for their salvation in the anthropological dualism of spirit and flesh, attributing all universality to the spirit and all particularity to the flesh, depreciating all differences—ethnic and gender—based on the particularity of the flesh, and ultimately reducing human existence to abstract identity devoid of all concrete particularity.

31. Second Vatican Council, *Dogmatic Constitution on the Church* (*Lumen Gentium*; Nov. 21, 1964), § 11; idem, *Constitution on the Sacred Liturgy* (Sacrosanctum Concilium; Dec. 4, 1963), § 10. For a comprehensive theological reflection on the many dimensions of the Eucharist, see Walter Kasper, *Theology and Church* (New York: Crossroad, 1989), 177–94.

32. For a profound discussion of the Trinitarian dimension of the body of Christ, see Mersch, *Theology of the Mystical Body*, 325–454.

33. Raimundo Panikkar, *The Cosmotheandric Experience: Emerging Religious Consciousness* (Maryknoll, N.Y.: Orbis, 1993).

34. Emile Mersch's two books, *The Whole Christ* and *The Theology of the Mystical Body*, were written with the Augustinian idea and conviction that the concept of the "whole Christ," which includes Christ's divinity and humanity, the head and members of his body, contains and sums up all Christian doctrines; see *Theology of the Mystical Body*, 47–74. From the perspective of the twenty-first century, we cannot avoid noticing the lack of the cosmic, historical, and liberationist dimensions of the body of Christ in his treatment, which tends to be excessively metaphysical. Still, I believe his work belongs among the most profound, classical discussions of the subject worth continuing study and discussion.

35. For example, Pope Pius XII's *Mystici Corporis Christi* (June 29, 1943), §§ 22, 95, 103, simply identified the body of Christ with the Catholic Church, excluding all others from that body.

36. An excellent example of a hierarchical ecclesiology without pneumatology is Karl Adam, *The Spirit of Catholicism* (orig. German ed., 1924; New York: Doubleday, 1954). For an Orthodox critique of the body-of-Christ ecclesiology without pneumatology, see Dumitru Staniloae, *Theology and the Church* (Crestwood, N.Y.: St. Vladimir Seminary Press, 1980), 45–71. Regarding Pius XII's *Mystici Corporis Christi,* it must be noted that while it is rather triumphalistic and hierarchically oriented (§§ 6, 17, 40, 44, 69) and even declares that Christ and the pope constitute "one only head" of the church (§ 40), it does also point out that the union of Christ and the church is not hypostatic and warns against treating the two as one person (§§ 54, 86).

37. On the theological necessity of separating the incarnation and the church, see Heribert Mühlen, *Una Mystica Persona: Die Kirche als das Mysterium der heilsgeschichtlichen Identität des heiligen Geistes in Christus und den Christen, eine Person in vielen Personen* (3d ed.; Munich: Ferdinand Schoningh, 1968), 173–215.

EIGHT

PRAXIS AND PLURALISM
*A Liberationist Theology of Religions**

In recent years, under the pressure of an increasingly interdependent world, the problem of religious pluralism, once the curiosity of a small number of missiologists and theologians of religions, has become central to Christian systematic theology. Given the nature of the challenge, this is hardly surprising. As Gilkey pointed out, the challenge is not just to "modernize," "demythologize," or "revise" Christian symbols as in the case of pre-pluralist theologies, which sought to relativize only the past *expressions* of traditional symbols in favor of modern ones; it is rather to relativize the *symbols themselves,* affecting *all,* not just some, theological doctrines.[1]

For those committed to Christian faith this challenge could be frightening in its implications. It rejects not only the older christocentric exclusivism but also christological inclusivism, the currently dominant position of mainline Christianity. It challenges the central dogma of faith: the universal, normative, and unique significance of Jesus Christ as the Savior of all humanity and history, and by implication all the creeds, dogmas, liturgical and sacramental systems, structures of authority, and private devotional practices founded on that belief. It challenges, in short, the very identity and the deepest core of Christian faith as traditionally practiced.

In this chapter I first present an outline of a liberationist approach to theology in general and the problem of pluralism in particular, based on the key concepts of concrete totality and praxis, and then offer some critical observations on some of the pluralist arguments for abandoning our belief in Jesus as the absolute Savior of all humanity. The discussion of pluralism will continue in the next chapter from the perspective of solidarity of others in the contemporary world.

* This is a revised version of a paper originally presented at the Southeastern Regional Meeting of the American Academy of Religion in Atlanta, on March 11, 1989. I thank the Faculty Development Committee of Belmont Abbey College for subsidizing my research on this article during the summer of 1988.

Basic Concerns of Liberation Theology

Theology of liberation,[2] like most modern theologies, is a theology of cor-relation, a product of synthesis of the message of revelation and the questions inherent in human existence. What distinguishes liberation theology from all other modern theologies as well as from the traditional is its conceptualiza-tion of the human correlative of divine revelation, that is, its anthropology. This anthropology is neither existentialist nor personalist nor Thomist nor dialogical. It is based on the notion of human existence as a concrete totality in the tradition of Hegel and Marx.

Human existence has many dimensions, notably those of transcendence and history, personal and social, material and spiritual, reason and experi-ence. These are mutually distinct and irreducible, yet also mutually constitu-tive and internally related. Precisely because human existence is a unity of these distinct yet mutually internal relations, a dialectic of conflict and con-tradiction is inherent in human life. Furthermore, this dialectical unity of internally differentiated yet related dimensions is a historical unity, a unity itself in the process of becoming in history. As a dialectical process, then, his-tory is also a teleological process in which humans struggle for the resolution of contradictions and strive toward a higher synthesis and reconciliation of the opposed elements. Human existence is a concrete totality, a totality inso-far as it is a unity of many differentiated elements, transcendence and his-tory, personal and social existence, materiality and spirituality, not just an individual or a purely spiritual being, not a mere juxtaposition or an extrin-sic aggregate of these dimensions. It is concrete insofar as it is a concrete his-torical process in which it seeks, through praxis, to achieve liberating self-unification out of the dialectic of these constitutive elements.

To put this in more concrete terms, humans are not isolated atoms or dis-embodied intellects. They are born into an already-existing world, and at all times they find themselves already involved in a particular world with its own historically specific and historically conditioned forms of economic and political organization and distribution of power, and corresponding forms of ideology and culture. It is in this world that they have to struggle to satisfy their basic material needs as *the* presupposition of everything else, establish humane relationships with one another as groups and individuals, and seek the transcendent meaning of their existence in and through their economic and political life. This struggle for the realization of human life as a concrete totality is both a struggle against the oppressiveness of the social status quo, a struggle in the context of its specific conflicts and possibilities, and a struggle for liberation, the establishment of humane relationships and reconciled communities.

It is in the midst of this struggle for liberation in a specific society and history—called praxis—that we become aware of, and develop, our individuality. It is also through such concrete struggles that our thought, self-consciousness, reason, will, and feeling are awakened, developed, and concretized through their sociohistorical objectification. These struggles are subordinate, although irreducibly distinct, aspects of our life as concrete totalities; they are moments of our praxis through which we experience ourselves and try to realize ourselves as concrete totalities. Humans are primarily subjects of sociohistorical praxis and only secondarily those of thought, self-consciousness, will, or feeling. Theory is born of the need for praxis in society and history; conditioned by the economic, political, and ideological conditions of that praxis; pursued for the sake of praxis and its goal, liberation; and verified by its contribution to that praxis. Human theory or human thought is that of a concrete historical totality, not that of an angelic spirit, and bears all the limitations and contradictions of historical existence. Theory is indeed the faculty of critical transcendence, has a measure of autonomy over against anything extrinsic, and is essential as a critical moment of praxis itself. At the same time such transcendence is always transcendence *within* history, not *over* history, except as its ideal goal, precisely as object of faith. Human reason, as Marx said, is anything but "pure," and it is never totally independent of human praxis and the sociohistorical conditions of that praxis. It is an essential, self-critical principle of praxis, but *within* praxis and *for* praxis.

Theology of liberation is based on the concrete praxis of liberation; with this anthropology of concrete totality born of that praxis as the human correlative of divine revelation, then, it performs its theoretical task by asking about the demand and meaning of the revealed message for human existence precisely as a concrete totality, not merely for a soul, an individual, an intellect, a moral will, or "existence" (Bultmann, Tillich), as traditional or modern theologies do. It does not merely ask, as existentialist and hermeneutical theologies do, about the *meaning* of the divine message for human understanding. More important than its meaning is the *demand* of that message for human praxis. What does God, Christ, revelation, grace, salvation, sin, justification, faith, or communion of saints demand *of* and mean precisely *for* human beings who are concrete sociohistorical totalities and who have to struggle for the healing, reconciliation, and fulfillment of such totalities, often against the oppressive "powers and principalities" of this world? Theology of liberation takes this concrete totality as the object of salvation and thus as "matter" of theology, and seeks to reflect on, and draw out, its explicitly theological "form" or meaning. It is thoroughly nondualist, as it is not abstractly monist. Salvation in its full sense is eschatological and *beyond* history, but the human response to the call of salvation is *through* the liberation of concrete totalities *in* history.

Without denying the eschatological transcendence of salvation, therefore, all theoretical questions of theology must be converted into terms of concrete totality, that is, concretized, socialized, and historicized into the practical problems of liberating praxis in society and history. It asks, therefore, What does God demand of, and mean for, the still-ruling classes of many Latin American countries and those huddled in the slums of Lima, San Paulo, and Buenos Aires? What does Christ demand of, and mean for, the ruling elites of many African countries and the millions of victims murdered in decades of mutual genocides on grounds of ethnic and religious differences in Rwanda, Angola, and the Congo? What does the "communion of saints" demand of, and mean for, the Christian members of the ruling elite in the United States, whose multinational corporations dominate the economics and politics of the third world? For the wealthy and powerful in the (over)developed nations of North America, Europe, Japan, and South Korea; and the "aliens," legal or illegal, whose labor is being exploited in those countries? That is, What is the practical demand and theological significance of this massive human alienation and suffering, unjust social structures, global economic and military rivalry, and the rush of history toward the destruction of nature?[3] I have already attempted to answer some of these questions in the three preceding chapters.

The Liberationist Approach to Pluralism

Finally, how should theology of liberation deal with the problem of pluralism? Pluralism as a *problem* does not lie in the mere coexistence of a plurality of different religions; it lies in the mutual *confrontation* and mutual *demand*—both practical and theoretical—of diverse religions, each with its own distinctive claim. It is not a purely theoretical question. We therefore must ask: (1) What is the historical origin and context of the confrontation of different religions? (2) What does the present confrontation demand by way of praxis? (3) What theoretical-theological questions does it raise? (4) What kind of theological answers are possible or desirable today? I suggest the following tentative responses to these questions.

Every theological question has its own historical *Sitz im Leben,* and it is crucial that we become clear about the historical origin and context of the problem of pluralism. Without this clarity all our answers are bound to be irrelevant, guilty of *ignoratio elenchi* (ignorance of the point to be proved). What are the historical forces and conflicts bringing different religions of the world together into mutual confrontation or cooperation today? The answer, I think, is that it is the struggle for oppression and liberation that brings religions together sometimes as enemies, sometimes as collaborators in the same cause. The struggle may be regional, as in the case of the struggles between Jews and Muslims in the Middle East, Catholics and Protestants in Northern Ireland, Buddhists and Hindus in Sri Lanka, Hindus and Sikhs in India, Catholics and Protestant fundamentalists in Latin America. There is also cooperation among religions in many regions, as, for example, between Catholics and Protestants in the common struggle against apartheid in South Africa, between Christians and Buddhists in the struggle against economic and political oppression in South Korea, between Catholics and Protestants in the common struggle for liberation in many Latin American countries. If we include Marxists in our discussion of pluralism, we see the same phenomenon repeated. There is the notorious confrontation of Christians and Marxists as in postwar Europe and China, just as there is collaboration between them in Latin America and China ("patriotic" Christians and the government). There is also the global aspect to these regional struggles, the pressure of the global capitalist economy that has created an increasingly interdependent world with all its momentous contradictions, and the political and military confrontations among the great powers who are involved in the regional conflicts either directly or often through their local cronies.

This historical context of the problem of pluralism should make clear at least two things. First, the problem of pluralism as the problem of the relationship among religions is not primarily a religious or theological problem in the sense of a conflict about ultimate religious beliefs, but a problem of historical praxis. In its historical content it is a political and economic problem. In its moral content it is a struggle for basic justice and human dignity in a world of conflicting interests. The task of theology is to reflect on, and give theological form to, this content. Second, no religion is a homogeneous group in this struggle; rather, every religion is internally divided because of the different political stands on the issue of oppression and liberation, which also leads to theological divisions in each religion (consider Alexander Haig and Daniel Berrigan, both Catholics). No serious dialogue among religions can ignore this fact of conflict in praxis and theology both *among* religions and *within* religions. Some members of a religion serve the cause of oppression, others the cause of liberation. A serious dialogue must do away with the assumption of the ultimate harmony of all religions and the plea for indiscriminate tolerance of all diversity. Not all religions are harmonizable with one another in their praxis or their theology. Not all diversities are constructive and unifying; some diversities are downright oppressive.

What does this historical context of the problem of pluralism demand by way of theological response? It demands, above all, interreligious cooperation in the praxis of liberation, or *diapraxis,* as distinct from dialogue: this means cooperation in the alleviation of unjust and unnecessary suffering of the *concrete human subjects* of religion. It is not simply that we cannot get to the problem of different religions except through the economic and political problems because they are all involved in such problems, or because the non-Christian religions are found mostly in the third world, where religion cannot be separated from politics and economics. This would be using liberation of the oppressed as only a means to the religious problem, as though the religious problem existed apart from the problem of liberation. The primacy of joint praxis of liberation arises from the fact that the problem of liberation and oppression, the problem of life and death, is in itself *the* theological or religious problem today. For it is precisely in this struggle for physical survival, basic justice, and minimum dignity against global and regional forces of oppression that humans experience, in the most concrete and painful way, the ultimate boundary questions of human existence (Jaspers, Tracy) and the absolute ontic, moral, and spiritual anxieties (Tillich) that many take to be the origin and essence of the religious question. It is also precisely to the concrete human subjects in these boundary situations that religions and theologies must speak and convincingly deliver the message of salvation or else condemn themselves to irrelevance. The intellectual dialogue and theoretical understanding among religions concerning ultimate questions, such as the nature of the ultimate reality and ultimate salvation, are important but secondary to this question of liberation.

Although the problem of liberation in its economic and political content is the problem of religious pluralism, the contemporary context of that problem still does raise transcendent and theoretical issues, such as the validity of the competing claims of different religions to ultimacy, universality, and absoluteness; and in particular the validity of the traditional Christian claim to the universal, normative, and unique significance of Jesus as the Savior of all humanity.[4] Compounding the problem is the increasing awareness, since Ernst Troeltsch, of the historical relativity of all human perspectives and claims. How could a particular historical religion claim a unique and normative universality for all humanity? Is it possible for God to reveal the divine will through a historical person in a way that is uniquely and normatively significant for all humanity? Is it possible for a historically finite being (e.g., Jesus of Nazareth) to be the unique and normative embodiment of the divine promise of salvation of all humans?

As historically oriented, theology of liberation does accept and insist on the historical conditioning and relativity of all human knowledge, and does so much more emphatically and self-consciously than does any other contemporary theology. It is crucial, however, to ask just what is entailed by this thesis of historical relativity. It means that human consciousness and knowledge are activities of human beings as concrete sociohistorical totalities, not those of pure spirits, and that human knowledge is, therefore, conditioned and limited by one's sociohistorical experience, his or her social location, and the particular intellectual horizon of a particular time. We cannot step beyond or outside of all history and claim intuitions into ahistorical, universal truths. The production of a universal theological system valid for all times and places is beyond the realm of human possibility. This is so not only because, as Kierkegaard said a century and a half ago, (individual) existence is irreducible to reason, but because human existence is primarily sociohistorical existence.

If the thesis of historical relativity is not to lapse into a self-defeating relativism and mechanistic determinism, however, it is important to maintain the element of dialectical flexibility in that thesis. Dialectically understood, the thesis does not claim that our thought is mechanistically determined by our historical conditions or that it is simply fixed on the ideas and perspectives of our historical present. As sociohistorical beings, we cannot indeed step beyond all history; but by the same token we are not passive objects of the historical situation. We also act and react, in praxis and thought, to contemporary history, often comparing it with the past, often attempting to transform it toward a future we project.

Furthermore, the thesis does not imply a sort of collective subjectivism, the claim that our knowledge at any particular time is simply a projection of collective subjectivity. Our knowledge is fundamentally conditioned by our historical experience, but it is not thereby rendered merely subjective. It is possible for our knowledge to be both historically conditioned and objective. We may see only a certain aspect of reality because we see it from our particular windows, but the aspect we see is really there.

It is likewise important here to recognize that historical conditions are not always negative. Historical conditions do not merely limit our knowledge; they can also expand our knowledge, such as our contemporary insistence on the moral equality of all humans, compared with the hierarchical and elitist ideologies of the past. We can come closer to the truth precisely because of our historical experiences. Certain truths in ethics, anthropology, even theology—not only in natural sciences—require a certain stage of historical development before they can be disclosed and appreciated; an example is the contemporary knowledge of our interdependence as an intrinsic condition of human existence. Our knowledge can be more objective, more adequate, and more universal precisely because of the larger perspectives and visions born of the historical process.

It is also crucial not to fix, reify, and absolutize the historical conditions of our knowledge. These conditions are themselves products of the historical process and always in process of self-cancellation and self-transcendence. We pose a false dichotomy when we think in terms of either purely objective, purely universal, ahistorical knowledge; or of purely subjective, purely particular, historical knowledge. Closer to the truth of our historical existence is to regard our knowledge as the product of the dialectic of particular and universal, as a process in which knowledge grows in universality while also rooted in particularity, that is, as something concretely universal, as both Hegel and Troeltsch understood. The "fusion of horizons" that Gadamer talks about is both possible and actual in our historical experience.

Given this dialectical understanding of historical relativity, it is also possible to appreciate the epistemological importance of the cooperative praxis of liberation mentioned earlier. Praxis is the matrix or source of theory. The interreligious cooperation in the praxis of human liberation, which entails exposure to and immersion in the historical conditions of human suffering, can give us a new perspective, often trivializing or at least relativizing our petty preoccupations and giving us a sense of what truly counts. This praxis can, therefore, dissolve certain theoretical issues as issues and reveal new ones. What cannot *theoretically* be resolved in the area of doctrinal differences at any particular time may be either *practically* dissolved as trivial or theoretically reformulated in light of later praxis and the wider horizon born of that praxis.

Here we can take lessons from the history of the relation between Catholicism and Protestantism. The scandal of mutual persecution and intolerance gave way over the centuries to a more peaceful and mutually respecting relationship, not primarily because of the dialogue among theologians but because historical changes have forced the separation of church and state, politically neutralizing the established churches to the point where no church is a practical threat to the other; and because such changes have also generated the need for theological dialogue and actually brought theologians, laity, and clergy of different denominations together on theological faculties, on the jobs, in the concentration camps and torture chambers, and in the general praxis of living. It is this praxis in history that has brought a new perspective on ancient dogmatic differences and animosities, to the point that many of the remaining differences are no longer seen today as "church-dividing."[5]

This also means that we must learn to live with theoretical tensions and unresolved issues for some time. Any ahistorical universality in human knowledge, including theology, is an impossible feat for humans who have to live in history and who are subject to all its limitations. Nor is it possible for humans to live without faith in the transcendent as mediated by human truths and concepts since they can best discover such truths and concepts within historical limits. We must learn to live the tension of the absolute and the relative, the universal and the particular, just as history itself embodies such tensions. This is so especially today when we are compelled to rise to a more universal perspective by the sheer historical dynamics of an increasingly interdependent world, without as yet having achieved theoretical clarity and consensus about many of the ultimate theological questions. We have to avoid both ahistorical absolutism, which in fact absolutizes a historically particular version of truth; and particularist relativism, which is either complacent about its own narrowness or despairing of any possibility to transcend itself to the call of greater objectivity and universality. Both are evasions of our historical responsibility.

Pluralist Arguments for Relativity of Christ: A Critique

Finally, where does this leave us with the most decisive issue in the pluralist debate, the question about the absolute significance of Jesus as the Savior of all humanity, and its corollary, the relative validity of other religions as ways of salvation? Does it mean that we have to abandon even the inclusivist understanding of Christ and accept the founders of other religions as equally saviors and "incarnations" of the divine, as Hick, Knitter, Swidler, and many others argue? Recent discussions have brought forth a number of arguments purporting to show why we have to abandon even christological inclusivism and fully embrace pluralism in religion just as we embrace pluralism in politics.

Let me summarize some of the important arguments, with observations on their underlying presuppositions. I cannot provide a detailed critique of each argument on its own merit.

Empirical Rationality

Hick and Knitter argue that the Christian claim to the finality of Christ violates the canon of empirical rationality. Such a claim is either unjustifiable, in light of the historical evidence of the moral quality of the praxis of Christians, which has failed to show the decisive superiority of Christian belief (Hick); or premature, in that we have not yet had a sufficiently long history of practicing discipleship in the context of a dialogue with other religions that would allow us to compare Christ with the founders of other religions and evaluate their respective significances on the basis of the praxis inspired by each.[6]

This argument makes two related assumptions, that faith—faith in the finality of Christ—is reducible to empirical rationality, and that praxis is the criterion and test of truth. The first denies the irreducible element of transcendence inherent in faith. It also ignores the inner resources of faith, as the history of Christian theology amply demonstrates, in coping with the theoretical difficulties posed by human rationality. The second assumption is true insofar as the truth and authenticity of faith must become concrete and actual through praxis (faith operating through charity), as Christian faith itself demands; but false insofar as it implies that truths of faith are definitively verifiable by means of historical praxis, which, like all things historical, is always particular and ambiguous even at its best, as though there were no transcendent dimension to faith. Here Knitter is appealing to a central thesis of liberation theology that praxis is "the proving ground of all theory."[7] We must, however, try to understand this thesis with more nuance and care than does Knitter, who seems to convert it into a principle of empirical verification in the short run.

The relation between theory and praxis is a dialectical relation, and like all dialectical relations—dialectical in the Hegelian, not the Kierkegaardian, sense—there are two interrelated aspects to the relation. On the one hand, a theory, which is always a product of human existence as a concrete sociohistorical totality, is teleologically oriented to serve that totality. It must, therefore, become concrete and effective through praxis, which is the only way of showing our subjective seriousness in holding such a theory, fulfilling its own inner demand—in case of Christian theory, the demand for justice, love of neighbor, new birth in Christ, reconciliation in a communion of saints—and thus "proving" its truth and relevance for human existence as a concrete totality. The dialectical theory of truth is a teleological theory, not a theory of simple correspondence in the objectivist sense. Effective concretization in liberating praxis, therefore, is a necessary condition for the truth of a human theory. It is clear, however, that in this sense praxis is the proving ground of theory only in the long run; a theory takes decades, often centuries, to arise and to show, or fail to show, its practical effectiveness in guiding our sociohistorical existence. Furthermore, it also takes a great deal of sociohistorical discernment—in fact, a whole sociology of "paradigm shift" and "ideology critique"—to determine whether a theory has proved true or false in a particular "test of time" or in the "court of history" (Hegel). Praxis in this dialectical, historical sense was not meant to be used as a simple method of empirical verification.

The other side of the dialectical relation is theory's critical, irreducible transcendence of praxis. A theory, and a fortiori a theological theory, is always universal and transcendent, whereas praxis is always particular and limited. It is precisely because of this transcendence that a theory exercises its critical and directing function for human praxis. A theory is not exhausted in a particular praxis or in a set of such practices, nor is it, therefore, definitively verifiable by praxis. This is true of any human theory with historical and social content, and a fortiori of the truths of faith, which have God as the content. God is not only the incomprehensible Transcendent—*semper major*—but also, in that very transcendence, the absolute judge of all human praxis in history, of all historical dialectic of theory and praxis. All human actions—however just and loving—stand under the eschatological proviso. God's presence in history is not only an "already" but also always a "not yet." The faith in God's eschatological kingdom cannot be definitively realized or "verified" in the history of human praxis without self-contradiction. In short, human praxis is a necessary, but not a sufficient, condition for the truths of faith by virtue of their irreducible transcendence. The only verification of faith may indeed be an eschatological verification, which is a far cry from verification by historical praxis.[8]

Dialogical Rationality

Knitter argues that the Christian claim also violates the canon of dialogical rationality, which requires "that no one enter the conversation with a prepackaged final word."[9] Dialogue, of course, does not forbid but requires expression of personal convictions and taking of positions; but it is one thing to make "universally relevant" claims, which is only reasonable, and quite another to make "definitively and normatively relevant" claims, which negates the very idea of dialogue.[10] Such a dogmatic posture prejudges other religions by one's own a priori criteria and disqualifies them from the very beginning, making it impossible to really listen to what others have to say.

Apart from the question of how far the distinction between "universally relevant" and "definitively and normatively relevant" could reasonably be pushed, this argument makes a rationalist and foundationalist assumption about the conditions of dialogue, as though a human dialogue, the dialogue among concretely historical beings, could occur in a vacuum of theoretical and faith commitments. What a priori convictions one is willing to suspend for the sake of dialogue would depend on what the convictions are about, not simply on the rationalistic a priori condition of dialogue for its own sake. Why was it so difficult even for otherwise very outstanding minds— such as Luther and Erasmus—to abandon their beliefs in the geocentric theory? Furthermore, the importance of a conviction can only be determined historically. Consider how impossible it was for the Catholic church to give up its claim to be the only true church of Jesus Christ; and how, under the changed circumstances of today, such a claim has been modified since the Second Vatican Council.

Soteriocentric Rationality

Knitter also argues that the christological affirmation is not only premature but also unnecessary. The prime necessity in the relations among religions today is the cooperative praxis of liberation, which can proceed without such an affirmation. What counts is orthopraxis of *sōtēria* (salvation), not orthodoxy of christological belief.[11]

I too argued earlier that the diapraxis of liberation is the most urgent item on the agenda of interreligious dialogue. However, I do not claim that the necessity of such praxis could be divorced from the necessity of theoretical commitments. After all, even the liberation theologians of Latin America have been arguing for the necessity of changing from an abstract, spiritualist Christology to a concrete, liberationist one as more adequate—not for doing away with all Christology. Furthermore, is it possible to separate the Christian praxis of liberation from their Christian, meaning christologically inspired, notion of liberation? What else would distinguish that praxis as Christian?

This, it seems to me, would falsify the relation between theory and praxis within a concrete totality. In reaction to the traditional tendency to emphasize theory and orthodoxy to the neglect of praxis and orthopraxis, Knitter goes, as the Latin American liberation theologians do not, to the other extreme of simply discounting the important role of theory for and within praxis. After all, it is essential for a Christian theology of liberation to regard the praxis of liberation as an essential historical mediation of eschatological salvation and thus in the context of our ultimate transhistorical destiny. The praxis of liberation, therefore, at least for the Christian, is inseparable from a commitment about the nature and source of this definitive salvation, without which we would indeed be guilty of "reducing" salvation to liberation. No human praxis occurs in a theoretical vacuum; such a praxis would be blind praxis without a guiding and critical principle. No "theology" of liberation could be committed to the praxis of liberation without a faith commitment about the nature and source of transcendent salvation, which requires such a praxis. I am not arguing, of course, that this necessity of faith commitment in itself and by itself justifies the particular Christian faith in Jesus Christ as the unique mediator of all salvation.

Hermeneutic Rationality

Knitter and others argue that to affirm the finality of Christ today is to violate the canon of hermeneutic rationality. The attribution of uniqueness and exclusivity to the saving role of Jesus belongs more to the *medium* of the early Christian message than to its *content*. This medium is constituted by the absolutist classical conception of truth, the Jewish eschatological-apocalyptic mentality, and the psychology of the early Christians as a besieged minority in a hostile world. Considering these cultural presuppositions, a contemporary hermeneutic need not take the early Christian affirmation at its own word, says Knitter.[12]

Without denying the influence of all these media of the Christian message, it must be pointed out that this cultural explanation would be decisive only if it could also show that the idea of a unique, normative, and universal savior has no intrinsic validity apart from such cultural conditions. Cultural explanations provide the context for the intelligibility of an idea, but they do not validate or invalidate that intelligibility as such, any more than the capitalist context for the exercise of freedom invalidates the intelligibility of freedom as such, which preexisted capitalism and certainly will survive its demise.

Mythological Language

Linguistically, as Stendahl and Hick argue, expressions such as "one" and "only" and the language of "incarnation" in the New Testament references to the saving role of Jesus are mythological language, the language of love and confession, an expression of subjective commitment, as is the declaration of a husband who says to his wife, "You are the most beautiful woman in the world. You are the only woman for me." They were not meant either to absolutize Christ or to exclude other religions in the objective, ontological sense. To take such statements literally is to confuse them with objective description and ontological language.[13]

This argument assumes that the early Christians did not know the distinction between the subjective language of confession and commitment and the objective language of metaphysics, an assumption I do not find very convincing. Furthermore, the qualitative difference between a woman one loves and the Jesus the early Christians worshiped as Lord and Savior, is too great to lend much validity to the analogy.

Theological Fundamentalism

Hick and Knitter argue that the metaphysical identification of Jesus and God (*homoousios*), the backbone of traditional Christology, is an incoherent and self-contradictory "theological fundamentalism."[14] They also argue that there is no reason to believe that what happened to Jesus—the fullness of the union of the divine and the human—as interpreted by Rahner, Cobb, and Hick, has happened "only" to him. There is no metaphysical necessity why the "incarnation" of God in Jesus of Nazareth could not also have taken place in other historical figures such as the Buddha, Muhammad, and founders and prophets of other religions. In fact, given the universal salvific will of God and the historical diversity of cultures that necessarily mediate the faith of individuals, it seems more reasonable to assume that there have been many such mediators and saviors besides Jesus, each adapted to the peculiarities of each culture; thus, just as Christians of the West truly encounter God through Jesus, so can non-Christians through their own saviors. In any event, from the fact that Jesus is an incarnation of God, we cannot conclude that he is the "only" such incarnation, that there are no others. Only a dialogue with other religions could settle that issue.[15]

This argument, if valid, would perhaps be the most decisive for abandoning christological inclusivism; it assumes a purely moral conception of salvation, a purely exemplary conception of savior, a purely contingent conception of the unity of humanity, and the inherent irrationality of the idea of a finite historical being so appropriated by God as to be God's *definitive* self-revelation in history. If we assume, on the other hand, as the Christian tradition always has, that salvation means not only moral transformation but the definitive, eschatological liberation from sin and death; that there is an essential unity and solidarity of all humanity in their need for this salvation; that a savior can save us not only by what he teaches and what we learn, but also by what he is in his solidarity with us through God's salvific will and what we can be by participation in him through divine grace; and that it is possible for God to empower a finite historical being to be her definitive self-revelation, although it is clearly impossible for a finite being to be such on its own power—then, the idea of one absolute savior for the one history of humanity need not be so implausible or unreasonable. I have argued these points elsewhere and intend to continue to do so in the future.[16] Here I only state that I do not find the arguments of Hick and Knitter very persuasive.

A Confessionalist Pluralism of Praxis

Earlier I stated that as historical beings we have to live the tension between universality and particularity, that we cannot presume to have intuitions into ahistorical universal truth on the one hand, and that we cannot live without commitment to truth as we can best discover it in the obscurities of history on the other. In the present context, where I do not see any compelling reasons to reject christological inclusivism, we must recall that such inclusivism has been supported by all sorts of reasons, rational, biblical, historical, and metaphysical. This means that it is premature to abandon our traditional commitment to the finality of Jesus Christ so central to the identity of Christian faith.

It is also necessary, however, to be clear about what this commitment means. The finality of Jesus is not an ahistorical, universal truth acceptable, or seen as acceptable, by all rational beings. Since there are no humans who are purely rational, so our commitment to the finality of Jesus is not an intuition into an ahistorical truth. It is a commitment to something that both transcends history and is mediated by history, by the history of a living historical community and the historical praxis of that community; and thus it is precisely a matter of faith, confession, and commitment.

By the same token, we cannot a priori dismiss the possibility that we may have to modify or abandon our christological belief at some point in the future. This risk, as Kierkegaard told us in the nineteenth century, and Tillich and Rahner did in the twentieth, is precisely what constitutes our faith as faith. It cannot be otherwise with us, who are concrete historical totalities, neither purely material nor purely spiritual. We must learn to live with tensions—tensions between the faith imperative for commitment and the demand of universal rationality, and between the past and the future. Nor can we deny the sincerity of the followers of other religions in their commitment to their own faiths. We cannot a priori dismiss the validity of their respective claims, which are also claims of confessing communities. A theoretical resolution of the issues of comparative evaluation of different religions will simply have to be left to the judgment of future history, where our historical praxis, it is hoped, will expand our perspectives and create a consensus of intellectual presuppositions that are more universal and thus enable us to resolve the remaining issues more adequately, and where the expanded perspectives may also simply dissolve certain present issues as issues altogether. I do not think a consensus of such presuppositions now exists. In short, a theology of religions is possible only as the future of our joint praxis of liberation.

The position presented here, then, may be called confessionalist pluralism of praxis. It is confessionalist in that it regards the claims of religions as confessions of communities. It is pluralist in that it respects the integrity of different religions, each with its own claim, including the Christian claim to the finality of Jesus. It involves praxis in that it considers the praxis of liberation both as the most urgent contemporary religious task and the ultimate historical condition for evaluating the relative validity of religious claims. This position is different from traditional inclusivism in that I am conscious of the historical and confessional character of Christian faith itself and reserve final judgment about the validity of other religions in their own right. It is also different from the confessionalist pluralism of Hans Küng in that I take the praxis of liberation, not theoretical dialogue and understanding, as the most urgent task in the contemporary relations among religions. It is likewise different from what I would call "universalist pluralism" as advocated by Swidler and W. C. Smith in that I am not too optimistic about the possibility of a universal theology built on universally intelligible insights, myths, and concepts. It is also different from the "theocentric pluralism" of Hick and Knitter in that I do not simply relativize the role of Jesus and advocate theocentrism as opposed to Christocentrism.

It is, finally, also different from the "Trinitarian pluralism" of Raimundo Panikkar, whose speculation I find the most profound among religious pluralists, in that I take the present conflicts among and within religions as a very serious matter and do not, as he does, transfer the harmony of religions at the *ultimate* metaphysical level to the relative level of historical existence. The diverse religions of the world may or may not be harmonious at the ultimate metaphysical level as part of *coincidentia oppositorum*; but we, existing as we do in history, can reach the ultimate only through its historical mediations. These mediations are harmonious at times, but also, sorry to say, often violently contradictory.[17]

How, then, can we both hold the traditional Christian conviction about Jesus Christ as the one absolute Savior of all humanity and creation and still respect other religions in all their integrity, including their final claims? Is it possible to serve two kings in a coherent way? What is the next step beyond inclusivism and toward genuine pluralism? In the next chapter I turn to these and other related issues.

Notes

1. Langdon Gilkey, "Plurality and Its Theological Implications," in *The Myth of Christian Uniqueness: Toward a Pluralistic Theology of Religions* (ed. John Hick and Paul Knitter; Maryknoll, N.Y.: Orbis, 1987), 41.

2. By the term "liberation theology" in this article, I am referring exclusively to the liberation theology of Latin America.

3. For a detailed elaboration of these basic ideas, backgrounds, and approaches of liberation theology, see my presentation: Anselm Kyongsuk Min, *Dialectic of Salvation: Issues in Theology of Liberation* (Albany, N.Y.: SUNY Press, 1989).

4. For an excellent survey of the theoretical problems of religious pluralism, see Paul F. Knitter, *No Other Name? A Critical Survey of Christian Attitudes toward the World Religions* (Maryknoll, N.Y.: Orbis, 1985); Hick and Knitter, *Myth of Christian Uniqueness*; Leonard Swidler, ed., *Toward a Universal Theology of Religion* (Maryknoll, N.Y.: Orbis, 1987).

5. See, for example, H. George Anderson, T. Austin Murphy, and Joseph A. Burgess, eds., *Justification by Faith: Lutherans and Catholics in Dialogue VII* (Minneapolis: Augsburg, 1985); Lutheran-Catholic Dialogue, "Joint Declaration on the Doctrine of Justification," *Origins* 28, no. 7 (1998): 120–27.

6. Hick and Knitter, *Myth of Christian Uniqueness,* 16–36 for Hick, and 191–92 for Knitter.

7. Gustavo Gutierrez, *A Theology of Liberation* (Maryknoll, N.Y.: Orbis, 1973), 32; and Min, *Dialectic of Salvation,* 51–53.

8. For a detailed discussion of the dialectic of theory and praxis in liberation theology, see Min, *Dialectic of Salvation,* 37–78.

9. Knitter, *No Other Name?,* 143.

10. Ibid., 142.

11. Hick and Knitter, *Myth of Christian Uniqueness,* 191–97.

12. Knitter, *No Other Name?,* 182–84.

13. Krister Stendahl, "Notes for Three Biblical Studies," in *Christ's Lordship and Religious Pluralism* (ed. Gerald H. Anderson and Thomas F. Stransky; Maryknoll, N.Y.: Orbis, 1981), 14; John Hick, ed., *The Myth of God Incarnate* (Philadelphia: Westminster, 1977), 178; Knitter, *No Other Name?,* 184–86.

14. Hick, *Myth of God Incarnate,* 184.

15. Hick and Knitter, *Myth of Christian Uniqueness,* 186–92.

16. See my article: Anselm Kyongsuk Min, "Christology and Theology of Religions: John Hick and Karl Rahner," *Louvain Studies* 11, no. 1 (spring 1986): 3–21.

17. For a brief survey of the different pluralist positions, see my article: Anselm Kyongsuk Min, "The Challenge of Radical Pluralism," *Cross Currents* 38, no. 3 (fall 1988): 268–75.

NINE

SOLIDARITY OF OTHERS IN A RELIGIOUSLY PLURAL WORLD
Toward a Dialectical Conception of Pluralism

Taking Pluralism Dialectically

"The deepest need" in our increasingly polycentric world, David Tracy tells us, is "the drive to face otherness and difference."[1] One example of this drive is religious pluralism, which has been proposed as an alternative to exclusivism and inclusivism, spawning for some two decades now a fascinating variety of competing positions and a lively debate among the disputants.

To apply a tentative typology, there are the phenomenalist pluralism of John Hick and Paul Knitter, which takes religions as diverse phenomenal responses to what is ultimately the same ineffable transcendent reality; and the universalist pluralism of Leonard Swidler, Wilfred Cantwell Smith, Ninian Smart, Keith Ward, and David Krieger, which stresses the possibility and necessity of a universal theology based on insights from the history of religions. Rosemary Ruether, Marjorie Suchocki, Tom Driver, and Paul Knitter propose an ethical or soteriocentric pluralism that insists on justice as measure of all religions.[2] Raimundo Panikkar advocates an ontological pluralism that asserts the pluralism not only of our knowledge of being but of being itself.[3] There is, finally, the confessionalist pluralism of Hans Küng,[4] John Cobb,[5] Jürgen Moltmann, J. A. DiNoia, John Milbank, Kenneth Surin,[6] and Mark Heim,[7] which insists on the legitimacy and necessity of each religion to confess itself precisely in its particularity, including the claim to finality.[8]

A flaw common to many of these positions is that they fail to take pluralism dialectically. Ignoring the historicity of pluralism itself, they tend to begin with the plurality of religions as something simply *given,* and argue about how and why we should or should not leave each religion alone in its particularity without reduction to a common essence or criterion; and how to deal with the *cognitive* implications of pluralism in terms of universality and particularity, absolutism and relativism. They do not take seriously the implications of the dialectic inherent in the contemporary phenomenon of the encounter of religions, the dialectic of world history that brought pluralism into being in the first place by making the entire globe increasingly interdependent, challenging each religion to readjust itself to the practical and theoretical demands of interdependence, and pressing all religions to find a mode of living together in reasonable solidarity of others. Some ask about the practical demands of the pluralist situation, many ask about the theoretical demands, but few ask about the dialectic of the practical and the theoretical, especially about the impact of the practical on the theoretical.

In this chapter I intend to add another type of pluralism, the dialectical confessionalist pluralism of solidarity or, simply, dialectical pluralism, by developing the historical dialectic inherent in the interaction of plural religions. I begin by outlining the high points of dialectical pluralism, then elaborate its conception of religion as a dialectical totality, discuss the paradox of pluralism itself, and go on to develop the implications of dialectical pluralism for three issues of current interest among pluralists: basic attitudes toward other religions, the relevance and limits of interreligious dialogue, and the imperative of justice. I'll conclude with reflections on the future of pluralism.

In brief outline, dialectical pluralism is confessionalist in that it understands religion to be a matter of existential commitment, discipleship, and transformation that includes but also transcends objective rationality; thus it is more a (salvific) way of existing to be confessed in faith and praxis than a theory to be understood in detached reflection.[9] As such, this pluralism encourages each religion to confess its distinctive beliefs and claims including the claim to finality. Unlike Hick, Swidler, and ethical pluralists, it does not relativize the absolute claims of religions, or demand, like Knitter, renunciation of such claims as condition of interreligious dialogue. Rather, in deference to the confessional character of religion, dialectical pluralism leaves it up to each religion to maintain or modify its ultimate claim on its own terms, in light of the dialectic of its inherited tradition and the challenge of the pluralistic situation.

Dialectical pluralism is pluralist in that it begins by accepting the mutual incommensurability of religions taken as concrete totalities and allows each religion to define itself without reduction and subordination. It is opposed to traditional exclusivism and inclusivism, both of which deny the historical relativity of human perspectives and subordinate other religions to their own criteria, either in judgmental exclusion or condescending inclusion. It is also opposed to any abstract universalism that subordinates the particularity of each religion to a common concept of the ultimate (Hick) or to a common theological Esperanto (Swidler), even if this is done in the pluralist name of peace and respect among religions.

Dialectical pluralism is dialectical in the Hegelian-Marxian sense in that it takes history, including the history of the concrete relations among diverse religions, to be a process of differentiation, contradiction among the different, and sublation or reconciliation of such a contradiction; and in that it regards concrete history, especially its political economic conditions, as the ultimate determinant of human perspectives and horizons. It begins by taking each religion seriously in its irreducible differentiation as a particular religion, but it does not stop at the affirmation of sheer particularity. In an increasingly interdependent and conflictual world, history does not leave each religion alone to pursue and enjoy its own particularity in peaceful indifference to one another. Rather, the movement of world history, which brings diverse religions together and sensitizes each to the diversity of the other, also subjects them to the conflict of particularities and the need to sublate the conflict into a reasonable form of reconciled life. It creates the practical challenge of living together with others in common political space in justice, dialogue, and mutual respect, producing new perspectives and horizons in the process, and imposing the theoretical challenge of redefining oneself and others in light of the practical challenge and the new perspectives.

Although dialectical pluralism accepts the necessity and legitimacy of religious particularity, it does not consider the preservation of any *given* particularity of each religion as its highest priority. Every religion is subject to the dialectic of history of which it is a part, and it undergoes changes, often revolutionary, in its self-understanding, or else it suffers historical irrelevance and oblivion. What counts is not the unchanging identity of each religion in its given particularity but the dialectic of the inherited identity of each religion, and the social necessity of religions to live together in, and despite, their diversity. Just as religions are more than systems of ideas, the challenge of the encounter of religions is not primarily intellectual but practical. Dialectical pluralism, therefore, asks of each religion whether and how it is able and willing, *from within its own resources,* to promote the solidarity of others by contributing to the cooperation of different cultures and religions in common space, and to reinterpret itself and others in light of that solidarity.

Dialectical pluralism is, therefore, a pluralism of solidarity in that it does not locate the ultimate historical significance of pluralism in the assertion of

particularity as such, as do most confessionalist and cultural-linguistic pluralists, but in the affirmation and promotion of the solidarity of others. This
solidarity is not "our" solidarity "with" "others," where "we" implicitly constitute the privileged center of reference to which "others" have to be
referred; instead, it is the solidarity "of" others, where no group is a privileged center, where all of us are "other" to one another in religion, culture,
language, and ethnic origin, yet also summoned as others to enter into the
solidarity of a "we" by working together to create common conditions of dignity by the dialectic of recent history. Neither the elimination of all differences nor the affirmation of sheer particularity is possible or desirable in an
increasingly interdependent world; the former would lead to totalitarianism,
the latter to the conflict of particularisms. What we need is affirmation of
otherness compatible with human solidarity, pursuit of solidarity compatible
with legitimate otherness, and the dialectic of the two in the solidarity of
others. Dialectical pluralism believes and hopes that the dialectic of history
will eventually transform and sublate radical pluralism and produce new
horizons and paradigms of solidarity.[10]

Dialectical pluralism, therefore, does not posit a common essence of religion like Hick's phenomenalist pluralism, although it shares in his hope of
complementarity; nor does it demand renunciation of final claims like Knitter's dialogical pluralism, although it shares in his soteriological concerns;
nor does it place as much confidence in the possibility of a global theology as
do Swidler, Krieger, Smith, Ward, and Smart, although it shares in their
hopes; nor does it remain simply relativist as many, although it shares in the
recognition of the relativity of perspectives. In contrast to both the confessionalist pluralism of Heim, DiNoia, and Milbank with its overriding interest
in the preservation of *particularity*; and in contrast to Panikkar's ontological
pluralism concerned to show the ultimate *harmony* of particularities by root-
ing it in the ontological structure of being itself as "discordant concor-
dance"[11]—the emphasis of dialectical pluralism is neither the particularity of
the other as such nor the ontological harmony of others, but the concrete
historical process that creates the *solidarity* of others and the implications of
that process for the transformation of our hermeneutic horizons.

In short, dialectical pluralism shares with all five types of pluralism—phenomenalist, universalist, ethical, ontological, and confessionalist—the rejection of exclusivism and inclusivism, respect for the distinctive identity of
each religion, and the urgency of dialogue and justice. Just as these types differ among themselves in terms of their respective emphases, so dialectical
pluralism differs from all of them in explicitly and constitutively bringing
the dialectical sense of change, conflict, and interaction, and the rejection of

abstract idealism, to every aspect of the dynamics of the relationship among religions. Let me now go on to elaborate on some of the features just outlined.

Religion as a Dialectical Totality

Dialectical pluralism regards each religion as a concrete totality, a system of symbols comprising beliefs, rituals, and practices that embody the collective self-understanding of its adherents within a "plausibility structure" (Berger), those objective sociohistorical conditions that render such self-understanding plausible. As a concrete totality of many dimensions such as intellectual, aesthetic, and practical, a religion is not reducible to the purely intellectual dimension. It can, therefore, only be "appreciated"—not conceptualized—and even then only on the basis of a long existential immersion in the depth of that totality and only from its own horizon or perspective acquired on that basis. No particular belief, ritual, story, or practice will make complete sense in isolation from its proper *Sitz im Leben* in the totality of which it is a part.

As living totalities of ultimate beliefs, symbols, and practices, religions remain irreducibly different and mutually incommensurable. There is no common perspective such as universal theology (Swidler), nor a common essence as phenomenally different responses to the same noumenal reality (Hick), nor, as Heim well points out, a common "end" such as salvation applicable to all religions. It is not possible even to say with Ruether that all religions have "equal integrity"[12] or with Knitter that they are all "equally" valid and meaningful and that no one religion has "*the* final or normative word for all the others."[13] Both affirmations and denials of equality, truth, superiority, and finality presuppose a common horizon of meaning and discourse, which is currently absent.[14]

It would only be possible to reduce the differences of religions, overcome pluralism, and compare religions if we could achieve a grasp of the religions as living totalities from within, and acquire a horizon higher and more comprehensive than those of the different religions at issue, so as to make a "fusion of horizons" possible (Gadamer). I do not think we possess such a grasp or such a comprehensive, suprapluralist horizon at the present time. What Charles Taylor says about cultures, I think, is also true of religions: "We are very far away from that ultimate horizon from which the relative worth of different cultures might be evident."[15]

In this sense a Christian theology of non-Christian religions, that is, an evaluation of the salvific role of non-Christian religions from the perspective of Christian theology, must be regarded as premature. To attempt a theology of religions now would inevitably mean artificially and prematurely subordinating the integrity of other religions to the particular criterion of Christianity.[16] For some time in the foreseeable future, Christians must get used to this irreducible plurality of religions and learn to explore both the positive significance and the challenges of that plurality.

To say, however, that the concrete totality of a religion is not reducible to the intellectual dimension or a common essence or measure, is not to deny the possibility of understanding parts of a religion, dimensions of its totality, or even certain common aspects of different religions. It means that such an understanding would be only partial, abstract, and always from a particular perspective, and that it does not substitute for the experience of a religion as a concrete whole.

Nor does the irreducibility of a religion mean that the totality is something historically frozen and fixed. No concrete totality is so self-contained as to be immune from the dialectic of history, or so insulated from change and otherness as to enjoy immutable identity. History has a way of generating and dissolving concrete totalities, whether nations, institutions, races, or religions. My pluralist insistence on the irreducible uniqueness of a religion must be taken in this dialectical sense. As a totality, a religion remains irreducible in the sense that it cannot be totally intellectualized or reduced to a common measure, not in the sense that it is immune from change, often revolutionary. It is precisely this intrinsic openness to historical change that makes a religion a *concrete* and differentiated totality, not an abstract and homogeneous one.

It is important to take dialectically, without reification, not only the concrete totality of a religion and the relationship among such totalities, but also pluralism itself as an intellectual perspective on the pluralistic situation. The existence of a plural*ity* of religions, even with limited but significant mutual interaction, is an ancient fact. Pluralism as a form of consciousness of such a reality, however, is a quite recent phenomenon, and will certainly go some day the way of all theories—either disappear altogether, disappear because realized and no longer relevant, or be subsumed and integrated into a more relevant and comprehensive theory. It is well now to insist with Panikkar that being or truth is of itself plural,[17] or to affirm with Knitter "the ontological priority of manyness."[18] It is equally important, however, to remember that the ongoing historical revolution of categories and horizons will one day render such pluralism not perhaps false but simply irrelevant in light of more pressing perspectives, as so many theologies, philosophies, and ideologies have been so rendered even in recent history. Who still cares about "kerygmatic" theology today except as a historical curiosity?

As a product of the dialectic of history, pluralism too has its own historicity. It is the post-World War II history and its political economy—the imperatives of neocolonialism and neoimperialism, the demands of the expanding global economy, and the concomitant expansion of communication, transportation, and information technologies—that have brought diverse religions into common space and made them painfully aware of the sheer diversity of cultures and religions, with their often conflicting horizons and ways of life. Without these radical changes in the political economic plausibility structures, pluralism would not have been possible as a distinctive intellectual position.

The same dialectic of history, however, also compels different religions to relate to one another at different levels of social existence and find ways of living together. It is simply not possible to live in common economic, political, and cultural space and yet leave one another alone with his or her own religion. The subjects of religion are human beings immersed in concrete history and its dialectic, which also necessarily involves their religions in the conflicts and tensions of history, making it absolutely incumbent on different religions to use all their resources to reduce such tensions. In this regard, as I discuss below, there are four imperatives of the social existence of diverse religions: pluralistic sensibility, mutual dialogue in religious matters, social justice with respect to one another, and solidarity of others beyond categorical differences. These exchanges do not require that we abrogate the irreducible difference of religions as *totalities*; but they do require that we engage one another about certain common aspects of our social existence and those *dimensions* of religions that bear on such social aspects, always leaving ourselves open to the unpredictable, deabsolutizing, dereifying impact of our social interaction on the religious totalities themselves. One may also hope that the challenge to open up to one another will force each religion to enter into its own depth and there discover its own deepest identity precisely in the solidarity of others in the transcendent Other. The kairological demand for pluralistic sensibility, mutual dialogue, mutual justice, and supracategorical solidarity is not only political but also profoundly religious in its content.

The Paradox of Pluralism

There is something paradoxical about pluralism, as there is about relativism and absolutism. This paradox is well pointed out by Raimundo Panikkar:

> The problem of pluralism arises when we are confronted with mutually irreconcilable worldviews or ultimate systems of thought and life. Pluralism

has to do with final, unbridgeable human attitudes. If two views allow for a synthesis, we cannot speak of pluralism. . . . We do not take seriously the claim of ultimacy of religions, philosophies, theologies, and final human attitudes if we seem to allow for a pluralistic supersystem. . . . This, I submit, is not pluralism. This is another system, perhaps a better one, but it would make pluralism unnecessary. We have a situation of pluralism only when we are confronted with mutually exclusive and respectively contradictory ultimate systems.[19]

The paradox is that pluralism cannot even define or assert itself without contradicting itself. Taken at its face value, even Panikkar's definition contradicts itself in two ways. First, as an ideology with a particular content, it excludes any position that claims to reduce all systems to one supersystem and thereby contradicts the validity of pluralism thus defined; but Panikkar's definition also claims to include all ultimate systems without reduction in its very definition. Second, his definition claims the irreducibility of ultimate systems of thought yet reduces all such systems to the uniformity of the definition with its inevitably particular content, making its own metaphysical assumptions about "ultimate" and "relative," "final" and "provisional," "irreconcilable" and "reconcilable," "system" and "nonsystem," and many others. Insofar as every definition of pluralism is itself from a particular perspective, although the intent of pluralism is to affirm the indefinable irreducibility of all ultimate perspectives, Panikkar is quite right in saying that pluralism is not possible as a *system* but only as an *attitude*—the attitude of respect for diversity, acceptance of the other without understanding, and hope in the ultimate harmony of the different.[20]

Speaking of religious pluralism truly pluralistically, then, involves the caution of not defining religious pluralism in such a way as to imply a particular view of what a religion should be. Any definition of religious pluralism that attributes a particular "content" to religion and thereby defines the "essence" of all religions, contradicts its declared intention to allow all religions to exist in their diversity and to define themselves. It would be monism in the guise of pluralism. This means that talk about pluralism is more consistent insofar as it becomes more formal and abstains more from all prescription of "content." The discourse on pluralism must remain as purely formal and metareligious as possible.

From this perspective of consistent pluralism that safeguards the genuine otherness of religions, criticisms have been leveled at Hick for subordinating all religions to a common essence as phenomenally diverse responses to the same noumenal reality; at W. C. Smith and Swidler for reducing the intrinsic differences of religions to a universal theology; and at Knitter and others for imposing a common ethical or soteriocentric requirement for all authentic religions. It has also been pointed out that the original question underlying the pluralist debate, whether there is salvation outside the faith in Christ, is itself misconceived; that question assumes the centrality of "salvation" for all religions and imposes a particular concept of salvation on all religions. As Mark Heim argues, the very "end" of religion must be conceived pluralistically.[21]

The interreligious situation thus puts us in a quandary: radical and ultimate pluralism seems to reduce all of us to total silence about the other; yet the very situation that has brought different religions together and generated the need for the pluralistic sensibility, also challenges us to enter into a relationship with one another and speak to one another *about* one another at various levels: cooperation in the sphere of res publica, dialogue in matters of religious content, and general respect for one another. We must continue to discourse about the other even at the risk of paradox or contradiction; living together in common economic, political, and cultural space disallows the luxury of apophatic radical pluralism. The imperative is to be able to talk and relate to one another about all relevant issues from politics to religion as much as necessary to meet the challenge and demand of the interreligious situation in the context of the broader dialectic of history, while also trying to respect the integrity and self-understanding of each religion as much as is feasible in that context. The heart of the matter is to negotiate the dialectic of mutual challenge between the demand of religious particularity and that of human solidarity.

My alternative is to keep all discourse about "all" or "other" religions as purely formal and metareligious as possible, abstaining from any substantive definition that prescribes a specific content or essence for all religions, while also clearly recognizing that such an alternative can never wholly succeed and that it always remains particular in its perspective. This is the alternative I follow in this chapter. In this sense, I gladly admit that my very description of religion as a concrete totality that as such is irreducible to a particular perspective, contains an implicit definition and is caught in the contradiction of claiming both irreducibility and reducibility for religion.

Pluralist Sensibility

Even if we are not in a position to judge or evaluate other religions as totalities, this does not leave us in the position of total silence or sheer agnosticism. In the absence of a suprapluralist horizon, it is both necessary and possible to *assume* a certain attitude toward other religions precisely in their totality. I call this attitude the "pluralist sensibility." This is the a priori attitude of primordial respect for other religions as religions and primordial willingness to leave oneself vulnerable to their challenge. In support of this attitude are three considerations: anthropological, historical, and theological.

Anthropologically, we believe in the basic equality of all human beings and basic respect for their equal dignity. This is a basic, a priori position regarding all human beings as human beings apart from and regardless of the validity or goodness of their particular behavior. This basic respect for the dignity of human beings should also lead us to respect, at least in principle, their collective achievements such as religions, literatures, the arts, and cultures in general, which both express and nurture their collective dignity. This primordial respect is not incompatible with the possibility, necessity, and validity of empirical judgments about particular dimensions of their cultures; it is rather a necessary condition of such judgments.

Historically, it is only reasonable to believe that there is something worthy and valuable about religions that have inspired, energized, and sustained the collective lives of millions of people over centuries and millennia. As Charles Taylor argues,

> It is reasonable to suppose that cultures that have provided the horizon of meaning for large numbers of human beings, of diverse characters and temperaments, over a long period of time—that have, in other words, articulated their sense of the good, the holy, the admirable—are almost certain to have something that deserves our admiration and respect, even if it is accompanied by much that we have to abhor and reject. Perhaps one could put it another way: it would take a supreme arrogance to discount this possibility a priori.[22]

The respectable ethical achievements of non-Christian religions have been precisely one of the arguments of Hick,[23] Knitter,[24] W. C. Smith,[25] Ward,[26] and others for pluralism over against exclusivism and inclusivism: on strictly empirical grounds, there seems to be no reason to privilege the achievements of Christianity over those of other religions.

Theologically, to put a pluralistic twist on Rahner's inclusivist argument, we hope that God, or the ultimate reality, loves all human beings and enables them to reach their ultimate fulfillment, whether such fulfillment is conceived as salvation, liberation, *moksha,* enlightenment, or otherwise. We also know that such fulfillment is essentially mediated through historical religious communities, however different these might be from one another. God's love of all humanity and the essential social mediation of our ultimate fulfillment

lead us to the a priori plausibility that each religion is the vehicle of that ultimate fulfillment for its own members.[27]

The a priori bias in favor of basic respect for the worth of other religions
as totalities entails that each religion should explore grounds for a positive
evaluation of other religions from the perspective of its own tradition. This is
one of the urgent challenges of the pluralistic situation to each of the religions. In the absence of a purely universal, common, suprapluralist horizon,
how far is each religion able and willing to go, *from its own perspective,* in
exploring the possibility of respecting and appreciating other religions without, of course, reducing and subordinating them? As Mark Heim insightfully
observes, the imperative of respect for religious diversity must be grounded
in the "foundational convictions" of each tradition and "become part of the
DNA of the traditions themselves," not merely part of "theories *about* the
religions," which would only make it marginal in the actual priorities of the
traditions.[28]

In this regard, we should not disparage the Trinitarian inclusivism of Vatican II, Karl Rahner, Jürgen Moltmann, Jacques Dupuis, Wolfhart Pannenberg, Carl E. Braaten, Rowan Williams, Gavin D'Costa, Christoph Schwöbel,
and others—those who are precisely trying to respond to the challenge of
finding positive reasons for appreciating the other by retrieving, expanding,
and transforming the Christian tradition. My difference from these inclusivists is not in their attempts to include others within their perspectives, but
in their refusal to accept the irreducible plurality of religions. They include
other religions on the basis of a confidence in the universality of their perspectives, ultimately subordinating others to their own universality. I begin,
on the other hand, with radical pluralism of horizons, proceed with respectful agnosticism about other religions, and try to find my own Christian reasons for including others in the hope for their ultimate fulfillment through
their own religions. I do so, not because I wish to subordinate and reduce
others to the same religion, which would be mine, but because I cannot
remain simply uncommitted in the matter but have to take a (positive) position even while maintaining pluralism and agnosticism, a position that could
only be from my own particular perspective. My pluralist position consists of
the dialectic of my twofold commitment: to my Christian particularity and
to the irreducible pluralism of religions.

The pluralist sensibility entails not only respect for the other but also the
readiness to take the other so seriously as to make oneself vulnerable to the
possibility of being transformed by the other. The pluralistic situation is not
simply an unrelated juxtaposition of self-contained religions; instead, it is the
dialectic of cultures and religions entering into manifold relations with one

another, each in its historically developed particularity. The pluralist sensibility is a full, self-conscious commitment to this dialectic of fidelity to one's own religion and vulnerability to the challenge of the other. It is a sensibility that is aware of the existence of other religions that are not only irreducible to my own religion but also challenging and questioning mine. Opposed to triumphalism and dogmatism, it does not reduce or subordinate the other as a totality to one's own intellectual and religious categories, nor does it trivialize its own faith into the indifference of relativism. It must live its own faith and convictions: but as a "diatopical" dialectic of different horizons,[29] it must do so in the permanent shadow/light of the other, the possibility of different ultimate horizons, with a self-conscious, cultivated vulnerability to their disturbing presence; and it must do so without falling into sheer relativism but always maintaining the tension between one's own commitment and the possibility of other horizons and the risk of change. As critical self-consciousness of the encounter of different religions in their very difference, the pluralist sensibility intensifies the tension of identity and otherness to the extreme.

Promises of Interreligious Dialogue

This primordial respect for the value and challenge of the other should also naturally lead us to relate to one another through dialogue, not violence. From the perspective of dialectical pluralism, I envision three purposes for interreligious dialogue. The first is not only to "know" the other in the intellectual sense, but more importantly to "appreciate" the other as a lived totality in the holistic sense. The point is to understand others from within as they understand themselves, and to acquire their horizon, perspective, and sensibility so as to be able to see and experience the world from that perspective. As W. C. Smith pointed out, "To understand the faith of Buddhists, one must not look at something called 'Buddhism.' Rather, one must look at the world, so far as possible, through Buddhist eyes."[30] For this sort of appreciation, it is necessary not only to master the philosophical and religious texts of the other, but also to penetrate its tradition to what Aloysius Pieris calls its "soteriological depth,"[31] and learn to participate in its originating experience. The knowledge acquired here would be what Thomists call "connatural knowledge" at its most profound.[32]

The second purpose of interreligious dialogue would be to learn from others so as to transform and expand ourselves in light of the dialogue. From the very beginning, Christian theology has been learning from secular culture and its philosophies. In recent decades, history as "signs of the times" has been considered a locus and source of theology. Certainly, the non-Christian religions, along with the cries of the oppressed, are part of the kairological signs of our time. By keeping ourselves open to such dialogical transformation, we do come closer to the ideal of a global theology that Smith, Hick, Krieger, Swidler, Knitter, Smart, Ward, Gordon Kaufman, Peter Hodgson, and others have been advocating.

In this regard, it is important to distinguish, as Thomas Dean suggests, between universality as "perspective" and universality as "data."[33] It is not possible to claim a simply universal perspective for our own theologies, which will always remain more or less particular in their perspectives. It is both possible and necessary, however, to make the data base—the locus and source—of our theology as global and universal as possible by incorporating the lessons of other religions, and thereby make Christian theology at least less parochial and more global in its context, sensibility, and concern. Given the necessary dialectic between perspective and data, we can be assured that this broadening of data will also lead to the broadening of our theological perspectives. In this regard, the resources of interreligious dialogue for constructive Christian theology, as for non-Christian theologies, have scarcely been tapped, although we see promising beginnings of such endeavor.

The third purpose of dialogue, I believe, should be to share our good news with the other. So much of the discussion about dialogue has been emphasizing learning about and from others as well as criticisms of traditional Christian relations with others, such as imperialism, triumphalism, and exclusivism. Precisely because it is pluralism, however, dialectical pluralism encourages not only the other but also my own religion to confess itself in its particularity, and prescribes the way and spirit in which such particularity is to be presented in the dialogue with the other. I should not try to impose my religious particularity on the other like an imperialist or even to convert the other like a zealous missionary.

Insofar, however, as I believe that my faith is not something arbitrary but something to which I feel called beyond my pure subjectivity, I cannot remain indifferent to its demand and appeal. I should also want to proclaim it to others, not as a threat to be imposed on them, but as the gift of the good news to be shared with them with joy and solidarity, precisely because I believe that it is good news not only for me but also for all humanity. Whether others will be converted or even learn anything from us should be left to the dialectic of grace and freedom. With full respect for the other, then, each religion should be encouraged to share with the other its own good news, its own particularity, and its distinctive genius. This dialogical sharing of the good news should characterize all proclamations of faith and missionary work.

To dialogue is not only to listen to the other in order to learn about and from the other, or to speak to the other in order to share with the other, but also, through this very dialectic of self and other, to "search *together* from our *different* vantage points."[34] To dialogue is to enter into an open-ended process in which one engages differences, experiences perplexity, enrichment, and transformation through that engagement, and thereby undergoes self-transcendence toward, and solidarity with, the other. It is to suffer and enjoy all the tensions and movements inherent in the simultaneous experience of otherness of difference and solidarity of togetherness. It is an exercise in the solidarity of others. Dialogical rationality thus overcomes the dichotomy of universalist logocentrism repressive of the other and particularist deconstructionism reveling in otherness without solidarity.[35] It also goes beyond abstract essentialism that denies concrete differences of the many, and static relativism that ignores the creative dynamism of the dialogical process itself for generating and expanding norms and values.[36]

Limits of Dialogical Idealism

Does dialogue require more than this pluralist sensibility, with its respect and openness, with its perpetual tension between one's own identity and the possibility of the other? Does it demand the renunciation of "final" claims as its condition?

The past decade has seen much discussion of the conditions of interreligious dialogue, such as openness, honesty, sincerity, trust, equality.[37] In particular, Knitter has been arguing that it is fine to claim that "one's own view of things is closer to the truth than one's partner's," but that it is "an obstacle" to dialogue to claim that "one possesses a God-given final and normative word." One can make "universal," "decisive," and "indispensable" claims for one's convictions and commitments, but not "full," "final," "normative," "absolute," or "one and only" claims. This would violate a condition for the possibility of authentic dialogue: the ability to "really listen to and be challenged by what one's partner is saying."[38] In order to fulfill conditions for such dialogue, therefore, one is asked to give up all definitive and final claims about one's own religion, especially—in the case of the Christian partner—the claim that Jesus Christ is the "one and only" Savior for all humanity.

I cannot go into all the issues relating to the conditions of dialogue and the possibility of pluralist Christology. Here I limit myself to the issue of whether the renunciation of final and absolute claims is a necessary condition of dialogue. There are four considerations against such renunciation:

First, dialogue does require readiness to be transformed, even with regard to one's final claims, which in turn requires temporary suspension of such claims so as indeed to be able to listen to the other. This *readiness* to change, however, is also all that is required as a condition, not actual change, not the antecedent admission that one is wrong in part or in whole. Whether and how one will be changed can only be determined as a *result* of actual dialogue, not as a *condition* of dialogue. As a result of extensive dialogue one may be converted to the other religion altogether, or one may be led to see aspects of one's own religion in a more critical light or to undergo a paradigm change in perspective while remaining within the same religion, or one may be so sensitized to the contrast between one's own and other religions as to rediscover and appreciate one's own religion even more than one used to. What the result will be should not and cannot be dictated a priori. I do not see why this readiness to listen and change requires more than the temporary or provisional suspension of "final," and in fact all, related claims while listening to the other, and demands a *permanent* renunciation of such claims as a condition of dialogue.

Second, to require a renunciation of final claims is to underestimate the existential nature of such claims. Final or absolute claims in religion concern precisely what is final and absolute: the ultimate reality, its ultimate relation to our existence, the ultimate fulfillment or failure of our life. Finality of subjective claim corresponds to the finality of the content claimed. It is a matter of ultimate, not relative, concern. It has not been achieved as a conclusion of purely rational reflection, like a philosophical theory, but arrived at as a result of faith that is indeed rationally responsible, not arbitrary, and yet also transcends rationality as such. It is not reasonable to require that we give up final claims with such existential ultimacy just to fulfill the purely formal condition of dialogue without providing us with an at least equally existentially compelling alternative. One does not exist for the sake of dialogue. Dialogue exists for the sake of human existence.

Third, to require the renunciation of final claims is to underestimate the central role they play in the historical constitution of religious particularity and to require renunciation of one's particularity as such. Most religions have their own nonnegotiable final or ultimate claims, such as the Buddhist claim about the Four Holy Truths and the Eightfold Paths. In the Christian case, the claim of Jesus Christ as the final, universal, normative Savior of humanity is not just one belief among others, but, contrary to Knitter,[39] an "essential" and central part of the Christian tradition. It is the foundational, animating principle of the Christian religion as a concrete totality and constitutes the very heart of Christian particularity. On it depends the whole edifice of Christian faith, the doctrine of the Trinity, liturgy, ecclesiology, spirituality, praxis. Twenty centuries of tradition have been invested in it. To demand that Christians now give up this claim would be to demand that they cease to be Christian. No group would or should commit such a collective suicide just for the sake of dialogue, without the promise of something more compelling than the belief they are asked to give up.

Fourth, to require the renunciation of final claims is to remove in principle the epistemological tension inherent in the pluralistic situation and sensibility. Dialectical pluralism differs in this regard from both the inclusivists and the pluralism of Knitter and Hick. The inclusivists remove the dialectical tension among competing "final" perspectives by subordinating them to one's own concrete particularity. Knitter and Hick likewise remove the tension by relativizing final perspectives as more or less equal by a metatheoretical standard and ultimately by subordinating them to their own formal and particular conception of that standard. Dialectical pluralism tries, on the other hand, to maintain the tension between ultimate perspectives by taking them as they are in all their concrete historical particularities, including their respective final claims, without reducing them to a common concept or requirement. It too has to resort to metatheoretical observations as an unavoidable necessity of pluralist discourse; but it also insists on recognizing them as expressions of a particular perspective and refuses to subordinate concrete religions to their purely formal requirements—as Hick does to his pluralist hypothesis and Knitter to his dialogical imperative.

Underlying these difficulties, I believe, is a more fundamental problem with Knitter's dialogical approach: his tendency to what I would call dialogical idealism, which reduces dialogue to a transaction carried out by purely rational, disembodied beings according to the ideal conditions of pure reason alone, and which fails to consider concrete *material,* historical conditions of powers, interests, and horizons as equally constitutive of human dialogue.

The subjects of dialogue are not disembodied, ahistorical angels but human beings fully situated in concrete history and society and subject to their material conditions. The *logos* of *dia-logos* is historically immersed human reason, not ahistorical, atemporal angelic reason. Human beings are not pure intellects whose contents (such as final claims) can be filled or emptied according to the rules of universal reason alone, any more than they are tabulae rasae whose content can be written or erased according to the demands of pure rationality. As concrete totalities of many historical relationships, human beings always already find themselves burdened with their particular needs and interests, immersed in determinate social contexts and their conflicts, rooted in specific traditions and communities, and committed to definite cultural horizons. As an event of human beings thus situated, the dialectic of dialogue has its historicity and is conditioned, shaped, and limited by the broader dialectic of concrete history. As such, the possibility of authentic dialogue requires not only universal, ideal conditions such as respect, openness, equality, readiness for change, and so on, but also particular, historical conditions; and it is necessarily subject to the tension between the ideal and the historical.

Consider the condition of openness. Openness is indeed one of the ideal conditions for the authentic exercise of dialogical rationality. However, whether, to what extent, to whom, and about what we should be open depend on concrete historical conditions, such as the distribution of political economic power, communal interests, and cultural horizons. The very selection of the ideal of undistorted communication and its conditions such as openness and equality, depends on the contemporary pluralistic political situation that makes such conditions relevant and necessary, and on the Enlightenment rationalist cultural horizon that appreciates openness as the hallmark of reason. By the same token, political economic oppression destroys mutual trust and renders openness difficult and often impossible, as in the many ethnic and religious conflicts throughout the world. Conflicting interests and horizons likewise severely limit, and often rule out the concrete possibility of open dialogue. Certainly, one should not expect ease of dialogue where our ultimate interests and ultimate horizons are at stake, as in interreligious dialogue.

The concrete possibility of openness and change is in inverse proportion to the gravity of interests at stake and the ultimacy of horizons at issue, and it is precisely these interests and horizons that are historically conditioned. Sometimes the concrete historical conditions (such as the material prosperity, liberal politics, and progressive culture of the 1960s) create the common interests and horizons for dialogue on certain issues (e.g., ecumenism, theology of secularity) and thus concretize the ideal condition of openness—in which case one can say that the kairos has arrived. Sometimes, however, historical conditions (such as political oppression and economic exploitation) destroy mutual trust and make openness impossible, contradicting the ideal condition of dialogical reason—in which case the overriding need is not dialogue but the creation of the appropriate historical conditions of dialogue through political praxis. As historically situated beings, no society or community can remain open to everything and about everything at all times. In this sense, Moltmann is quite right in saying that dialogue "is not universally possible among all peoples and communities"; a fruitful dialogue needs "a special kairos."[40] In many instances, we may remain open for some time but also have to close the issue so as to be able to be open to and about other more urgent issues.

The crucial question, therefore, is not whether the participants in a dialogue are willing to observe the formal, a priori conditions of pure dialogical reason, such as openness and equality, but whether we live in a society with a shared basic horizon and a shared dominant interest that make it a concrete, not merely an abstract, possibility—a "living" option, according to William James—to give up absolute claims regarding one's ultimate concerns. Without the sharing of a horizon higher than the absolute claim at stake, and of a dominant interest more ultimate than one's ultimate concern in question, it would not be reasonable to demand the renunciation of absolute claims as a condition of dialogue, or to expect it as a conclusion of one. I do not believe we have reached the stage where we share the horizon and interest appropriate to a dialogue about ultimate concerns, although we are increasingly being challenged by the global situation to change our current horizons and interests.

In short, dialogical idealism, a legacy of the European Enlightenment, isolates logos, thought, speech, and dialogue from the concrete totality of human existence, and tries to impose the abstract, purely formal, universal, ideal conditions of thought or speech on the concrete totality. The result is the reduction of concrete existence, with its own concrete rationality, to the demand of the abstract rationality of disembodied logos, absolutizing dialogue for its own sake, as classical rationalism and intellectualism tended to absolutize (abstract) reason and intellect at the expense of the concrete totality of human existence. This criticism would also apply to any approach (Kant, Lonergan, Habermas) that argues for certain universal, a priori conditions of the possibility of reason, dialogue, public discourse, or understanding; and argues solely from an analysis of the intrinsic nature of each taken in isolation from the concrete historical totality of human existence; and argues without also considering the material conditions of historically situated reason and socially located dialogue.[41]

The Imperative of Justice

The dialectic of pluralism within the larger dialectic of history not only demands respect and dialogue, which are largely matters of discourse, attitude, sensibility, and thought. It also throws the much tougher challenge of a pluralistic praxis, of *living together* with others, practicing what we believe in the most concrete circumstances of conflicting economic and political interests and the struggle for survival. As concrete totalities, religions are not self-contained islands but enter into the social dialectic of an increasingly interdependent world. History has brought together Arabs and Jews in Palestine;

Buddhists and Hindus in Sri Lanka; Catholics and Protestants in Northern Ireland; Muslims, Orthodox, and Catholics in Bosnia; Confucianists, Buddhists, Hindus, Muslims, Protestants, and Catholics in Los Angeles, New York, London, and Toronto. They are brought together into common economic and political space and compelled to work out ways of living together by means of a reasonable consensus on rights, opportunities, basic economic and political structures, and a common responsibility for the earth. This is not a question of leaving the other alone with his or her otherness, or welcoming the other in dialogue, or even committing oneself to the other in praxis; it is a question of a practical solidarity *of* others, of *together* creating the concrete social conditions of mutual justice and solidarity.

How will these religionists behave toward one another in the face of the common historical problems? Will they remain indifferent to one another, join one another in the political praxis of alleviating human suffering, or confront one another as ancient enemies? Will they respect one another's right to life and security in peaceful coexistence, or try to wipe out one another in an apocalyptic struggle? Will they try to dominate one another or to create a society that guarantees at least the basic human needs and rights? They will be compelled to establish rules for living together (laws), and to impose them on all through the public power of the state. Will the laws be exploitative and oppressive, or will they embody at least a minimum degree of respect for life and security and other basic human needs and be fairly applied?

What kind of resources does a religion have in dealing with these essentially political challenges of living together in a pluralistic society? Will it shun the struggle in the name of eternal salvation or nirvana, and thereby condone all the bloody murders of history, or commit itself to the struggle for justice and peace as part of its own mission? Will it have the historical sense to recognize the gravity of the emerging situation, the political courage to confront it, and the spiritual discernment to interpret the signs of the times? Will it be a force for liberation and solidarity, or a force for oppression and division? Will it have the courage and wisdom to rethink its inherited doctrines in light of the kairos and be involved in history, or refuse to do so and retreat from history?

Mark Heim and John Milbank fault ethical or soteriocentric pluralists such as Knitter for understanding justice on the Western model and then making it the absolute measure of all religions, thus falling into Western ethnocentric exclusivism.[42] I am afraid that here Heim and Milbank are missing an important point: however different the *concepts* of justice may be in different religions and cultures, there is a common longing for the *reality* of justice in the sense of basic fairness in treatment and basic freedom from genocide and externally imposed material suffering and political oppression.

What is at stake is an absolutely elementary reality accessible to all religions. If the bloody struggles now going on between different religionists in the world signify anything, it should be that neither Buddhists nor Hindus nor Muslims nor Protestants nor Catholics want to be murdered and dominated; all of them demand a minimum of justice: security of life and basic fairness in the distribution and exercise of economic and political power. The theory of justice, its concept and justification, may indeed be different from religion to religion, but one can hardly imagine a religion that would defend the *reality* of such gross injustices as genocide and outright exploitation regarding its own people.

In arguing for the suffering of injustice as the common context and ground for interreligious dialogue, Knitter insightfully appeals to two characteristics of suffering: its universality and immediacy. Suffering is found everywhere throughout the world due to similar causes such as poverty, abuse, victimization, and violence.[43] It is also so immediate that "while interpretations about the cause or the remedy of suffering will abound, the sense of suffering as a reality that calls us to some kind of resistance is, I dare say, almost given in the very experience of suffering itself." Like the Cartesian cogito whose self-evidence keeps it immune from the attack of doubt—but in the practical, not theoretical, sphere—suffering is "too immediate to be suffocated under the pillow of a hundred interpretations." This immediacy is "available to all cultures and all religions."[44] In the immediate, felt necessity of resistance to evil and injustice, there is a disclosure of an unconditional, absolute obligation that cannot be evaded in the name of universal relativity; as Gilkey points out, the praxis of resistance reveals a concrete, relative absolute.[45]

Furthermore, precisely because justice is such an elementary reality, all forms of society, and a fortiori a pluralistic society, have to come to grips with the problem of securing justice not only for one's own group, but also for all others in its laws and institutions. Justice in this sense is not an optional matter, as Heim and Milbank seem to imply, but a practical necessity inherent in all forms of social existence,[46] a necessity made even more compelling today by the dialectic of history that has been adding the tensions of religious and cultural pluralism to our already existing class, race, and gender contradictions. No society, and certainly no contemporary pluralistic society, can exist without some norm of justice, even though the concrete content of justice may vary from one context to another.

This is why Nicholas Rescher's "orientational pluralism," upon which Heim depends so crucially,[47] must be judged less than adequate as a way of grappling with the issue of pluralism. Orientational pluralism reduces the issue of pluralism to the theoretical and intellectual question of the pluralism of perspectives and truth, and remains indifferent to the problem of the social, practical context and consequences (justice) of conflicting orientations or perspectives. When Orthodox, Catholics, and Muslims murder one another in Bosnia, can we really say, with Rescher, "Never mind about the others; they may follow a different drummer. Our job is to follow ours"?[48] Such an attitude would be historically most irresponsible. All religions are compelled to enter into the practical dialectic of justice in a pluralistic society and propose a positive solution by retrieving the best of their respective traditions, or else be ready to be dismissed from history as simply irrelevant. As Tom Driver well pointed out, without doing justice, pluralism degenerates into "mere tolerance" and "a mere contemplation of variety."[49]

Is this not to "judge" another religion by the criterion of justice? It is, but it would be necessary to distinguish between absolute and relative judgments. An absolute judgment is the condemnation of a religion as a (concrete) totality; a relative judgment is a criticism of certain aspects of a religion without condemning the religion as a whole. If ever there is a religion to whose identity the condoning of genocide, political murders, and artificially caused starvation, homelessness, slavery, and so on, belongs essentially, not accidentally, such a religion should indeed be condemned as a totality. Any responsible pluralism would set limits to what it could tolerate. On the other hand, most religions may have condoned such things at one time or another in their sinful history, but they may also be capable of repenting of such deeds, in which case a relative judgment would be appropriate. Not judging a religion as a concrete totality (except in the hypothetical case just mentioned) does not exclude partial, relative judgments regarding the failures of a religion in a particular historical context. I do not intend here to settle the complicated and delicate issue of the moral culpability of religions for various historical crimes, but only to claim the possibility and even necessity of criticizing them even when they are taken as concrete totalities.

Solidarity of Others as the Future of Pluralism

Dialectical pluralism is cautiously optimistic about the future of religious pluralism. If it is true, as Marx said, that our social existence conditions our consciousness more than our consciousness conditions our social existence, we could be certain that the recent epochal changes in our social existence would also bring about corresponding changes in our horizons and perspectives.

Engaging in dialogue with respect and openness, cooperating in matters of political and economic justice, and above all living together in common space subject to the same political, economic, and cultural institutions and pressures such as same languages, same laws, same schools, same media, and same markets—such experiences will certainly heighten and expand our sensitivity to the other but also accentuate the need for cooperation and introduce uniformities, standardizations, similar ways of thinking, and eventually common culture. The impact of all these changes in our social conditions upon the respective self-understanding of the religions is sure to be decisive, although difficult to specify at this point.

Certainly, this dialectic of history will pressure all religions to rethink old theological paradigms, revise traditional conceptions of our collective identities, including "final" claims, and remove parochial and destructive preconceptions of one another. Religions will feel increasingly compelled not only to think and act particularity, but also to think and act solidarity; not only to think others, but also to think the solidarity of others. History would thus sublate the negativities of sheer pluralism and introduce forms of pluralism more compatible with coexistence and solidarity.

In the meantime, we can promote not only the pluralistic sensibility, dialogical sharing, and the pluralistic praxis of justice, but also a pluralist spirituality, the cultivation of the solidarity of others beyond all categorical differences. For the foreseeable future, essential differences will remain among the world religions. The imperative of solidarity seems to require that we learn to think and act *beyond* such differences by, as Panikkar puts it, "accepting" one another without necessarily "understanding" one another.[50] We do not have to wait until all the differences have been resolved before we can enter into spiritual, not only intellectual and political, solidarity with one another.

This would entail breaking with logocentrism and intellectualism, which are always interested in reducing the other to the same, and shifting our ultimate concern from the intellectual to the aesthetic. What we are looking for, as Panikkar suggests, is not an agreement of intellects but the convergence of hearts, un*animity,* con*sensus,* or con*cord* at the transintellectual level, a communion of others beyond the categories, in the "translogical realm of the heart."[51]

Notes

1. David Tracy, *On Naming the Present: God, Hermeneutics, and Church* (Maryknoll, N.Y.: Orbis, 1994), 4.

2. John Hick and Paul F. Knitter, eds., *The Myth of Christian Uniqueness: Toward a Pluralistic Theology of Religions* (Maryknoll, N.Y.: Orbis, 1987).

3. Raimundo Panikkar, "The Jordan, the Tiber, and the Ganges: Three Kairological Moments of Christic Self-Consciousness," in *Myth of Christian Uniqueness* (ed. Hick and Knitter), 89–116; idem, "The Invisible Harmony: A Universal Theory of Religion or a Cosmic Confidence in Reality?" in *Toward a Universal Theology of Religion* (ed. Leonard Swidler; Maryknoll, N.Y.: Orbis, 1987), 118–53.

4. Hans Küng, "What Is True Religion? Toward an Ecumenical Criteriology," in *Toward a Universal Theology* (ed. Swidler), 231–50.

5. John Cobb Jr., "Toward a Christocentric Catholic Theology," in *Toward a Universal Theology* (ed. Swidler), 86–100; idem, "Beyond 'Pluralism,'" in *Christian Uniqueness Reconsidered* (ed. Gavin D'Costa; Maryknoll, N.Y.: Orbis, 1990), 81–95.

6. J. A. DiNoia, "Pluralist Theology of Religions: Pluralistic or Non-Pluralistic?" in *Christian Uniqueness* (ed. D'Costa), 119–34; Jürgen Moltmann, "Is 'Pluralistic Theology' Useful for the Dialogue of World Religions?" in ibid., 149–56; John Milbank, "The End of Dialogue," in ibid., 174–91; Kenneth Surin, "A 'Politics of Speech': Religious Pluralism in the Age of the McDonald's Hamburger," in ibid., 192–212.

7. S. Mark Heim, *Salvations: Truth and Difference in Religion* (Maryknoll, N.Y.: Orbis, 1995); and idem, *The Depth of the Riches: A Trinitarian Theology of Religious Ends* (Grand Rapids: Eerdmans, 2001).

8. I would include Ernst Troeltsch among the confessionalist pluralists; see his 1923 essay "The Place of Christianity among the World Religions," in *Christianity and Other Religions* (ed. John Hick and Brian Hebblethwaite; Philadelphia: Fortress, 1980), 11–31.

9. Küng, "What Is True Religion?" 245–46.

10. See my essays: Anselm Kyongsuk Min, "Christology and Theology of Religions: John Hick and Karl Rahner," *Louvain Studies* 11, no. 1 (1986): 3–21; idem, "Praxis and Pluralism: A Liberationist Theology of Religions," *Perspectives in Religious Studies* 16, no. 3 (1989): 197–211.

11. Anselm Kyongsuk Min, "The Challenge of Radical Pluralism," *Cross Currents* 38, no. 3 (fall 1988): 268–75.

12. Rosemary Radford Ruether, "Feminism and Jewish-Christian Dialogue," in *Myth of Christian Uniqueness* (ed. Hick and Knitter), 142.

13. Paul F. Knitter, "Key Questions for a Theology of Religions," *Horizons* 17 (1990): 93.

14. Charles Taylor, *Multiculturalism and "the Politics of Recognition"* (Princeton, N.J.: Princeton University Press, 1992), 71–73; Panikkar, "Invisible Harmony," 128–29; Wilfred Cantwell Smith, *Towards a World Theology: Faith and the Comparative History of Religions* (Maryknoll, N.Y.: Orbis, 1981), 109–13; Cobb, "Beyond 'Pluralism,'" 81–95; DiNoia, "Pluralist Theology," 119–34; Milbank, "End of Dialogue," 174–91; Surin, "Religious Pluralism," 192–212.

15. Taylor, *Multiculturalism,* 73.

16. Smith, *Towards a World Theology,* 107–29.

17. Panikkar, "Invisible Harmony," 128; and idem, "Jordan, Tiber, and Ganges," 109.

18. Knitter, "Key Questions," 94.

19. Panikkar, "Invisible Harmony," 125.

20. Panikkar, "Jordan, Tiber, and Ganges," 110.

21. Heim, *Depth of the Riches,* 17–45; John Cobb Jr., "Dialogue," in *Death or Dialogue?* (ed. Leonard Swidler et al.; Philadelphia: Trinity Press International, 1990), 1–18; essays by DiNoia, Milbank, and Surin in *Christian Uniqueness Reconsidered* (ed. D'Costa).

22. Taylor, *Multiculturalism,* 72.

23. John Hick, "The Non-Absoluteness of Christianity," in *Myth of Christian Uniqueness* (ed. Hick and Knitter), 16–36; idem, *An Interpretation of Religion* (New Haven, Conn.: Yale University Press, 1989), 316–37; idem, *A Christian Theology of Religions* (Louisville, Ky.: Westminster John Knox, 1995), 13–18.

24. Paul F. Knitter, *One Earth, Many Religions: Multifaith Dialogue and Global Responsibility* (Maryknoll, N.Y.: Orbis, 1995), 30–33.

25. Smith, *Towards a World Theology.*

26. Keith Ward, *Religion and Revelation* (Oxford: Clarendon, 1994), 15–21.

27. See my essay: Min, "Christology and Theology of Religions"; Smith, *Towards a World Theology,* 171–73; Knitter, *One Earth, Many Religions,* 33.

28. Heim, *Salvations,* 190.

29. Panikkar, *Myth, Faith, and Hermeneutics* (New York: Paulist, 1979), 8–9.

30. Smith, *Towards a World Theology,* 47.

31. Aloysius Pieris, *An Asian Theology of Liberation* (Maryknoll, N.Y.: Orbis, 1988), 64.

32. On the concept of "knowledge through connaturality," see Jacques Maritain, *The Range of Reason* (New York: Charles Scribner's Sons, 1952), 22–29.

33. Thomas Dean, "Universal Theology and Dialogical Dialogue," in *Toward a Universal Theology of Religions* (ed. Swidler), 173.

34. Panikkar, "Invisible Harmony," 141, emphasis added.

35. Peter C. Hodgson, *Winds of the Spirit* (Louisville, Ky.: Westminster John Knox, 1994), 100–112, 304–11.

36. Cobb, "Beyond 'Pluralism,'" 86–87; idem, "Dialogue."

37. Leonard Swidler, "Interreligious and Interideological Dialogue: The Matrix for All Systematic Reflection Today," in *Toward a Universal Theology of Religions* (ed. Swidler), 13–16; Paul F. Knitter, "Interreligious Dialogue: What? Why? How?" in *Death or Dialogue?* (ed. Swidler), 19–44; Leonard Swidler, "A Dialogue on Dialogue," in ibid., 56–78; Paul F. Knitter, *No Other Name? A Critical Survey of Christian Attitudes toward the World Religions* (Maryknoll, N.Y.: Orbis, 1985), 142–44, 207–13; idem, "Key Questions," 96; idem, *One Earth, Many Religions,* 16, 29, 78, 86–87.

38. Knitter, "Key Questions," 96.

39. Knitter, *No Other Name?* 143.

40. Moltmann, "Is 'Pluralistic Theology' Useful?" 153.

41. See my work: Anselm Kyongsuk Min, *Dialectic of Salvation: Issues in Theology of Liberation* (Albany, N.Y.: SUNY Press, 1989), 75–77. Thus far, I have been arguing that it is not reasonable to require renunciation of absolute claims for dialogical reasons. Knitter and Hick have also been giving other reasons such as theological, ethical, biblical, hermeneutical, metaphysical, and linguistic, which I have not considered here. I have dealt with some of them in my essays, "Christology and Theology of Religions" and "Praxis and Pluralism," and plan to do so again in the future.

42. Heim, *Salvations,* 91–98; Milbank, "End of Dialogue," 174–91.

43. Knitter, *One Earth, Many Religions,* 58–67.

44. Ibid., 89.

45. Langdon Gilkey, "Plurality and Its Theological Implications," in *Myth of Christian Uniqueness* (ed. Hick and Knitter), 44–50.

46. Ward, *Religion and Revelation,* 319.

47. Nicholas Rescher, *The Strife of Systems: An Essay on the Grounds and Implications of Philosophical Diversity* (Pittsburgh: University of Pittsburgh Press, 1985), 98ff.; idem, *Pluralism: Against the Demand for Consensus* (Oxford: Clarendon, 1993), 98–126; Heim, *Salvations,* 133–44.

48. Rescher, *Strife of Systems,* 201.

49. Tom Driver, "The Case for Pluralism," in *Myth of Christian Uniqueness* (ed. Hick and Knitter), 217.

50. Panikkar, "Invisible Harmony," 124.

51. Panikkar, *Myth, Faith, and Hermeneutics,* 9; idem, "Invisible Harmony," 142–48.

TEN

DIFFERENCE AND SOLIDARITY
Pneumatologies of Moltmann, Welker, and Hodgson

Like any other area of contemporary theology, pneumatology too must pay due attention and sensibility to the issues of liberation, solidarity, and difference. In this chapter I propose to engage three prominent theologians who have recently published on the theology of the Holy Spirit. They are Jürgen Moltmann, author of *The Spirit of Life*;[1] Michael Welker, author of *God the Spirit*;[2] and Peter C. Hodgson, author of *Winds of the Spirit*.[3] I devote much more space to a discussion of Moltmann, surveying and analyzing his pneumatological developments, than to the discussion of the other two, because he has been the pioneer without peer in renewing the theology of the Holy Spirit during the last three decades.

Jürgen Moltmann

There have been plenty of breakthroughs and new approaches in many areas of theology in the last three decades, notably in methodology, Christology, ecclesiology, and theology of non-Christian religions. Compared with these areas, the areas of the Trinitarian doctrine and pneumatology have not been as significantly rethought, despite the increasing emphasis on relationality, communion, and the economic Trinity as opposed to the immanent Trinity. During this period there have not been too many significant works published in pneumatology, to begin with, and those few significant works that have appeared have been either apologetic in defense of a particular type of spirituality, as are works emanating from the pentecostal movement, or historical in the sense of a revisitation of the history of pneumatology in biblical and postbiblical periods, as are works coming from mainline denominations.

What is typical of these works, apologetic or historical, is that they generally confine the "economic" role of the Spirit to the history of salvation narrowly conceived, to the inspiration of prophets and biblical authors, the life of Christ from conception to resurrection, the sanctifying and guiding presence of the Spirit in the church in its teaching and sacramental ministries, and the various "gifts" and "fruits" of the Spirit in the lives of individual Christians. These works are traditional in that they contain no awareness of the contemporary concerns for the liberation of history and the renewal of all creation and see no necessity, therefore, to expand the role of the Spirit and rethink the whole of pneumatology accordingly. Typical of the traditional approach is the case of Yves Congar, who had nothing to say about the wider role of the Spirit outside the church, in history and the cosmos while writing his otherwise impressive three-volume work *I Believe in the Holy Spirit*;[4] he had to add a short, seven-page chapter "The Holy Spirit in the Cosmos" in his later work *The Word and the Spirit* only after, and in response to, Moltmann's criticism.[5] Creative systematic reconstructions of the doctrine of the Holy Spirit with appropriate contemporary sensibilities and horizons have been rather rare.

Not many theologians of recent decades perhaps can match Jürgen Moltmann in making conceptual breakthroughs in so many areas of theology and expanding theological horizons beyond the confines of the individual, the church, and the Judeo-Christian history of salvation, even while remaining loyal to the biblical tradition. His pneumatological works in recent years show no less of that pioneering spirit. His works from *Theology of Hope*[6] to *The Trinity and the Kingdom*[7] are christological in theological focus and political in concern; his works from *God in Creation: A New Theology of Creation and the Spirit of God*[8] through *The Spirit of Life: A Universal Affirmation* have been pneumatological and ecological. If a Christology of the cross seemed most appropriate to the urgencies of political liberation, it is now a pneumatology of the cross that seems most appropriate to the newly emerging imperatives of ecological liberation, the cry of *all* creation for freedom from violence and death. The paradigm of "history," the ruling horizon of the earlier works, is now integrated into the paradigm of "nature," just as "anthropocentrism" is to be replaced by a "new cosmological theocentrism."[9] Despite this shift in paradigm, however, his recent works still remain quintessentially Moltmannian in that they preserve his characteristic Trinitarian, messianic, and eschatological thrusts.

In order to appreciate Moltmann's pneumatological-ecological turn, it is perhaps well to begin with his *God in Creation*. This work presents a pneumatological doctrine of creation, with emphasis on a theology of creation dealing with such topics as creation, time, space, evolution, anthropology, embodiment, and the Sabbath as the feast and crown of creation; in comparison, the later *Spirit of Life* presents an ecological doctrine of the Holy Spirit, with emphasis on a theology of the Spirit, on her specific role in the liberation, justification, regeneration, and sanctification of life as well as in charismatic and mystical experiences, and on her essential nature as fellowship. Nevertheless, the first complements the second in an important way. The doctrine of creation in the power of the Spirit lays down the basic content of an ecological theology, which is then creatively elaborated into a theology of the Spirit from the ecological perspective.

From *God in Creation* one can observe three basic moves Moltmann makes in his ecological turn: (1) the recognition of the ecological crisis as the central crisis of our time, (2) the elaboration of a new philosophical paradigm (holism) and a new set of categories (those of relation) with which to look at the world in a way required by the ecological crisis, and (3) a theological approach (pneumatological) appropriate to the ecological urgencies and the holistic paradigm. The first requirement of an ecological theology, as of any theology, is the discernment of its *Sitz im Leben,* which consists, for ecological theology, in the recognition of the ecological crisis as *the* crisis of our time. It is not one crisis among others, such as poverty and oppression, but the *central* crisis of the modern industrial world in which "the whole system with all its part-systems" is at stake.[10] It is not due to either capitalism or socialism but to "scientific and technological civilization," "undoubtedly the most terrible monster ever to appear on earth."[11]

The second requirement is the systematic cultivation of a "holistic" way of thinking and holistic categories. The present crisis is a "crisis of domination"[12] brought about by modern anthropocentrism and built into our analytical, mechanistic, hierarchical, and positivistic ways of thinking that isolate, dichotomize, objectify, particularize, and reduce for the purpose of control and domination. The cure is a holistic way of thinking that relates, integrates, harmonizes, shares, and includes for the sake of letting others be and meditating on, and participating in, them with respect and love.[13] The basic categories of holistic thinking are wholeness, relationship, interaction, cooperation, reciprocity, complementarity, harmony, symbiosis, community, sociality, solidarity, participation. To be is not to be an isolated substance or subject confronted with other such substances or subjects, but to enter into relationships with others and achieve a harmonious community of interdependent beings who can exist only *in, with, from,* and *for* one another.[14]

The holistic paradigm, therefore, seeks to move away from all modes of competitive, confrontational, and exclusivistic dualisms to a wholeness or totality in which each can be both itself and also related to others without domination, exploitation, and subordination. God and the world, nature and history, soul and body, male and female, individual and social—these inherited dualisms must be transformed into forms of reciprocity and perichoresis. Perhaps the most pernicious dualism of all to be overcome is the anthropocentric dualism of nature and history. History must be integrated into nature, not nature into history.[15] We must transcend the master-slave relationship between history and nature and learn to consider nature not only as object and material of "work" but more importantly as the place of our "home."[16] Holism thus provides its own spirituality to strive for, the spirituality of the Sabbath: it is the spirituality of being rather than acting, rest rather than work, equilibrium rather than growth, letting be rather than dominating, Daoist nonaction rather than aggressive intervention.[17]

The third requirement of an ecological theology, then, is a theological approach that would overcome the many traditional dualisms responsible for the denigration of nature and provide a holistic theology of nature. For Moltmann, there are in particular two sorts of dualisms and their corresponding theologies that have justified the anthropocentric domination of nature and require special attention.

The first is the dualism of God and the world, and the monotheism that opposes the two in an external relationship of sovereignty and obedience. As in Karl Barth, *the* theologian of sovereignty, the relationship of the ruling Father and the obedient Son in the Trinity is reflected in the master-slave relationship between God as the absolute subject and the world as God's object, between the ruling soul and the serving body, and between dominating man and dominated woman. As long as God is pictured as the sovereign Lord of the world, the human being too, as the image of such a God, will seek to confront and dominate the world as its ruler. Monotheism leads not only to political and clerical domination but also to domination of nature. In order to overcome this dualism, therefore, we have to shift the basic paradigm from domination to reciprocity, which is to say that we have to shift from the monotheism of sovereignty to a social doctrine of the Trinity that defines the unity of God in terms of reciprocal perichoresis among three equal persons, which in turn would serve as the "archetype of all the relationships in creation and redemption."[18] By virtue of the presence and activity of the Spirit in the world, God is *in* the world and the world is *in* God in mutual perichoresis. An ecological theology is possible only as a Trinitarian, especially pneumatological, theology.[19]

The second dualism is that of nature and history, and its theological justification is in terms of nature and grace in Catholic theology, and in terms of creation and covenant in Barth. In this regard, both Catholic theology and Barth are guilty of three things. They are guilty of triumphalism in that by failing to distinguish between grace and glory, between history and new creation, they tend to consider glory as already inherent in grace and the kingdom as already present in the covenant.[20] They are also guilty of a dualistic, fixed opposition between creation and covenant, seeing in them only an extrinsic relation. Finally, they are guilty of theologically justifying the modern hubris of subordinating creation and nature to history, the history of God's covenantal relationship with human beings.

What Moltmann proposes, then, is first to substitute a three-term dialectic for the two-term dogmatics and think in terms of creation (nature), covenant (salvific grace in history), and the kingdom of God, or the new creation of all things in the eternal kingdom of glory, rather than in terms of creation and covenant alone. Second, we have to regard the three as intrinsically related, complementary aspects of a common movement, rather than as terms of a fixed opposition with at best an extrinsic relationship with one another. Third, in order to remove all theological ground for anthropocentric, triumphalistic subjection of nature to history, we have to subordinate both creation and covenant to the eschatological kingdom of glory as the "internal" ground of both rather than, as Barth does, denigrating creation as the "external" basis of the covenant and exalting the covenant as the "internal" ground of creation.[21]

The task of a new, holistic theology of nature, then, is to find a way of dynamizing the three terms of nature, history, and the new creation in the kingdom in a manner that is also integrating and unifying. It is here that Moltmann's characteristic approach comes into play. It is, first of all, the messianic orientation to liberation unleashed by Jesus the Messiah that provides the content for a common, integrating movement. Grace is not the perfection of nature, as medieval theology used to say, but the "messianic" preparation of the world for the kingdom.[22] In light of the resurrection of Jesus, the beginning of new creation, creation too is revealed as "groaning" for redemption from transience and death.[23] From the Christian perspective creation too, not only human history, is oriented toward messianic liberation from the very beginning. Creation is indeed aligned toward history and taken up into the dynamics of historical redemption; but it is more than an external theater or stage for history, for its ultimate destination, like that of history itself, is the final consummation in the kingdom. If messianic liberation provides a common movement for nature and history, the eschatological hope in the final liberation and renewal of all things in the kingdom provides the unifying telos for both creation and history; the ultimate fulfillment of their messianic liberation is possible only eschatologically.[24]

It is, however, the Holy Spirit who provides the divine agency that actually empowers the messianic movement of both history and nature and brings them to their eschatological fulfillment in the kingdom. The power of God, who justifies and redeems in history, is the same power that "gives life to the dead and calls into existence the things that do not exist" (Rom 4:17 NRSV). It is "through the Son" that God creates, redeems, and perfects his creation, but God does so "in the power of the Spirit" who "first brings the activity of the Father and the Son to its goal."[25] It is the same Spirit "indwelling" her creation by a sort of *kenōsis* of self-limitation, self-humiliation, and self-surrender who creates by giving life; empowers both nature and history to transcend themselves toward the final kingdom, suffering and sighing for liberation in both; and brings about the eschatological renewal of all things as the power of the resurrection.[26]

More concretely, the Spirit operates in creation as the principle of evolution by creating new possibilities, as the holistic principle by creating interactions and harmonies, as the principle of individuation by differentiating, and as the principle of intentionality by opening up all systems of matter and life toward a common future. The common future of all creation is "the future of the new creation: the rebirth of the cosmos to glory, the blessed community of creation which joins all separated creatures, and the direct fellowship with God of the creation united in Christ and renewed in the Spirit."[27] Thus, "the history of creation is the history of the efficacy of the divine Spirit."[28] "In the operation and indwelling of the Spirit, the creation of the Father through the Son, and the reconciliation of the world with God through Christ, arrive at their goal."[29]

The Spirit of Life continues the ecological turn of *God in Creation.* In a world increasingly threatened with a global destruction of life in all its forms, its primary concern is to promote "a comprehensive reverence for life"[30] or, as the subtitle indicates, *A Universal Affirmation* of life. It too seeks to overcome destructive dualisms, especially the dualism of the experience of God and the experience of life, by means of the holistic paradigm (the "Spirit of life") and a Trinitarian, pneumatological approach. To be sure, *Spirit of Life* also deals with many topics not explicitly developed in *God in Creation,* notably the whole area of "spirituality" and the personhood of the Spirit. Nevertheless, the basic approach and central issues and themes of *God in Creation* recur in *Spirit of Life.*

If *Spirit of Life* indicates no new, radical departures from *God in Creation,* it does involve illuminating, new developments of some of the central themes of the latter and complements it in important ways. These developments occur in four respects: in its concern for holism in pneumatology, its execution of that holism through its retrieval of the nonchristocentric biblical traditions in pneumatology, its (theological) ontology of "life" as the most comprehensive and holistic category, and its pneumatology of fellowship in which the essential activity of the Holy Spirit is to create life precisely by creating community.

First of all, *Spirit of Life* is an attempt at a "holistic pneumatology,"[31] whereas *God in Creation* was an attempt at a holistic theology of nature. Both are committed to a holistic approach, seeking a nondualistic understanding of God, the world, and their relationship: neither God nor the world would be conceivable apart from the other. However, *God in Creation* was more a theology of nature, using the Holy Spirit as the holistic, integrating principle, than a theology of the Holy Spirit as such; *Spirit of Life,* then, is more a theology of the Holy Spirit, using the perceived threat to the wholeness or integrity of nature as a basis for a holistic pneumatology, than a formal theology of nature. The concern of the former was how to conceive of nature in a holistic way, that of the latter how to so conceive of the Holy Spirit.

This holistic concern is shown in Moltmann's critique of the manifold forms of captivity to which the doctrine of the Spirit has been subjected throughout history, of which there are three main forms: the anthropocentric, the ecclesiocentric, and the christocentric. The *anthropocentric* captivity sees the Holy Spirit operating only in the interiority of the human subject and excludes the whole realms of the body, social relations, and nature as pneumatologically irrelevant.[32] The *ecclesiocentric* captivity confines and ties the role of the Spirit to "the church, its word and sacraments, its authority, its institutions and ministries,"[33] and dismisses history and nature as possible loci of the activity of the Spirit. The *christocentric* captivity, ultimately responsible for the two preceding forms of captivity, sees the Spirit only as the Spirit of Christ and thus limits and "subordinates" her role to the "subjective" side of God's self-revelation in Christ (Barth), to that of redemption in the narrow sense as opposed to creation and new creation.[34] In each case the role of the Spirit has been severely restricted.

The urgent theological imperative is to liberate the Spirit from these confinements and restore her as *the liberating power of the whole.* Insofar as such confinements were consequences of a restrictive and dualistic anthropology, a holistic and liberating pneumatology presupposes a holistic anthropology and a holistic theology of creation that comprehend human beings in their "total" being, soul and body, the conscious and the unconscious, personal life and social institutions, and embrace the "wholeness" of the community of creation, that is, both humanity and nature.[35]

For Moltmann, the first task of a holistic pneumatology is to rehabilitate the Holy Spirit to the position of reciprocity with the Son in the context of the Trinity by freeing her from her christocentric subordination, and to recover her universal, integrating role in God's creative, redemptive, and re-creative relationship with the world. First of all, it is essential to recall that, in the eternal perichoresis and simultaneity of the immanent Trinity, there is a thoroughgoing reciprocity of relationship between the Son and the Spirit. The generation of the Son and the procession of the Spirit are simultaneous processes without priority, without subordination. The Spirit accompanies the generation of the Son: the Son is begotten by the Father through the Spirit. The Son accompanies the procession of the Spirit: the Spirit proceeds from the Father and rests in the Son. The problem with the *Filioque* is precisely that it ignores this reciprocity of relationship and subordinates the Spirit to the Son.[36]

This view of the immanent Trinity, for Moltmann, better accords with what we know about the economic Trinity as revealed in Scripture. Under the influence of certain strains in Paul and John, the Holy Spirit has been reduced to the Spirit of Christ; but if we look at Scripture as a whole, the Spirit is also the Spirit of the Father who creates, the *ruakh* of God that gives life, the Spirit of the messianic impulses in history, the Spirit in whose power Jesus is conceived, proclaims the kingdom of God, heals as a sign of that kingdom, surrenders his life to the Father on the cross, and is raised from the dead. The Spirit not only is sent by the Father and the Son as in the christo-logical pneumatology of Paul and John, but also empowers the Son from conception to resurrection, according to the pneumatological-christological strains of the Synoptics. It is not only that the Spirit is the Spirit of Christ; it is also that Christ is the Christ of the Spirit.

In a typically Moltmannian "pneumatology of the cross," where the cross is at the same time a revelation of the Trinity as in *The Crucified God*,[37] Molt-mann pays special attention, in this reciprocity of the Son and the Spirit, to the suffering presence of the Spirit in Jesus' passion and death on the cross. The Spirit not only accompanied the Son in his messianic life but also par-ticipated in his suffering from within. The role of the Spirit in the self-surrender of the Son to the Father was not extrinsic in the sense of merely enabling such a self-surrender of the Son from a position outside his suffer-ing, but intrinsic in that the Spirit was involved in that suffering as God's empathy through whose indwelling in the Son the Father suffered *with* and *in* the Son. Inasmuch as we speak of the *kenōsis* (emptying) of the Son and a Christology of the cross, we can also speak of the *kenōsis* of the Spirit and a pneumatology of the cross. "It is precisely his suffering with the Son to the point of death on the cross which makes the rebirth of Christ from the Spirit inwardly possible. The Spirit participates in the dying of the Son in order to give him new 'life from the dead.' Because he accompanies Christ to his end, he can make this end the new beginning."[38] Thus the Spirit of God became the Spirit of the Son.

Second, it is essential to recover a sense of unity in God's threefold relationship to the world designated by creation, redemption, and re-creation of all things, and the integrating and unifying role of the Spirit in that relationship. Here it is imperative to overcome the traditional Platonic dualism of creation and redemption that construes redemption as the other-worldly salvation of the soul separated from the body, society, and nature, and posits radical discontinuity between creation and redemption. From a properly Christian perspective, redemption lies in the resurrection of the body and the new creation of all things, not in the salvation of the isolated soul. The goal of the history of Christ is the coming of the Spirit, and the goal of the history of the Spirit is "the eschatological restoration of all things and their new creation for eternal glory,"[39] for communion with the triune God, the origin and goal of creation. Redemption as new creation presupposes old creation and is the eschatological fulfillment of the latter as a totality, not just as souls; it is "the final new creation of all things out of their sin, transitoriness and mortality, for everlasting life, enduring continuance and eternal glory." This mutual relationship between creation and redemption is derived from "the unity of God's work in the creation, redemption and the sanctification of all things."[40] The redeeming Spirit of Christ cannot be any Spirit other than the Spirit of the Father, the creative *ruakh* of God, or the Spirit of the cosmic Christ. As the Spirit of the resurrection and new creation of all things, the redeeming Spirit is the creative and life-giving Spirit of God.

The work of the Holy Spirit, then, is truly universal. The Spirit is involved in creation as Spirit of the Father, in redemption as Spirit of the Son, and in the eschatological re-creation of all things as the Spirit of the resurrection, which brings both creation and redemption to their final consummation, making Christ's redemptive work universally effective and mediating Christology and eschatology. As "the newly creative efficacy in everything that lives,"[41] as "the divine energy of life animating the new creation of all things,"[42] the Spirit is at work not only in the interiority of the "heart" or ministries of the "church" but also in history and the whole of creation. Indeed, wherever there is a positive experience of rebirth to true life as anticipation of the rebirth of the whole cosmos, as well as wherever there is the negative experience of "restless" dissatisfaction with the way things are— there the Spirit is operative as the universal eschatological power, the power of hope for ultimate liberation, making critical negation possible in the hope of the final negation of negation, rejoicing and "sighing" in all things. The work of the Spirit both precedes and transcends the work of Christ; in doing so, it also precedes and transcends the boundaries of both human subjectivity and the Christian church. The work of the Spirit is truly universal.[43]

The work of a holistic pneumatology does not stop with the theological establishment of the Trinitarian reciprocity of the Son and the Spirit or the universal eschatological presence of the Spirit. It still remains to concretize the mode of the presence of the Spirit in all creation, so as to make manifest its universal operation as a holistic power. It is here that Moltmann seeks to complement his eschatological pneumatology with a pneumatology of life that is also a pneumatology of fellowship.

Drawing from the philosophers of "life" such as Nietzsche, Bergson, Dilthey, and Simmel, Moltmann takes the concept of life as the all-comprehensive category and explores its holistic potential for overcoming traditional dualisms, seeing the world as a unity in diversity, and affirming life over against the many destructive forces of the modern world. The Spirit is taken, above all, as "the divine wellspring of life—the source of life created, life preserved and life daily renewed, and finally the source of the eternal life of all created being."[44] The life-giving Spirit is experienced in every experience of life and is immanent wherever there is life, making possible the panentheistic vision of all things *in* God as an alternative to the monotheistic vision of God *against* the world.

It is especially noteworthy that Moltmann uses the concept of life as a way of overcoming the traditional dualism of the natural and the supernatural, vivification and sanctification, creation and redemption. Without denying the validity of such a distinction, he sees redemption and sanctification in the "intensification of life," the "exhilaration of existence," "new vitality," and "new delight" in living brought about by life in the Spirit. The sanctifying Spirit is to be perceived *in* and *as* the vivifying Spirit, not separately. The Spirit sanctifies life precisely with the Creator's "passion" for the life of what she has created. "At the edge of the abyss, the integrity of creation and rebirth to life become so intermingled that it is as the life-giving Spirit that the sanctifying Spirit is experienced."[45] In this sense, the *ordo salutis* (order of salvation) is "entirely aligned toward the *concept of life*." Liberation, justification, regeneration, sanctification, and mystical experience: these are not stages in the experience of the Spirit but "different aspects of the one single gift of the Holy Spirit."[46]

True spirituality does not lie in the cultivation of the other-worldly, in the mysticism of the soul and the repression of the body; as life in the Spirit, spirituality is the same as vitality, love of life, which also links humans with all other living beings. Humans are images of God not as souls but in their whole being.[47] To experience the Spirit as the Spirit of the new creation of all things is to experience already here and now something of the life given to our mortal, sick, and repressed bodies. The life-giving Spirit is also the liberating Spirit. The experience of the Spirit is always an experience of liberation for life, of new possibilities of life not only in our inwardness but also in history: in faith liberating us from the compulsions of sin and works, in love liberating us for solidarity, and in hope liberating us for shared projects of the future.

Furthermore, the Spirit who liberates for life is also the Spirit who justifies life by making love of life possible through not only justifying the sinner as in the Reformation doctrine, but also creating justice for those deprived of justice and rectifying unjust social structures. In this sense, for Moltmann, "the full and complete Protestant doctrine of justification is a liberation theology."[48] The Spirit is present in the pain of those without rights and their struggles for justice, as Christ's solidarity with them; speaks in the guilty conscience and restlessness of those who commit violence, as Christ's atoning power for them and in them; and operates in world history as the divine justice, "destabilizing" unjust structures and institutions.[49]

The Spirit that justifies life is the same Spirit that regenerates. Justification is not separable from regeneration as something objective and extrinsic from something subjective and intrinsic. Justification includes not only forgiveness of sins but also new life; the former is only the backward-looking act, the latter the forward-looking act, of justification itself. The dualism of justification and regeneration is due to the separation of the cross and the resurrection, Christ and the Spirit. Both are christologically based (including the resurrection), pneumatologically accomplished, and eschatologically orientated. The same Spirit is operative in both. Furthermore, as "the life of all the living," the Spirit has already sanctified life, and our job is to live life with love and joy. Sanctification of life does not mean religious and moral restriction of life but "learning to see life and love it as God sees and loves it: as good, just and lovely."[50]

For Moltmann, the Spirit of life is also always the Spirit of fellowship. Fellowship does not seek to possess or dominate the other but to draw the other into a relationship, opening ourselves to the other and giving the other a share in ourselves in reciprocal participation and mutual recognition. In this sense, fellowship is not only a special gift of the Spirit but also her essential, eternal nature. Just as the Spirit issues from her fellowship with the Father and the Son, so the role of the Spirit is to create fellowships among beings and ultimately a community or fellowship of the entire creation, and to bring that community into the fellowship she shares with the Father and the Son, into the Trinitarian fellowship, the origin and goal of all creation.[51]

Life without fellowship leads to domination, isolation, and death. It is only *as* fellowship that life can fulfill its holistic function. For Moltmann, the Spirit gives life precisely by creating relationships, fellowships, or communities. To live is to be related, social, interdependent. "To form community is the life principle of created beings."[52] *Bios* is always symbiosis. This community or fellowship is at the same time a differentiated community, a unity in diversity, uniting what is different and differentiating what is united, neither unity nor diversity holding primacy over the other. Wherever there are relationships and communities, there the Spirit is operative as "the dynamic of the universe and the power that creates community in the widening, differentiating network of the living."[53] It is the Spirit that creates relationships between body and soul, between human beings and groups, and between human culture and the ecosystems of nature. "The life-creating Spirit is the Spirit of community,"[54] aimed at "the full community of the Creator, Reconciler and Redeemer with all created being, in the network of all their relationships."[55]

It is not easy to read Moltmann without being immensely impressed. His messianic, Trinitarian, and eschatological thrust will touch the evangelical chord in many a Christian heart. His historical sensibility to current human crises will be congenial to all concerned with the fate of humanity. The soaring eschatological vision of all creation reconciled and united with the triune God is simply uplifting to us living and suffering in what must appear to be an impossibly divided and broken world. In particular, his attempt to highlight the universal activity of the Holy Spirit as a vitalizing, socializing, and liberating power, and his use of the concept of life, at once differentiating and unifying, as a central holistic category, are certainly admirable enough from the systematic point of view.

One can take issue with different aspects of Moltmann's theology. Here, confining myself to his holistic turn, especially discernible in his pneumatological developments, I must confess to one fundamental reservation, his noticeable retreat from the negative dialectic of *Crucified God* since *God in Creation* and his subsequent tendency to stress only the positive-wholeness, fellowship, and harmony. In legitimate reaction to the domination and destruction of nature and all dualistic thinking considered responsible for such domination, Moltmann, along with many recent ecological theologians, has increasingly turned to the holistic paradigm. The struggle of the negative, of course, is not totally absent from *Spirit of Life*; it does talk about the penumatology of the cross and insists that without the cross the panentheistic vision of God becomes "pure illusion."[56] Yet the role of the negative has become accidental and has ceased to be systematic.

I see three basic problems with Moltmann's holism and the generally prevailing paradigm of holism, all of them having to do with the suppression of the political. The first problem of apolitical holism is that it tends to be harmonistic and either abstracts from, or ignores, the sociohistorical reality of conflict and negation, falling into what I would call "the fallacy of misplaced eschatology," which considers as already real what is only to be achieved in the future, precisely through painful and often bloody political struggles. In overcoming the many dualisms plaguing us, apolitical holism seeks to be as inclusive as possible, speaking of "soul *and* body," "individual *and* social," "history *and* nature," "political *and* psychological," "male *and* female," and so on, as opposed to the traditional "*against.*" However, these polarities are not all of the same kind, and all of them contain conflicts. The polarity of "male and female" is based on equality, which cannot be said of the polarities of history and nature, or the individual and the social. Furthermore, all of them contain conflicts and tensions, and they need education, discipline, and plenty of struggle to achieve any sort of harmony. The dualisms expressed in these pairs—like those of soul and body, the individual and social—are both expressions of the real experience of conflict and historically given ways of coping with those dualisms, although no longer acceptable today. History of such experiences shows that the harmony of "and" between the two sets of poles, which are in fact constitutive of human existence as such, is a *result* of struggle, not something simply *given*—a *post*dialectical, not *pre*dialectical, harmony.

Second, apolitical holism tends to be idealistic in that it locates the source of the destruction of nature primarily in our dualistic way of *thinking,* anthropocentrism, not in the economic and politic structures that both oppress other human beings and destroy nature in one and the same process. It thus seeks to change *reality* by changing our *thinking* from anthropocentrism to holism rather than by transforming the destructive and oppressive structures through political *praxis*—for which indeed change in thinking is necessary but not sufficient. The way to establish harmony with nature is precisely through the political praxis that abolishes the economic and political structures dominating other human beings even at the cost of destroying nature through depletion of nonrenewable resources and production of toxic goods and destructive weapons. The harmony of nature and history is not possible by *thinking* harmony but only by the political praxis that removes the conditions that destroy nature; such harmony is not something given in nature but a task to be achieved by historical praxis. An ecological theology is possible only through liberation theology or only as a political theology of the environment. Anthropocentrism as a mere idea wreaks no havoc; only the anthropocentrism objectified into structures does.

Third, apolitical holism tends to falsely universalize anthropocentrism, the worldview of a particular minority, especially the modern Western elite, and thus serve the ideological interest of the privileged and powerful. Historically, the vast majority of human beings have been too poor and helpless to indulge in the illusion of anthropocentrism, the idea that human beings are the center and end of all things. Such an illusion can be entertained only by those with power and wealth, i.e., the economic and political elites of the world. To attribute the ecological crisis to abstract and generalized anthropocentrism may be an effective way of masking the real, structural sources of such a crisis and justifying the domination by the few of both nature and the many.

On all three counts, Moltmann's holistic pneumatology remains a pneumatology without political praxis.

Michael Welker

The contrast between Moltmann's *Spirit of Life* and Welker's *God the Spirit* cannot be sharper. Moltmann and Welker—a former student of Moltmann, who in fact dedicates his book to his teacher—share the general contemporary concern for liberation and ecology, but their approaches are strikingly different.

Moltmann remains the systematic theologian par excellence, with a penchant for wholeness and totality; even if he has become, in recent years, more sober in his expectations of what a "systematic" theology could do, and more open to the pluralistic dimension of diversity, still he remains the systematician at heart, wholly at home with the categories of totalizing metaphysics and quite ready to venture into discussions of the inner-Trinitarian mysteries. *Spirit of Life* was such a systematic attempt at an ecological pneumatology based on the holistic paradigm and the holistic categories of life, relation, harmony, and wholeness.

In contrast, the battle cry of *God the Spirit* is the pluralism of difference. As Welker makes clear at the beginning, it seeks to be "a guide past the mistaken paths of totalistic metaphysics, merely speculative Trinitarianism, abstract mysticism, and irrationalism undertaken by conventional understandings of the Holy Spirit."[57] What we have is neither a full-blown theological ontology of "life" nor an abstruse discussion of the inner-Trinitarian relations among the three divine persons, but the first "postmodern," "pluralist," "emergent" account and interpretation of the biblical experiences of the liberating Spirit in their specificity and difference. Provocative in its challenge to traditional pneumatologies, enviable in its multidisciplinary erudition, and admirably sophisticated in its assessment of the contemporary world—*God the Spirit* is an impressive achievement that no pneumatology can ignore in the many post-modern years to come.

Beginning with a critical survey of the worldwide charismatic movement—which he faults for sensationalism, subjectivism, and escapism—Welker goes on to point out how the fullness of the Spirit is manifested in the diversity of contemporary liberation and feminist movements, even though these theologies have failed to recognize the centrality of the liberating Spirit. Welker makes an important distinction between "debilitating" and "invigorating"[58] forms of pluralism, and avoids the dichotomy between the false pluralism of atomistic, abstract individuals and the equally false totalism of undifferentiated unity. He sees the Spirit precisely as the "pluralizing" force of the invigorating sort that cultivates differences so long as they do not contradict justice, mercy, and the knowledge of God, and that seeks to create a differentiated community inclusive of the widest possible plurality of categories of persons and groups. This recognition of the Spirit as a pluralizing force is especially relevant today, when modern societies are endangering themselves by the extreme functional differentiation of society into a pluralism of subsystems, by their respective self-absolutization at the expense of the whole, and by the irreducibly "polycentric" organization and perception of society; thus modern societies leave the "whole" impossible either to envision or to control. If "postmodern" means the abandonment of all monistic assumptions about reality and experience, we are indeed living in such a world, where only "emergent" changes are possible and desirable.

This postmodern sensibility to difference and plurality, for Welker, is more congenial to a pneumatology than is the traditional assumption about the unity of reality and experience. The Spirit, in the biblical account, is precisely a power that creates solidarity out of mutually alienated and separated peoples and situations. There are, however, three dominant forms of theological reflection whose Babylonian captivity stands in the way of such a postmodern pneumatology: universalizing, totalizing metaphysics that abstracts from concrete particularity; dialogical personalism that abstracts from the sociohistorical dimension; and social moralism that confuses secular progress with divine action. Against these obstacles, postmodern pneumatology must become a "realistic" theology that takes seriously the diversity of biblical experiences of the Spirit and is constantly open to new ways of experiencing

God, paying as much attention to differences and discontinuities as to similarities and continuities (chap. 1).

Welker's account of the liberating role of the Spirit in the Bible is especially perceptive and illuminating. By examining the role of the Spirit in the concrete lives of such public figures as Othniel, Gideon, Jephthah, Saul, Samson, and Micaiah, Welker demonstrates the power of the Spirit to restore order and solidarity in times of collective distress, and to empower communities to act, preserve, and transform themselves in times of despair (chap. 2). In a detailed review of the messianic passages of Isaiah[59] and Joel, Welker goes on to present the Spirit as the Spirit of universal justice, mercy, and knowledge of God in their strict interconnection; to describe the scandal of the suffering, nonviolent, nonpolitical messianic bearer of the Spirit; and to elucidate the role of the Spirit whose "pouring out" subverts the monocultural imperialisms of age, sex, and power (chap. 3). In the analyses of the Synoptic accounts of the role of the Spirit, he calls attention to the empowering presence of the Spirit in the public installation of Jesus as the suffering Messiah (birth, temptations, baptism) and in his ministry of healing and the proclamation of the reign of God, showing a connection between Jesus and the Spirit in the Synoptics much deeper than is generally realized (chap. 4).

In contrast to the preceding three chapters, which are systematic reflections on the biblical accounts of the Spirit, the remaining two chapters are much more speculative and constructive. Explaining the pentecostal phenomenon of "pouring out" in Acts in terms of the creation of a "force field," Welker goes on to reinterpret faith, hope, love, charisms, especially speaking in tongues, law and spirit, flesh and spirit, and inspiration in terms of the Spirit's creation of such a force field and a socially dynamic conception of the Spirit (chap. 5). In the final chapter Welker contrasts the spirit of the Western world and the Spirit of God. In a typically postmodern account of Western civilization, he describes the spirit of the West, culminating in Hegel's thought, as the spirit of egolatry, with its cult of the abstract person, the monocentric institution, and oppressive imperialism. All the problems of the modern world, with its global self-endangerment and oppressiveness, as well as all the obstructions and distortions in our perception and experience of the Spirit of God, are ultimately traceable to this spirit of egolatry. In contrast, the Spirit of God is the Spirit of communion in selfless service of others, the Spirit who calls diverse peoples to share in the crucified and risen Christ and thereby to create forms of mutual solidarity, a power that overcomes individualistic isolation, dissolves systemic enslavement, relativizes monocultural imperialisms, and liberates us from the many self-destructive compulsions of the modern world. As the Spirit of Christ, the Spirit constitutes the "public person," the "domain of resonance," or the "webs of relationships" whose "individual center of action" remains Jesus Christ. Welker goes on to give perceptive accounts of the forgiveness of sins, resurrection of the flesh, and eternal life, according to the third article of the Apostles' Creed.

In short, Welker's thoroughly researched retelling of the biblical story of the Spirit—with its always meticulous attention to "differences" of persons, events, and situations—not only is an impressive scholarly achievement but also poses an open and timely challenge to both traditional and contemporary abstract, metaphysically oriented, totalizing pneumatologies. Furthermore, the social and dynamic conception of the Spirit as a "force field" or "public person" must be regarded as an important conceptual contribution when the temptation still remains strong to reduce the Spirit to the numinous, the incomprehensible, and the private.

I have two reservations about Welker's postmodern, pluralistic pneumatology of difference, both derived from his and postmodernists' tendency to absolutize difference as such and fall into a new kind of dualism, the dualism of the same and the other.

First, Welker tends so to stress the otherness of the Spirit that she could be found only in the unpredictable, the uncontrollable, the surprising, the new. Like the qualitatively different God of Barth, Welker's Spirit is found only in moments of negation and contradiction. As Hegel pointed out in his critique of bad infinity, and as Rahner pointed out in his critique of Barth, such a procedure is implicitly reductionist; it reduces the Spirit by limiting the Spirit to the unusual, in much the same way that Welker also accuses the charismatic movement of doing. If the Spirit is truly universal, there should be a way of finding her in our most ordinary and predictable experiences as well, especially in organized political attempts to introduce controlled but decisive liberating changes into repressive institutions and structures. One of the tasks of pneumatology would be precisely to disclose the pneumatological significance of the ordinary or reveal the pneumatological other in the same. In this regard, Moltmann's attempt to locate the experience of the Spirit in all dimensions of human experience should be complementary to Welker's pneumatology of difference.

Second, Welker's tendency to absolutize difference leads him to concentrate on what the Spirit does, not only saying absolutely nothing about what human beings should do but also disparaging the human praxis of liberation. He does emphasize the fact that the Spirit always works on human beings, through human beings, and with human beings, but also distinguishes the work of the Spirit precisely by the "resistance to all attempts to assert the power of 'making it happen.'"[60] Hence, the human mediator's role in the action of the Spirit is really only to be borne by the Spirit. Any conscious, organized, and controlled attempt to respond to her liberating action would be suspect as an attempt to "manage" the Spirit.[61] As a result, on the one hand, Welker nowhere works out a pneumatology of human praxis of liberation; on the other, he casts suspicion, often totally gratuitous, on all human political actions and programs,[62] always emphasizing the difference between the liberating action of the Spirit and the human praxis of liberation.[63]

For example, in commenting on Isaiah 42:2, which speaks of the messianic bearer of the Spirit as someone who "will not cry or lift up his voice, or make it heard in the street" (NRSV), Welker calls attention to the fact that the suffering Messiah "does not engage in a public relations campaign. He does not 'plug' himself and his action. . . . He forgoes the usual forms for solidifying and pushing through political rule. . . . He also forgoes the strategies of so-called politics from below."[64] Again, in discussing Jesus' mighty works of casting out unclean spirits, Welker again deliberately, gratuitously, and disparagingly adds that he "does not act by means of an 'organized' liberation action, nor by means of a process that would be analogous to structural changes of a political, judicial, or moral sort. Instead, he enters into a variety of individual, concrete stories and experiences of suffering. . . . No 'great army' of the delivered goes out to a messianic public relations event."[65] The action of the Spirit rules out "'total, unbeatable solutions to problems.'"[66] Liberation "cannot be brought about by merely moral or merely political means. It cannot be brought about by only one time, one nation, one culture, one race, or one class of people."[67] Welker's is not only a liberation pneumatology without liberating praxis but a deliberately *apolitical* or *antipolitical* pneumatology of liberation, which I am afraid verges on a contradiction in terms.

Peter Hodgson

Peter C. Hodgson's *Winds of the Spirit* is a work of both courage and creativity: courage because this work is unabashedly systematic and Hegelian when both are not only identified but eschewed like the plague: creativity because it masters and incorporates so much contemporary theological material into a new synthesis. The most systematic yet among his works, it is a significant development beyond his *God in History*[68] and a fitting addition to his always open-ended *itinerarium mentis*. The book is divided into three parts. The first part ("Interpreting") discusses the nature, resources, dimensions, and challenges of constructive theology. The second part ("Contextualizing") deals with the challenges of the contemporary world in a valuable survey of recent theological concerns such as postmodernism, liberation, ecology, and religious pluralism. The third part ("Revisioning"), which occupies more than two-thirds of the book, provides the systematic revisioning of the standard topics of Christian dogmatics, from the triune God through the incarnation to eschatology. The book, ostensibly intended for the introductory student, must be no less challenging to the established scholar.

Hodgson's many years of work on Hegel's philosophy of religion has left its mark not only on the structure of the third part, which follows the Trinitarian structure of Hegel's own *Lectures,* but more importantly, on Hodgson's conceptual revisions of the traditional dogmatics, especially the doctrine of God. He reconceptualizes the "persons" of the classical doctrine as "moments" of the ongoing process of divine life: identity, difference, and mediation; incorporates the immanent Trinity into the first moment of the economic; and renames the three relations of the Trinity "God, The One" (identity), "World, Love" (difference), and "Spirit, Freedom" (mediation). Perhaps most important, he regards the Spirit as a designation not only of the third person but also of the totality of God, which the Spirit mediates. As for Hegel, God truly exists as God, neither as God in isolation from the world nor as God in the otherness of the world, but precisely as the living mediation "between God as God and God in the world, emerging out of the interaction between them, completing God by bringing God back to Godself enriched and enlivened by worldly difference."[69] That is, God exists truly only as Hegel's (Absolute) Spirit or "World Spirit."[70]

Hodgson's "dialogical" pluralism "includes a deconstructive moment since it rejects totality and is generated out of difference." But whereas thoroughgoing deconstruction "does not recognize a way through difference but *only* difference," dialogue is "a way of speaking (*logos*) through and between (*dia*) difference."[71] Sheer irreconcilable and conflicting diversity is not satisfactory and contradicts "the eros for unity"[72] inherent in all the great religions. Assuming the willingness to be transformed by openness to others while remaining faithful to one's own heritage, dialogue can not only expose our own idolatries by exposing ourselves to the criticism of others, but also lead, beyond both essentialism and relativism, to a "convergence" or "coalescence" around certain fundamental values, principles, and practices among different religions—a convergence that is itself pluralistic, not unitary, not yet found in any one religion but to emerge in the future, and to which each religion will contribute. Such a convergence, based on the human capacity for transcendence and universality, itself a gift of the Spirit, builds solidarity among different religions, and constitutes the emerging content of a "global theology of religions." In this sense Hodgson's pluralism is a "unitive" pluralism, a pluralism of "solidarity," not that of "separation" (DiNoia, Milbank, Surin) that posits sheer diversity of religions in their irreconcilable particularity without presenting an alternative to dialogue.[73]

It is this dialogical pluralism with its hopes in the "emergence" of a "convergence" that leads Hodgson to characterize his model of the Trinity as "a triadic, social holism."[74] In conceiving the relation between God and the world, the driving concern is how to preserve both *relation* and *difference*. God cannot be considered in isolation from the world but only in relation to it; yet this relation is not in the mode of domination but of "releasement" that allows the world to be irreducibly other. The result is a "whole" that preserves both identity and difference, relation and otherness; it is beyond monism, which denies all difference, dualism which denies all relation, and even panentheism, which tends to reduce the *pan* to the self-othering of *theos*; it is "a trans-theistic vision of a whole that is . . . theo-cosmic-pneumatic."[75] Hodgson's holism, like Moltmann's, is not that of a closed totality but that of "an open, dynamic, relational whole,"[76] a vision that holds unity and difference to be equally primordial. The universe "is a whole without a single center, yet it works together as a system through an interplay of centers." The plurality and solidarity of religions are reflections of, and hints at, "the wholeness of God, who is one in and through the most radical diversity."[77]

Like all significant works of creative synthesis, *Winds of the Spirit* will have its share of controversies, notably in the areas of Hegelian interpretation, Trinitarian theology, and theological method. Here I confine myself to the relation between difference and dialogue.

Hodgson's own discussion presents two examples of differences of opinion on "difference" as such, that between Hegelians and radical pluralists, and that between Christians and Buddhists. On the one hand, Hodgson's holistic pluralism perhaps takes us as far to meet the demand of pluralism as it is possible within the limits of Hegelian thought; yet one wonders whether they would assuage the concerns of Michael Welker and other postmodern pluralists. What is at stake here, it would seem, is a conflict of two interpretive horizons: that of Hegel, who for all his emphasis on difference cannot tolerate a universe without a unity that holds it together; and that of radical pluralism that is suspicious of any form of unity including "wholeness" (*Whose* whole? it may ask) as a disguised form of domination. On the other hand, Hodgson's own Hegelian emphasis on difference—which is not emphatic enough in the postmodern eyes of Levinas, Derrida, and Welker, but which Hodgson seeks to preserve in order to avoid sheer, abstract monism—may appear to be the result of an a/ontological *avidya* in Buddhist eyes or *maya* in

Hindu eyes, both of which seek to rise above the differentiated phenomenal consciousness of the individualistic ego. This difference on "difference" reflects another fundamental difference Hodgson himself points to, the Christian's *historical* concern for the reign of God and the Buddhist's *ahistorical* concern for *nirvana*.

Hodgson's pluralism, like that of many theologians engaging in recent interreligious dialogues, does put much hope in the capacity of dialogue to bridge these differences and produce the "fusion of horizons" necessary for a global theology of religions. Given the radicality of the conflict between these horizons (difference on "difference" itself), however, I am not as sanguine about the possibility of sublating those differences by means of dialogue. Perhaps a more sustained attention to the very *conditions* of dialogue—discussed in the preceding chapter of this book—would put the dialogue on dialogue on a more concrete footing.

Dialogue indeed requires openness, respect, honesty, and willingness to learn from, and be transformed by, others. This is (1) the personal, ideal condition of dialogue. There is, however, (2) a social, ideal condition of dialogue, the availability of a higher and more comprehensive intellectual horizon from which to "sublate" the competing and often conflicting horizons in the Hegelian sense of negating them at their own level but preserving them at a higher. There is also (3) a social, material condition of dialogue, the concrete structure and distribution of economic and political power that concretely encourages or obstructs personal openness to dialogue and that also decisively contributes to the production of the horizon that may or may not be adequate to sublating the competing horizons.

Dialogical pluralists generally attend only to the personal, ideal condition of dialogue and ignore the other social conditions. The personal, ideal condition does already obtain among the theologians and scholars of religion now engaging in interreligious dialogue; but their number, I am afraid, is sociologically too insignificant to have a major transforming impact on the very horizons of various religious communities whose ultimate claims are at stake in the dialogue. Likewise, we do not as yet possess a common intellectual horizon comprehensive enough to sublate our existing, conflicting views. Worse, different religions are locked up in economic and political conflicts hardly conducive to dialogue, still less to the production of a common horizon (e.g., conflicts between Jews and Muslims in Palestine, Buddhists and Hindus in Sri Lanka, Hindus and Muslims in Kashmir, Catholics and Protestants in Northern Ireland and Latin America). This is not to say that attempts at dialogue are not fruitful, at least in places not affected by conflicts; they are, but they would remain inadequate, I believe, as long as they do not come to grips with the fundamental structural problems of power affecting the different religions.

Given this situation of dialogue, it seems plausible to say two things: On the one hand, it is indeed necessary to continue the work of dialogue among scholars and theologians even though they have as yet neither their religious communities with them nor the social-intellectual horizon to sublate their differences; their work is that of the pioneers on the frontiers of history that will be appreciated only decades or even centuries later. On the other hand, it is also necessary to be realistic in our expectations of dialogue and to attend, perhaps even more importantly, to the establishment of the concrete historical conditions conducive to dialogue and convergence: economic and political liberation. That is to say, the dialogical quest for interreligious convergence or a pluralism of solidarity is concretely possible only through the emancipatory quest for structures of justice. The global theology of religions, which Hodgson stresses is to emerge only in the future, is indeed possible only as the future of the interreligious praxis of liberation aimed at the solidarity of others. As pointed out throughout this book, perhaps the transcategorical "solidarity" of others at the level of ultimate convictions is possible only on the basis of categorical "totalities" of liberating structures of power. Furthermore, in the common praxis of liberation from injustice, each religion is not only preparing the appropriate condition of dialogue; it is also fulfilling the very goal of all religions and all dialogues, the alleviation of suffering or *dukka*.

Notes

1. Jürgen Moltmann, *The Spirit of Life : A Universal Affirmation* (trans. Margaret Kohl; Minneapolis: Fortress, 1992).

2. Michael Welker, *God the Spirit* (trans. John F. Hoffmeyer; Minneapolis: Fortress, 1994).

3. Peter C. Hodgson, *Winds of the Spirit* (Louisville, Ky.: Westminster John Knox, 1994).

4. Yves Congar, *I Believe in the Holy Spirit* (trans. David Smith; 3 vols. New York: Seabury, 1983).

5. Yves Congar, *The Word and the Spirit* (trans. David Smith; San Francisco: Harper & Row, 1986).

6. Jürgen Moltmann, *Theology of Hope: On the Ground and the Implications of a Christian Eschatology* (New York: Harper & Row, 1967).

7. Jürgen Moltmann, *The Trinity and the Kingdom: The Doctrine of God* (trans. Margaret Kohl; San Francisco: HarperSanFrancisco, 1991).

8. Jürgen Moltmann, *God in Creation: A New Theology of Creation and the Spirit of God* (trans. Margaret Kohl; San Francisco: HarperSanFrancisco, 1985).

9. Ibid., 139.

10. Ibid., 23.

11. Ibid., 28.

12. Ibid., 23.

13. Ibid., 1–4.

14. Ibid., 11, 17.

15. Ibid., 125.

16. Ibid., 46, 139.

17. Ibid., 5, 139, 276–87.

18. Ibid., 258.

19. Ibid., 1–2, 17, 252–62.

20. Ibid., 7.

21. Ibid., 8–9, 55.

22. Ibid., 8.

23. Ibid., 56.

24. Ibid., 56–57.

25. Ibid., 9, 15, 243.

26. Ibid., 12, 14, 56, 69, 102.

27. Ibid., 100.

28. Ibid., 14.

29. Ibid., 96.

30. Moltmann, *Spirit of Life,* xiii.

31. Ibid., xiii, 38.

32. Ibid., 31–38.

33. Ibid., 2.

34. Ibid., 7.

35. Ibid., 37.

36. Ibid., 71–73, 232, 306–8.

37. Jürgen Moltmann, *The Crucified God: The Cross as the Foundation and Criticism of Christian Theology* (London: SCM, 1974).

38. Moltmann, *Spirit of Life,* 68.

39. Ibid., 234.

40. Ibid., 9.

41. Ibid., 74.

42. Ibid., 9.

43. Ibid., 58–71, 73–77.

44. Ibid., 82.

45. Ibid., 178.

46. Ibid., 82.

47. Ibid., 94.

48. Ibid., 128.

49. Ibid., 142–43.

50. Ibid., 176–77.

51. Ibid., 217–19.

52. Ibid., 225.

53. Ibid., 227.

54. Ibid., 229.

55. Ibid., 221.

56. Ibid., 213.

57. Welker, *God the Spirit,* ix.

58. Ibid., 23.
59. Ibid., 11, 42, 61.
60. Ibid., 319.
61. Ibid., 319.
62. Ibid., 125–26, 128,131, 133.
63. Ibid., 46, 48, 120, 134, 318, 321, 336.
64. Ibid., 125.
65. Ibid., 202.
66. Ibid., 215.
67. Ibid., 321.
68. Peter C. Hodgson, *God in History* (Nashville: Abingdon, 1989).
69. Hodgson, *Winds of the Spirit,* 283.
70. Ibid., 285.
71. Ibid., 100.
72. Ibid., 111.
73. Ibid., 304–9.
74. Ibid., 157.
75. Ibid., 157.
76. Ibid., 111.
77. Ibid., 307.

CONCLUSION

Solidarity of Others as the Future of Theology

As the much-awaited third millennium opens, we continue to hear of conflicts and disasters in all parts of the world. For all the progress we have made in recent decades in political liberalization and economic growth, we are not about to look forward to a rosy twenty-first century. The picture of the new century is not all bleak, but in terms of justice, peace, and integrity of creation—our only perspective in this book—there still remain serious problems and formidable tasks straining and challenging all our human resources, especially our capacity for solidarity across the conventional boundaries of identity and difference. My projection is that solidarity of others will not only remain a compelling central theme in North American theologies but also become one in other parts of the world, ultimately making itself the fundamental theme of a global theology in the singular in an increasingly interdependent and unifying world. How to live *together* with a reasonable degree of solidarity despite our differences will become and remain a central, life-and-death issue, for all in the global village in the decades to come.

Let us look at some important facts of the world. As of August 1, 2001, there are about 6.2 billion human beings living in 194 sovereign nations. The gross world product for 1999 amounted to some $40.7 trillion, a phenomenal increase from $31 trillion in 1990. The unemployment and underemployment rate for the whole world was 30%, while it ranged between 4 and 12% for the industrialized nations. Vast disparities continue to exist in standards of living among the nations, from the 1998 per capita gross national product (GNP) of $32,350 in Japan to $4,630 in Brazil, $2,260 in Russia, $750 in China, $640 in Indonesia, and $440 in India. Vast disparities exist not only among nations but also within nations; in the United States the top 10% have six times the income of the lowest 20%, but the ratio in Brazil is 19 to one. In the world 2.8 billion people, almost half the human race, live on less than two dollars a day, 1.2 billion on less than a dollar a day. Africa, the poorest continent, contains 9 of the 10 countries of the world with the lowest GDP, 9 of the 10 countries with the highest infant mortality rate, all 10 countries with the lowest life expectancy—from 36 years of age in Mozambique to 42 in Niger—and all 25 "least livable" countries of the world. All this is according to the United Nations Development Index 2001, which calculates the quality of life in terms of life expectancy, adult literacy, school enrollment, educational attainment, and per capita GDP.

The underdeveloped nations owe a total of $2 trillion to the wealthy ones; one of the poorest countries, Zambia, spent 40% of its national budget on foreign debt payments in 1997, compared to only 7% it spent on social services for the poor.

In 2000 the HIV infection rate has reached 20% in South Africa, 25% in Zimbabwe, and 36% in Botswana.

The year 2000 saw 40 armed conflicts being fought in 35 countries, an armed conflict meaning an armed combat involving at least one state or one armed faction killing at least 1,000 people. Of these conflicts, 17 (42.5%) occurred in Africa, 14 (35%) in Asia, 5 in the Middle East, 2 in Europe, and 2 in the Americas. As of December 31, 2000, there were 14.5 million refugees in the world, produced by some 46 countries, largely in the Middle East and Africa, but also in other parts of the world.

In 1999 the industrialized nations—the United States, Canada, Mexico, Japan, France, Germany, Italy, the Netherlands, and United Kingdom—consumed 209.6 quadrillion BTUs, or 55% of the total world consumption of 381.8 BTUs, and 7,517 billion kilowatt-hours of net electricity, or 59% of the total world consumption of 12,833 billion kilowatt-hours. In the same year the same nations were responsible for 3,122 million metric tons of carbon emissions, or 51% of the total world carbon emissions.

According to the 2001 Transparency International Corruption Perception Index measuring a country's propensity to accept bribes as perceived by business people, risk analysts, and the general public, among the top 30 nations with the least corruption problem out of 91 participating countries, there are only four Asian countries: Singapore (4th), Hong Kong (14th), Japan (21st), and Taiwan (27th); only one Latin American country, Chile (18th); and only two African countries, Botswana (26th) and Namibia (30th); the rest are Western nations, including Western Europe, the United States, Canada, Australia, New Zealand, Finland (first), Israel, and Estonia. According to the 1999 Bribe Payers' Index measuring 19 leading exporting countries whose companies are likely to pay bribes abroad to senior public officials, the most likely (in order) are China, South Korea, Taiwan, Italy, Malaysia, Japan, France, Spain, Singapore, and the United States.[1]

On a typical day of the year, the January 4, 2002, edition of the *Los Angeles Times* carries several different stories that together provide a good intuitive picture of the dilemmas and challenges facing the world implicit in the preceding statistics. On that day, the United States warplanes were hitting hard at the last strongholds of Taliban and Al Qaeda forces in eastern Afghanistan. The same front page also headlined the story of Federal inspectors reviewing AIDS prevention programs, especially sexually explicit ads and workshops, in a country where those infected with HIV now amount to almost one million. Also, on the front page was the tragedy of an overloaded refugee boat sinking off the island of Java, killing 373 people, of which 147 were children and 141 women; they were fleeing from Afghanistan, Iraq, and other Islamic countries by way of Malaysia and Indonesia to seek political asylum in Australia, which was also doing its utmost to make such asylum as difficult as possible. The front page also headlined the story of an Arab American Secret Service agent put off the American Airlines Flight 363, which was supposed to take him to Texas to guard President Bush during Christmas. Being an Arab American and carrying arms on his person in the months following the September 11, 2001, attack, even when he was a Secret Service agent, made him suspect.

Off the front page in the same edition, an article celebrated the avoidance of the much-feared huge famine through the surge of food aid deliveries that winter in Afghanistan, a country that has suffered 22 years of war and many years of drought. The "World" section of the same edition headlined the conflict between India and Pakistan over Kashmir, followed by a story of how the economic instability and insecurity brought on by capitalism are now surfacing potentially explosive problems in China in terms of rising social tension and violence, ending in the astonishing annual suicide rate of 200,000. Another story in the same section tells of an ethnic clash in the Congo in a civil war that has been going on since 1998 and that has been made worse by the intervention of neighboring countries. On the same day, Argentina, long held up as a model of neoliberal economy, was swearing in its fifth president in two weeks in a national crisis triggered by its default on a foreign debt of $132 billion. Limited to $1,000 a month for bank withdrawals, many Argentines were angry, disgusted, and cynical at the prospect of recovery, blaming the crisis on inept, corrupt, hypocritical politicians. In Zimbabwe, a white judge resigned from the High Court, leaving only two whites among 25 judges of the Court, which has been under increasing pressure from the government to rule in its favor. In Nigeria, the family of the late dictator Sani Abacha has been forced to pay back $148 million out of an estimated $3 billion salted away from the nation's oil production during his five-year repressive rule.

The picture of the world at the turn of the twenty-first century, then, is not pretty. The gap between rich and poor nations is quite pronounced. The rich, largely Western, industrialized nations dominate the world, its politics, economics, and culture, through its information technology, its military power, and its banks and corporations. They consume a scandalously disproportionate share of earth's resources as well as produce an irresponsibly disproportionate share of environmental damage. And yet, compared with the poor nations, they appear to be models of democratic legitimacy and internal stability.

The poor countries, which means most countries of the world, are not only poor but also suffer all the consequences of poverty: short life, illiteracy, widespread epidemic, governmental corruption, lack of governmental legitimacy, human rights abuses, tribal and ethnic conflicts, and refugees, all of which cry to heaven and humanity for redress and response. Some, like India and Pakistan, still suffer, half a century later, the legacy of the British decision to partition the Indian subcontinent into two nations along religious lines, creating the largest migration in human history, with seventeen million people crossing the borders in both directions to escape persecution. The rich countries, especially the United States, the lone superpower at the present time, are not unrelated to the political instability of the poor nations and regions. They are involved directly or by proxy in the political and economic fortunes of many strategically important nations, often training and supplying one faction against another, sometimes assassinating their presidents and prime ministers, and always selling weapons of destruction to the rest of the world. All the rich nations are directly involved in the fortunes of poor nations by consuming disproportionately and immorally high shares of the resources of the earth, our common heritage, and causing disproportionately and immorally high shares of environmental damage to the planet, our common home.

Whether rich or poor, we are all living in a demonstratively and experientially interdependent world. It is no longer possible for imperialist nations to push other nations around overseas but remain domestically unaffected by what it does to other nations. The September 11, 2001, attack on the World Trade Center and the Pentagon, the heart of U.S. capitalism and military power, has shown that no country is immune from the consequences of its foreign policies when these are perceived to be blatantly biased; that the technologies of destruction, once invented by the West, are in principle available to all who want them, including aggrieved parties; and that such devastating attacks have their economic consequences in terms of deepening the domestic recession already in progress, which in turn throws a damper on the recovery of the global economy. Another telling example of growing global interdependence was provided in June 2000 when a twenty-four-year old Filipino named Onel de Guzman, a computer whiz, sent a "love bug" throughout the world, crashing the computer systems of governments and corporations from the Pentagon to the British Parliament and causing a damage of some $10 billion.

These global conditions compel the following questions: Will the different groups and tribes within nations, especially the poor ones, achieve the enlightenment, the minimum sense of mutual solidarity, and the collective will to cross the traditional boundaries of identity and cooperate in building a social system that will both ensure basic human rights for all and prevent one another from exploiting one another? It is no wonder that poor nations also seem more prone to ethnic, tribal, and religious conflicts and to governmental corruption than the rich nations. After all, what is at stake is survival itself, the most imperious demand of human existence. For the sake of survival, we are compelled and ready to sacrifice all things, including our very life, as well as to engage every available resource, including our ethnic, tribal, and religious loyalties that are often parochial, fundamentalist, and absolutistic.

Will the different groups and tribes in the poor nations achieve enough sense of solidarity of others to forget about their differences and cooperate in creating justice for all, obeying the rule of law, and resisting the temptation to exploit the organs and resources of the common good in the interest of solidarity? Most poor nations in Africa, Asia, and Latin America are in fact in the throes of nation building, constructing a political community that will survive the strains and temptations of ethnic, tribal, factional, and religious rivalries. The challenge to the poor nations is the political challenge of constructing a tradition of modern democracy quite absent from their own histories. The poor nations also face the further, more difficult challenge of finding sufficient unity and solidarity not only at home but also with one another as poor nations to join together in resisting the political, economic, and cultural imperialisms of the rich nations.

To the extent that many of these problems are in some sense permanent problems of all societies, they also apply to the rich nations, who may have more experience in democracy, but who are likewise prone to the problems of exploitation of minorities, factionalism, ethnic and religious rivalries, and corruption. These problems may in fact be just as intense in the rich nations not because what is at stake is sheer survival as in the poor nations, but because the prize at stake—economic and political power—is so much the greater than in the poor nations. At the same time, insofar as the rich nations bear more responsibility for the content and quality of the growing interdependence of nations, they too are subject to certain critical challenges.

Will the rich nations respect the common good of the international community, obey existing international laws, and resist the temptation to exploit the common resources of all humanity for their own selfish ends? Will they exercise a preferential justice, a kind of international affirmative action, for the poor nations, and resist the imperialist temptation to interfere in, and exploit, their domestic politics, often under threat of cutting off aid? Above all, will they stop selling destructive weapons to the poor nations, forcing austerity measures on them that will hurt the poor the most whenever they are in economic trouble, consuming and wasting an immorally high share of the resources of the planet, destroying the environment through reckless production and consumption, and trivializing important cultural and religious values by imposing the materialism and commercialism of Hollywood on the rest of the world through various information technologies?

The growing interdependence of the world means the growing interaction in common space of different groups, tribes, nations, religions, and cultures, and necessarily poses the most serious challenge of all: justice. In a world where there is no equality of political and economic power among different human groups, interdependence means the dependence of the weak on the strong, with all that dependence implies in exploitation, oppression, and marginalization, more than the dependence of the strong on the weak. Tensions and conflicts occur most often because the stronger seek to dominate the weaker, but also often because the weaker seek justice and liberation from that domination. There are wars of domination, just as there are wars of liberation. In either case, what is at stake is justice in the relation between different groups. As has been said during the last three decades of liberation theology, there is no peace without justice. Peace is the fruit of justice. Growing interdependence is not an unmixed good in itself. As many popular demonstrations have shown in many parts of the world against "globalization," the integration of the world into the one economic system of the free market also poses serious dangers of economic, political, and cultural subjection of many nations to the domination of the industrialized elite. The great challenge today and in the near future, therefore, remains whether the growing interdependence of the world will wear a human face or whether it will turn out to be a monster of global size.

Justice means justice to the transcendent dignity of the other, and entails the humanizing transformation of unjust systems and structures into liberating ones, and the moblilization of others in their solidarity at the service of such transformation as condition for the justice and dignity they all share. The dignity of the other is transcendent and supracategorical insofar as the other is not reducible to a purely empirical "price" and "means" (Kant), and in this regard all human beings share the same transcendent dignity. Doing justice to this dignity means the praxis of constructing a social system, structure, or totality—laws, policies, institutions—that apply to all and actualize and concretize that dignity under particular historical conditions, with all human beings likewise sharing the obligation of this praxis.

Hence, justice means a trinitarian relation among the transcendence or infinity of dignity, construction of an appropriate totality, and solidarity of destiny in dignity and praxis. As human beings we are born with a common destiny, whereby we depend on one another for establishing the social conditions appropriate to our shared dignity. Justice thus entails a trinitarian dialectic of infinity, totality, and solidarity. Without the infinity of the other as other, totality and solidarity tend to become totalitarian and collectivist. Without totality, infinity and solidarity become sentimental moralism and ineffective idealism. Without solidarity, infinity and totality become individualistic and libertarian. We need a constant trinitarian dialectic and tension among infinity, totality, and solidarity, which are permanent "existentials" of human destiny.

In this sense, solidarity of others in their dignity and praxis is not a new demand of our time. It has always been an implicit challenge to our social, historical existence: how we live *together* with those who are *different* from us has been the permanent crux of our coexistence in history. What is distinctive of our time is that globalization has heightened our sensibility to the other as other, to the many differences in class, gender, ethnicity, tribal origin, nationality, religion, and culture to a degree unprecedented in history. Globalization compels us, with a likewise unprecedented urgency, to cooperate in the construction of a totality, a system of laws and institutions that would do justice to our shared dignity as others, under pain of a mutually destructive spiral of violence and alienation. The supreme challenge of our time and century is that of solidarity, solidarity of others that recognizes our common infinity and collaborates in the building of a totality that will do justice to that infinity at this particular stage of historical existence.

My principal concern in this book has been to sublate sheer difference into a solidarity of the different, and to sublate identity theologies into a theology of solidarity of others. And I have been arguing this often against the background of proliferating identity theologies in North America of the last thirty years. What I am now saying in this conclusion is that solidarity of others is not only compelling and appropriate in the context of North America but also in the rest of the world. Given the dialectic of differentiation and interdependence inherent in the globalization process, solidarity of the different with regard to justice, peace, and integrity of creation remains an equally compelling challenge from the global perspective of the community of nations. Insofar as North America bears a lion's share of responsibility for the fate of the human and natural community, no theology in North America can remain indifferent, in the name of difference, to the role North America plays in the global dialectic of liberation and oppression in the name of its citizens. If the Christian theological horizon is the universal horizon of all creation and all humanity in the process of creation, redemption, and re-creation—according to the model of the Word in the reconciling and renewing movement of the Holy Spirit to the glory of the Father and Mother of us all—then no Christian theology today can remain a purely regional, identity theology without ceasing to be Christian; and no North American theology a fortiori today can remain such without complicity in colossal human suffering as well.

It is, then, the compelling task of Christian theology in the twenty-first century to explore all the biblical and theological resources of its tradition that contribute to the global sense of solidarity, solidarity of human others in the cosmic solidarity of all creation. I have done some of this in the theological chapters of this book. It is not the role of theology as theology to directly engage in the practical solution of the problems; but it is its role to make its share of contribution by enlightening the Christian churches and their faithful—some two billion of them, about one-third of the entire human population—on the compelling theological implications of the signs of the times and inspiring them with energetic Christian motivation to commit themselves to participate in God's own mission of reconciling the different in cosmic solidarity and bringing that solidarity into the divine solidarity of others, which is the triune God.

What I have presented thus far, then, is a Christian vision primarily meant for the Christian faithful, for their enlightenment and their motivation. This is a Christian theological way of making room for the other from within the church's own vision, so necessary today. It is primarily a challenge to the Christian community to broaden its vision and its sympathy so as to make that vision and that sympathy as universal as the triune God is universal. It uses the challenge of our time, solidarity of others, to remind the Christian community of its own essentially universalist founding vision which, for various historical reasons, has been narrowed in recent decades to the tribal horizon of different identity groups.

In addition to this domestic Christian purpose, I also propose my discussion as a challenge to other religions likewise to broaden their visions and sympathies from within their own horizons so that they too, without ceasing to be themselves, can participate in this global solidarity of the different. Considering the often destructive role religions have been playing against bridging differences and building solidarity, it is absolutely crucial that each religion also explore the best of its own tradition that will contribute to the global solidarity of the different. Then, and only then, will religion cease to be "the last refuge of human savagery" (Whitehead) and become "the last best hope of humanity" (Whitehead). I present this book as a modest contribution to this task.

Notes

1. All the preceding statistics are taken from The Worldwatch Institute, *State of the World 2001* (New York: Norton, 2001), 6, 8, 144; and Borgna Brunner, ed., *Time Almanac 2002* (Boston: Time, Inc., 2001), 560, 592–93, 638, 706–7, 714–16.

WORKS CITED

Adam, Karl. *The Spirit of Catholicism.* Orig. German ed., 1924. New York: Double-day, 1954.

Anderson, H. George, T. Austin Murphy, and Joseph A. Burgess, eds. *Justification by Faith: Lutherans and Catholics in Dialogue VII.* Minneapolis: Augsburg, 1985.

Aquinas, Thomas. *Selected Writings.* Edited and translated by Ralph McInerny. London: Penguin Books, 1998.

———. *Summa Theologiae.* 4 vols. Matriti, Italy: Biblioteca de Autores Cristianos, 1955–58.

Barnett, Richard J., and John Cavanagh. *Global Dreams: Imperial Corporations and the New World Order.* New York: Simon & Schuster, 1995.

Bauman, Zygmunt. *Postmodern Ethics.* Oxford: Blackwell, 1993.

Baumann, Gerd. *The Multicultural Riddle: Rethinking National, Ethnic, and Religious Identities.* New York: Routledge, 1999.

Bellah, Robert N. "Changing Themes in Society: Implications for Human Services: Social Change and the Fate of Human Services." Speech to Lutheran Social Services, San Francisco, Apr. 28, 1995.

Benhabib, Seyla. "Epistemologies of Postmodernism: A Rejoinder to Jean-François Lyotard." *New German Critique* 33 (fall 1984): 103–26.

Bernasconi, Robert, and David Wood, eds. *The Provocation of Levinas: Rethinking the Other.* London: Routledge, 1988.

Bernstein, Richard J. "An Allegory of Modernity/Postmodernity: Habermas and Derrida." Pages 204–29 in *Working through Derrida.* Edited by Gary B. Madison. Evanston, Ill.: Northwestern University Press, 1993.

Best, Steven, and Douglas Kellner. *Postmodern Theory: Critical Investigations.* New York: Guilford, 1991.

Boff, Leonardo. *Church, Charism and Power: Liberation Theology and the Institutional Church.* Translated by John W. Diercksmeier. New York: Crosssroad, 1985.

———. *Trinity and Society.* Translated by Paul Burns. Maryknoll, N.Y.: Orbis, 1988.

Boyarin, Daniel. *A Radical Jew: Paul and the Politics of Identity.* Berkeley: University of California Press, 1994.

Brunner, Borgna, ed. *Time Almanac 2002.* Boston: Time, Inc., 2001.

Calhoun, Craig. *Critical Social Theory: Culture, History, and the Challenge of Difference.* Oxford: Blackwell, 1995.

Camus, Albert. *The Rebel: An Essay on Man in Revolt.* Translated by Anthony Bower. New York: Knopf, 1956.

Caputo, John D. *The Prayers and Tears of Jacques Derrida: Religion without Religion.* Bloomington: Indiana University Press, 1997.

Chardin, Teilhard de. *The Phenomenon of Man.* New York: Harper, 1959.

Coakley, Sarah, ed. *Religion and the Body.* Cambridge: Cambridge University Press, 1997.

Cobb, John B. Jr. "Beyond 'Pluralism.'" Pages 81–95 in *Christian Uniqueness Reconsidered.* Edited by Gavin D'Costa. Maryknoll, N.Y.: Orbis, 1990.

———. "Dialogue." Pages 1–18 in *Death or Dialogue?* Edited by Leonard Swidler et al. Philadelphia: Trinity Press International, 1990.

———. "Toward a Christocentric Catholic Theology." Pages 86–100 in *Toward a Universal Theology of Religion.* Edited by Leonard Swidler. Maryknoll, N.Y.: Orbis, 1987.

Coffee, Patrick. "The Holy Spirit as the Mutual Love of the Father and the Son." *Theological Studies* 51, no. 2 (June 1990): 193–229.

Cohen, Richard A., ed. *Face to Face with Levinas.* Albany, N.Y.: SUNY Press, 1986.

Comblin, Jose. *The Holy Spirit and Liberation.* Translated by Paul Burns. Theology and Liberation. Maryknoll, N.Y.: Orbis, 1989.

Congar, Yves. *I Believe in the Holy Spirit.* Translated by David Smith. 3 vols. New York: Seabury, 1983.

———. *The Word and the Spirit.* Translated by David Smith. San Francisco: Harper & Row, 1986.

Coward, Harold, and Toby Foshay, eds. *Derrida and Negative Theology.* Albany, N.Y.: SUNY Press, 1992.

Critchley, Simon. *The Ethics of Deconstruction: Derrida and Levinas.* Oxford: Blackwell, 1992.

Crook, Stephen, Jan Pakulski, and Malcolm Waters. *Postmodernization: Change in Advanced Society.* London: Sage Publications, 1992.

Dalferth, Ingolf U. "Wissenschaftliche Theologie und kirchliche Lehre." *Zeitschrift für Theologie und Kirche* 85 (1988): 98–128.

Davis, Colin. *Levinas: An Introduction.* Notre Dame, Ind.: University of Notre Dame Press, 1996.

D'Costa, Gavin, ed. *Christian Uniqueness Reconsidered.* Maryknoll, N.Y.: Orbis, 1990.

Dean, Jodi. *Solidarity of Strangers: Feminism after Identity Politics.* Berkeley: University of California Press, 1996.

Dean, Thomas. "Universal Theology and Dialogical Dialogue." Pages 162–74 in *Toward a Universal Theology of Religion.* Edited by Leonard Swidler. Maryknoll, N.Y.: Orbis Books, 1987.

Derrida, Jacques. "Deconstruction and the Other." Pages 107–26 in *Dialogues with Contemporary Continental Thinkers.* Edited by Richard Kearney. Manchester, U.K.: Manchester University Press, 1984.

———. *Deconstruction in a Nutshell: A Conversation with Jacques Derrida.* Edited by John D. Caputo. New York: Fordham University Press, 1977.

———. "Faith and Knowledge: The Two Sources of 'Religion' at the Limits of Reason Alone." Pages 1–78 in *Religion.* Edited by Jacques Derrida and Gianni Vattimo. Stanford, Calif.: Stanford University Press, 1998.

———. *The Gift of Death.* Translated by David Wills. Chicago: University of Chicago Press, 1995.

———. "How to Avoid Speaking: Denials." Pages 73–142 in *Derrida and Negative Theology.* Edited by Harold Coward and Toby Foshay. Albany, N.Y.: SUNY Press, 1992.

———. *Margins of Philosophy.* Translated by Alan Bass. Chicago: University of Chicago Press, 1982.

———. *Of Grammatology.* Baltimore: Johns Hopkins University Press, 1974.

———. *On the Name.* Edited by Thomas Dutoit. Translated by David Wood, John P. Leavey Jr., and Ian McLeod. Stanford, Calif.: Stanford University Press, 1995.

———. *The Specters of Marx.* Translated by Peggy Kamuf. New York: Routledge, 1994.

———. *Writing and Difference.* Translated by Alan Bass. Chicago: University of Chicago Press, 1978.

——— and Giovannie Vattimo, eds. *Religion.* Stanford, Calif.: Stanford University Press, 1998.

DiNoia, J. A. "Pluralist Theology of Religions: Pluralistic or Non-Pluralistic?" Pages 119–34 in *Christian Uniqueness Reconsidered.* Edited by Gavin D'Costa. Maryknoll, N.Y.: Orbis, 1990.

Driver, Tom. "The Case for Pluralism." Pages 203–18 in *The Myth of Christian Uniqueness: Toward a Pluralistic Theology of Religions.* Edited by John Hick and Paul Knitter. Maryknoll, N.Y.: Orbis, 1987.

Dunn, James D. G. *Baptism in the Holy Spirit.* Philadelphia: Westminster Press, 1970.

———. *Jesus and the Spirit.* Philadelphia: Westminster, 1970.

Dupuis, Jacques. *Toward a Christian Theology of Religious Pluralism.* Maryknoll, N.Y.: Orbis, 1997.

Escoffier, Jeffrey. "The Limits of Multiculturalism." *Socialist Review* 21, nos. 3–4 (July–Dec. 1991): 61–73.

Fee, Gordon D. *God's Empowering Presence: The Holy Spirit in the Letters of Paul.* Peabody, Mass.: Hendrickson, 1994.

Flavin, Christopher. "Rich Planet, Poor Planet." Pages 3–20 in *State of the World 2001: A Worldwatch Institute Report on Progress Toward a Sustainable Society.* Edited by Worldwatch Institute. New York: W. W. Norton, 2001.

Fox, Matthew. *The Coming of the Cosmic Christ.* San Francisco: Harper & Row, 1988.

Fromm, Erich. *The Sane Society.* Greenwich, Conn.: Fawcett Publications, 1955.

Gilkey, Langdon. *Message and Existence: An Introduction to Christian Theology.* New York: Seabury, 1979.

———. "Plurality and Its Theological Implications." Pages 37–52 in *The Myth of Christian Uniqueness: Toward a Pluralistic Theology of Religions.* Edited by John Hick and Paul Knitter. Maryknoll, N.Y.: Orbis, 1987.

Gilpin, Robert. *The Political Economy of International Relations.* Princeton, N.J.: Princeton University Press, 1987.

Gutierrez, Gustavo. *A Theology of Liberation.* Maryknoll, N.Y.: Orbis Books, 1973.

Hand, Sean. *The Levinas Reader.* Oxford: Blackwell, 1989.

Heim, S. Mark. *The Depth of the Riches: A Trinitarian Theology of Religious Ends.* Grand Rapids: Eerdmans, 2001.

———. *Salvations: Truth and Difference in Religion.* Maryknoll, N.Y.: Orbis, 1995.

Herms, Eilert. "Die Lehre im Leben der Kirche." *Zeitschrift für Theologie und Kirche* 82 (1985): 192–230.

Heron, Alasdair I. *The Holy Spirit.* Philadelphia: Westminster, 1983.

Hick, John. *A Christian Theology of Religion.* Louisville, Ky.: Westminster John Knox, 1995.

———. *An Interpretation of Religion.* New Haven, Conn.: Yale University Press, 1989.

———. "The Non-Absoluteness of Christianity." Pages 16–36 in *The Myth of Christian Uniqueness: Toward a Pluralistic Theology of Religions.* Edited by John Hick and Paul F. Knitter. Faith Meets Faith. Maryknoll, N.Y.: Orbis, 1987.

———. ed. *The Myth of God Incarnate.* Philadelphia: Westminster, 1977.

——— and Paul F. Knitter, eds. *The Myth of Christian Uniqueness: Toward a Pluralistic Theology of Religions.* Faith Meets Faith. Maryknoll, N.Y.: Orbis, 1987.

Hilberath, Bernd Jochen. "Identity through Self-Transcendence: The Holy Spirit and the Fellowship of Free Persons." Pages 265–94 in *Advents of the Spirit: An Introduction to the Current Study of Pneumatology.* Edited by Bradford E. Hinze and D. Lyle Dabney. Milwaukee: Marquette University Press, 2001.

Hodgson, Peter C. *God in History.* Nashville: Abingdon, 1989.

———. *Winds of the Spirit.* Louisville, Ky.: Westminster John Knox, 1994.

James, William. *The Will to Believe and Other Essays in Popular Philosophy.* New York: Dover Publications, 1956.

Jay, Martin. *Marxism and Totality.* Berkeley: University of California Press, 1984.

Käsemann, Ernst. *Perspectives on Paul.* Translated by Margaret Kohl. Mifflintown, Pa.: Sigler, 1996.

Kasper, Walter. *The God of Jesus Christ.* Translated by Matthew J. O'Connell. New York: Crossroad, 1984.

———. *Theology and Church.* New York: Crossroad, 1989.

Kee, Howard Clark. *Good News to the Ends of the Earth: The Theology of Acts.* Philadelphia: Trinity Press International, 1990.

Kennedy, Paul. *Preparing for the Twenty-First Century.* New York: Random House, 1993.

Knitter, Paul F. "Interreligious Dialogue: What? Why? How?" Pages 19–44 in *Death or Dialogue?* Edited by Leonard Swidler et al. Philadelphia: Trinity Press International, 1990.

———. "Key Questions for a Theology of Religions." *Horizons* 17 (1990): 92–102.

———. *No Other Name? A Critical Survey of Christian Attitudes toward the World Religions.* Maryknoll, N.Y.: Orbis, 1985.

———. *One Earth, Many Religions: Multifaith Dialogue and Global Responsibility.* Maryknoll, N.Y.: Orbis, 1995.

Kovel, Joel. *History and Spirit: An Inquiry into the Philosophy of Liberation.* Boston: Beacon, 1991.

Küng, Hans. "What Is True Religion? Toward an Ecumenical Criteriology." Pages 231–50 in *Toward a Universal Theology of Religion.* Edited by Leonard Swidler. Maryknoll, N.Y.: Orbis, 1987.

LaCugna, Catherine. *God for Us: The Trinity and Christian Life.* San Francisco: HarperSanFrancisco, 1991.

Levinas, Emmanuel. *Ethics and Infinity.* Translated by Richard A. Cohen. Pittsburgh: Duquesne University Press, 1985.

———. *Existence and Existents.* Translated by Alphonso Lingis. Dordrecht: Kluwer Academic Publishers, 1988.

———. *Otherwise than Being or Beyond Essence.* Translated by Alphonso Lingis. The Hague: Nijhoff, 1981.

———. *Totality and Infinity: An Essay on Exteriority.* Pittsburgh: Duquesne University Press, 1969.

———. "The Trace of the Other." Pages 345–59 in *Deconstruction in Context: Literature and Philosophy.* Edited by Mark C. Taylor. Chicago: University of Chicago Press, 1986.

Llewelyn, John. *Emmanuel Levinas: The Genealogy of Ethics.* London: Routledge, 1995.

Lyotard, Jean-François. *The Postmodern Condition: A Report on Knowledge.* Translated by Geoff Bennington and Brian Massumi. Minneapolis: University of Minnesota Press, 1984.

Maritain, Jacques. *The Range of Reason.* New York: Charles Scribner's Sons, 1952.

Marty, Martin E. *The One and the Many: America's Struggle for the Common Good.* Cambridge: Harvard University Press, 1997.

Marx, Karl. *The Holy Family, or Critique of Critical Criticism.* Moscow: Progress Publishers, 1975.

McCarthy, Thomas. "The Politics of the Ineffable: Derrida's Deconstructionism." *The Philosophical Forum* 21, nos. 1–2 (fall-winter, 1989-90): 146–68.

McDonnell, Killian. "The Determinative Doctrine of the Holy Spirit." *Theology Today* 39 (1982): 142–61.

———. "A Trinitarian Theology of the Holy Spirit." *Theological Studies* 46 (1985): 191–227.

McFague, Sallie. *The Body of God: An Ecological Theology.* Minneapolis: Augsburg Fortress, 1993.

Mersch, Emile. *The Theology of the Mystical Body.* St. Louis: Herder, 1951.

———. *The Whole Christ.* Milwaukee: Bruce, 1938.

Milbank, John. "The End of Dialogue." Pages 174–91 in *Christian Uniqueness Reconsidered.* Edited by Gavin D'Costa. Maryknoll, N.Y.: Orbis, 1990.

Min, Anselm Kyongsuk. "The Challenge of Radical Pluralism." *Cross Currents* 38, no. 3 (fall 1988): 268–75.

———. "Christology and Theology of Religions: John and Karl Rahner." *Louvain Studies* 11, no. 1 (spring 1986): 3–21.

———. *Dialectic of Salvation: Issues in Theology of Liberation.* Albany, N.Y.: SUNY Press, 1989.

———. "Dialectic of Salvation in Solidarity: Philosophy of Religion after Kant and Kierkegaard." Pages 278–94 in *Kant and Kierkegaard on Religion.* Edited by D. Z. Phillips and Timothy Tessin. New York: St. Martin's, 2000.

———. "Dialectical Pluralism and Solidarity of Others: Towards a New Paradigm." *Journal of the American Academy of Religion* 65, no. 3 (fall 1998): 587–604.

———. "From Autobiography to Fellowship of Others: Reflections on Doing Ethnic Theology Today." Pages 135–59 in *Journeys at the Margin.* Edited by Peter Phan. Collegeville, Minn.: Liturgical, 1999.

———. "From Tribal Identity to Solidarity of Others: Theological Challenges to a Divided Korea." *Missiology* 27, no. 3 (July 1999): 333–45.

―――. "Liberation, the Other, and Hegel in Recent Pneumatologies." *Religious Studies Review* 22, no. 1 (Jan. 1996): 29–30.

―――. "The Other without History and Society: A Dialogue with Derrida." Pages 167–85 in *Philosophy of Religion in the Twenty-First Century.* Edited by D. Z. Phillips. New York: Macmillan, 2001.

―――. "The Political Economy of Marginality." *Journal of Asian and Asian American Theology* 1, no. 1 (summer 1996): 82–94.

―――. "Praxis and Liberation: Toward a Theology of Concrete Totality." Ph.D. diss., Vanderbilt University, 1989.

―――. "Praxis and Pluralism: A Liberationist Theology of Religions." *Perspectives in Religious Studies* 16, no. 3 (1989), 197–211.

―――. "Renewing the Doctrine of the Spirit: A Prolegomenon." *Perspectives in Religious Studies* 19, no. 2 (summer 1992): 183–98.

―――. "Solidarity of Others in the Body of Christ: A New Theological Paradigm." *Toronto Journal of Theology* 12, no. 2 (fall 1998): 239–54.

―――. "Solidarity of Others in the Power of the Holy Spirit: Pneumatology in a Divided World." Pages 416–43 in *Advents of the Spirit: An Introduction to the Current Study of Pneumatology.* Edited by Bradford E. Hinze and D. Lyle Dabney. Milwaukee: Marquette University Press, 2001.

―――. "Toward a Dialectic of Totality and Infinity: Reflections on Emmanuel Levinas." *The Journal of Religion* 78, no.4 (Oct. 1998): 571–92.

Minear, Paul S. *Images of the Church in the New Testament.* Philadelphia: Westminster, 1960.

Moltmann, Jürgen. *The Church in the Power of the Spirit: A Contribution to Messianic Ecclesiology.* Translated by Margaret Kohl. San Francisco: HarperSanFrancisco, 1991.

―――. *The Crucified God: The Cross as the Foundation and Criticism of Christian Theology.* Translated by R. A. Wilson and John Boyden. London: SCM Press, 1974.

―――. *God in Creation: A New Theology of Creation and the Spirit of God.* Translated by Margaret Kohl. San Francisco: Harper Collins, 1985.

―――. "Is 'Pluralistic Theology' Useful for the Dialogue of World Religions?" Pages 149–56 in *Christian Uniqueness Reconsidered.* Edited by Gavin D'Costa. Maryknoll, N.Y.: Orbis, 1990.

―――. *The Spirit of Life: A Universal Affirmation.* Translated by Margaret Kohl. Minneapolis: Fortress, 1992.

―――. *Theology of Hope: On the Ground and Implications of a Christian Eschatology.* New York: Harper & Row, 1967.

―――. *The Trinity and the Kingdom: The Doctrine of God.* Translated by Margaret Kohl. San Francisco: HarperSanFrancisco, 1991.

―――. *The Way of Jesus Christ: Christology in Messianic Dimensions.* San Francisco: HarperSanFrancisco, 1990.

Moltmann-Wendel, Elisabeth. *I Am My Body: New Ways of Embodiment.* London: SCM Press, 1994.

Mühlen, Heribert. *Una Mystica Persona: Die Kirche als das Mysterium der heilsgeschichtlichen Identität des heiligen Geistes in Christus und den Christen, eine Person in vielen Personen.* 3d ed. Munich: Ferdinand Schoningh, 1968.

Murphy, Peter. "Postmodern Perspectives and Justice." *Thesis Eleven* 30 (1991): 117–132.

The Nation 263, no. 3 (July 15/22, 1996). On globalization.

National Endowment for the Humanities, ed. *A National Conversation on American Pluralism and Identity: Scholars' Essays.* Washington, D.C.: National Endowment for the Humanities, 1994.

Nicholson, Linda. "Interpreting Gender." Pages 39–67 in *Social Postmodernism: Beyond Identity Politics.* Edited by Linda Nicholson and Steven Seidman. Cambridge: Cambridge University Press, 1995.

Norris, Christopher. *The Truth about Postmodernism.* Oxford: Blackwell, 1993.

O'Donnell, John J. *The Mystery of the Triune God.* Mahwah, N.J.: Paulist, 1989.

Olson, Alan. *Hegel and the Spirit: Philosophy as Pneumatology.* Princeton, N.J.: Princeton University Press, 1992.

Panikkar, Raimundo. *The Cosmotheandric Experience: Emerging Religious Consciousness.* Maryknoll, N.Y.: Orbis, 1993.

———. "The Invisible Harmony: A Universal Theory of Religion or a Cosmic Confidence in Reality?" Pages 118–53 in *Toward a Universal Theology of Religion.* Edited by Leonard Swidler. Maryknoll, N.Y.: Orbis, 1987.

———. "The Jordan, the Tiber, and the Ganges: Three Kairological Moments of Christic Self-Consciousness." Pages 89–116 in *The Myth of Christian Uniqueness: Toward a Pluralistic Theology of Religions.* Edited by John Hick and Paul F. Knitter. Faith Meets Faith. Maryknoll, N.Y.: Orbis, 1987.

———. *Myth, Faith, and Hermeneutics.* New York: Paulist, 1979.

Pannenberg, Wolfhart. *Systematic Theology.* Translated by Geoffrey W. Bromiley. 3 vols. Grand Rapids: Eerdmans, 1991–98.

Park, Andrew Sung. *Racial Conflict and Healing: An Asian-American Theological Perspective.* Maryknoll, N.Y.: Orbis, 1996.

Pfaff, William. *The Wrath of Nations: Civilization and the Furies of Nationalism.* New York: Simon & Schuster, 1993.

Phan, Peter C., and Jung Young Lee, eds. *Journeys at the Margin: Toward an Autobiographical Theology in American-Asian Perspective.* Collegeville, Minn.: Liturgical, 1999.

Pieris, Aloysius. *An Asian Theology of Liberation.* Maryknoll, N.Y.: Orbis, 1988.

Pius XII, Pope. *Mystici Corporis Christi.* Encyclical, June 29, 1943.

Rahner, Karl. *The Content of Faith: The Best of Karl Rahner's Theological Writings.* New York: Crossroad, 1992.

———. *Foundations of Christian Faith: An Introduction to the Idea of Christianity.* New York: Seabury, 1978.

———. *Jesus, Man, and the Church.* Translated by Margaret Kohl. Vol. 17 of *Theological Investigations.* London: Darton, Longman & Todd, 1981.

———. *More Recent Writings.* Translated by Kevin Smyth. Vol. 4 of *Theological Investigations.* London: Darton, Longman & Todd, 1966.

———. *Prayers and Meditations.* New York: Seabury, 1980.

———. *The Spirit in the Church.* New York: Seabury, 1979.

———. *The Trinity.* New York: Crossroad, 1974.

Rescher, Nicholas. *Pluralism: Against the Demand for Consensus.* Oxford: Clarendon, 1993.

———. *The Strife of Systems: An Essay on the Grounds and Implications of Philosophical Diversity.* Pittsburgh: University of Pittsburgh Press, 1985.

Rorty, Richard. *Contingency, Irony, and Solidarity.* Cambridge: Cambridge University Press, 1989.

————. *Objectivity, Relativism, and Truth.* Cambridge: Cambridge University Press, 1991.

Ruether, Rosemary Radford. "Feminism and Jewish-Christian Dialogue." Pages 137–48 in *The Myth of Christian Uniqueness.* Edited by John Hick and Paul F. Knitter. Maryknoll, N.Y.: Orbis, 1987.

Schnackenburg, Rudolf. *The Church in the New Testament.* Translated by W. J. O'Hara. New York: Seabury, 1965.

Schrag, Calvin O. "Rationality between Modernity and Postmodernity." Pages 81–106 in *Life-World and Politics: Between Modernity and Postmodernity.* Notre Dame, Ind.: University of Notre Dame Press, 1989.

Schüssler Fiorenza, Elisabeth. "The Politics of Otherness: Biblical Interpretation as a Critical Praxis for Liberation." Pages 311–25 in *The Future of Liberation Theology: Essays in Honor of Gustavo Gutierrez.* Edited by Marc H. Ellis and Otto Maduro. Maryknoll, N.Y.: Orbis, 1989.

Schweizer, Eduard. *The Church as the Body of Christ.* Richmond: John Knox Press, 1964.

————. "Spirit of God." Pages 1–7 in vol. 3 of *Bible Key Words.* Edited by Gerhard Kittel. Translated by Dorothea M. Barton, P. R. Ackroyd, and A. E. Harvey. New York: Harper & Row, 1961.

Second Vatican Council. *Constitution on the Sacred Liturgy* (Sacrosanctum Concilium). Dec. 4, 1963.

————. *Dogmatic Constitution on the Church* (Lumen Gentium). Nov. 21, 1964.

————. *The Pastoral Constitution on the Church in the Modern World* (Gaudium et Spes). Dec. 7, 1965.

Seidman, Steven. *The Postmodern Turn: New Perspectives on Social Theory.* Cambridge: Cambridge University Press, 1994.

Smith, Steven G. *The Concept of the Spiritual: An Essay in First Philosophy.* Philadelphia: Temple University Press, 1988.

Smith, Wilfred Cantwell. *Towards a World Theology: Faith and the Comparative History of Religions.* Maryknoll, N.Y.: Orbis, 1981.

Staniloae, Dumitru. *Theology and the Church.* Crestwood, N.Y.: St. Vladimir Seminary Press, 1980.

Stendahl, Krister. "Notes for Three Biblical Studies." Pages 7–18 in *Christ's Lordship and Religions Pluralism.* Edited by Gerald H. Anderson and Thomas F. Stransky. Maryknoll, N.Y.: Orbis, 1981.

Strasser, Stephan. *Jenseits von Sein und Zeit: Eine Einfuhrung in Emmanuel Levinas' Philosophie.* The Hague: Nijhoff, 1978.

Surin, Kenneth. "A 'Politics of Speech': Religious Pluralism in the Age of the McDonald's Hamburger." Pages 192–12 in *Christian Uniqueness Reconsidered.* Edited by Gavin D'Costa. Maryknoll, N.Y.: Orbis, 1990.

Swidler, Leonard. "A Dialogue on Dialogue." Pages 56–78 in *Death or Dialogue?* Edited by Leonard Swidler et al. Philadelphia: Trinity Press International, 1990.

————. "Interreligious and Interideological Dialogue: The Matrix for All Systematic Reflection Today." Pages 13–16 in *Toward a Universal Theology of Religions.* Edited by Leonard Swidler. Maryknoll, N.Y.: Orbis Books, 1987.

————. ed. *Toward a Universal Theology of Religion.* Maryknoll, N.Y.: Orbis Books, 1987.

Taylor, Charles. *Multiculturalism and "the Politics of Recognition."* Princeton, N.J.: Princeton University Press, 1992.

Taylor, Mark C. *Erring: A Postmodern A/theology.* Chicago: University of Chicago Press, 1984.

Thistlethwaite, Susan Brooks. *Sex, Race, and God: Christian Feminism in Black and White.* New York: Crossroad, 1989.

———. and Mary Potter Engel, eds. *Lift Every Voice: Constructing Christian Theologies from the Underside.* San Francisco: Harper & Row, 1990.

Tillich, Paul. *The Courage to Be.* New Haven, Conn.: Yale University Press, 1952.

Tracy, David. *The Analogical Imagination: Christian Theology and the Culture of Pluralism.* New York: Crossroad, 1981.

———. *On Naming the Present: God, Hermeneutics, and Church.* Maryknoll, N.Y.: Orbis, 1994.

Troeltsch, Ernst. "The Place of Christianity among the World Religions." Pages 11–31 in *Christianity and Other Religions.* Edited by John Hick and Brian Hebblethwaite. Philadelphia: Fortress, 1980.

United States Conference of Catholic Bishops, The. *Economic Justice for All: Pastoral Letter on Catholic Social Teaching and the U.S. Economy.* Washington, D.C.: U.S. Catholic Conference, 1986.

Von Balthasar, Hans Urs. *Creator Spirit.* Vol. 3 of *Explorations in Theology.* San Francisco: Ignatius, 1993.

———. *Mysterium Paschale.* Grand Rapids: Eerdmans, 1993.

———. *Spirit and Institution.* Vol. 4 of *Explorations in Theology.* San Francisco: Ignatius, 1995.

Walzer, Michael. *On Toleration.* New Haven, Conn.: Yale University Press, 1997.

Ward, Keith. *Religion and Revelation.* Oxford: Clarendon, 1994.

Waters, Malcolm. *Postmodernization: Change in Advanced Society.* London: Sage Publications, 1992.

Welker, Michael. *God the Spirit.* Translated by John F. Hoffmeyer. Minneapolis: Fortress, 1994.

West, Cornel. *Race Matters.* New York: Random House, 1993; Vintage Books, 1994.

Williams, Robert R. *Recognition: Fichte and Hegel on the Other.* Albany: State University of New York Press, 1992.

Wolff, Walter. *Anthropology of the Old Testament.* Translated by Margaret Kohl. Philadelphia: Fortress Press, 1974; paper, 1981.

Worldwatch Institute, The. *State of the World 2001.* New York: Norton, 2001.

Wuthnow, Robert. *Christianity in the Twenty-First Century: Reflections on the Challenges Ahead.* New York: Oxford University Press, 1993.

Young, Iris Marion. "Gender as Seriality: Thinking about Women as a Social Collective." Pages 187–215 in *Social Postmodernism: Beyond Identity Politics.* Edited by Linda Nicholson and Steven Seidman. Cambridge: Cambridge University Press, 1995.

———. "Polity and Group Difference: A Critique of the Ideal of Universal Citizenship." Pages 117–41 in *Feminism and Political Theory.* Edited by Cass R. Sunstein. Chicago: University of Chicago Press, 1990.

Zizioulas, John D. *Being as Communion: Studies in Personhood and the Church.* Crestwood, N.Y.: St. Vladimir's Seminary Press, 1985.

INDEX